Thomas G. (Thomas George) Gentry

Family Names from the Irish, Anglo-Saxon, Anglo-Norman and Scotch

Considered in Relation to their Etymology

Thomas G. (Thomas George) Gentry

Family Names from the Irish, Anglo-Saxon, Anglo-Norman and Scotch
Considered in Relation to their Etymology

ISBN/EAN: 9783337121655

Printed in Europe, USA, Canada, Australia, Japan

Cover: Foto ©ninafisch / pixelio.de

More available books at **www.hansebooks.com**

Family Names

FROM THE

IRISH, ANGLO-SAXON, ANGLO-NORMAN AND SCOTCH

Considered in Relation to their Etymology,

—WITH—

Brief Remarks on the History and Languages

—OF THE—

Peoples to Whom we are Indebted for their Origin.

BY THOMAS G. GENTRY,

Author of "Life-Histories of Birds of Eastern Pennsylvania," "The House Sparrow," "Nests and Eggs of Birds of the United States," etc.

PHILADELPHIA:
BURK & McFETRIDGE.
1892.

PREFACE.

In all ages and localities of the world names, implying some one or more characteristics of person, feature, faith, place or event, were conferred by people, especially by those of defective education and rude, unpolished manners. The nations of antiquity appear to have set the example, for the Hebrews had their "Adam," which meant "red earth," their "Elizabeth," "the oath of God," and the Greeks their "Theophilus," "the friend of God." Scriptural names, and those of a purely classical character, have been studied with less difficulty. Every Hebrew name has been fully discussed and examined by the best scholars, and the Greek have received the same amount of careful consideration. Not so with the Latin. While much of value and interest have been gleaned through patient study and investigation, yet there is a great deal that must forever remain doubtful and inexplicable.

Ripe German philologists have given full attention to the numerous race of German appellations, the Scandinavian class having been most ably treated in a series of articles to the *Norsk Maandeskrifts* from the pen of Prof. Munch, of Christiania. Turner, Kemble, Thierry, and others, have studied, but not comparatively, Anglo-Saxon names, and thrown considerable light upon the subject.

Keltic names have presented far greater difficulties. The changes through which the name passes must be considered, and not merely the sound when translated into English. Books of travels, histories, and popular tales, are here indispensable aids to the dictionary, especially when writers have been good enough to give with anything like tolerable accuracy the genuine word rather than their Anglicised construction.

While surnames and local names have often been discussed, and that very poorly in the large majority of cases, the Christian name has generally been considered too fortuitous to merit notice. Camden did indeed review the current ones of his day, giving many correct explanations, but Verstegen, who followed him up, was more speculative, and, consequently, less correct. Since his day, no English author seems to have given any reliable information to the subject. It is true that a few lists of names and meanings have appeared in magazines and popular works, but they have generally been copies of Verstegen, with puerile and incorrect additions. One paper, which was published a long time ago in Chamber's Journal, was the only truly valuable paper on English names *en masse* that has appeared since he wrote.

But little attention has been paid to the history of names. Why one should be popular and another forgotten, why one should flourish throughout an entire country, another in one section alone, and another around some petty district, has not, it would seem, been of sufficient importance to invite examination. History has answered some of these questions, genealogy others, and the patient tracing of patron saints, their relics, and their legends, many others. In this department of investigation, philology owes a lasting debt of gratitude to Charlotte M. Yonge, a well-known English authoress, who has had the time, the patience, the ability, for so herculean a task. A careful perusal of her work, while it shows a few defects, the results of preconceived notions and false reasoning, brings to the light of knowledge much that is valuable and important.

The writer's interest in the subject began with his study of the Irish language more than two decades ago. That interest has never wavered, but has gathered strength and force with the advancing years. A desire that his fellows should know something of the etymology and meanings of names, for few people have any other idea than that names, family names especially, are the results of chance, has led to the publication of this work. In its preparation he has drawn his facts from primitive sources. Few names, and these originally Christian in character, have been taken at second hand, but in most instances even these have been modified in derivation and meaning to adapt them to his conceptions of what the genius of the languages, from which they were drawn, would require. Bourke's *Self-Instruction in Irish*, O'Reilly's *Irish-English Dictionary*, Foley's *English-Irish Dictionary*, and *The Irish Echo*, a monthly paper published in Boston, and devoted to Irish history and genealogies, are the sources from which have been obtained the facts for the Irish names. March's *Comparative Grammar of the Anglo-Saxon Language*, March's *Anglo-Saxon Reader*, and Bosworth's *Anglo-Saxon and English Dictionary* have been invaluable so far as the Anglo-Saxon are concerned, and for the Anglo-Norman and Scotch considerable information has been gleaned from the writings of Chaucer, edited by Wright, from Percy's *Reliques of Ancient English Poetry*, and from scores of other sources.

It is not pretended that the list of names herein given is anything like complete. Hundreds of others could have been included, but they would only have augmented the size of the book beyond the author's intention. He has endeavored to select names presumably familiar to English-speaking people, and to give their probable derivation and significance. The keen eye of the critic may detect some faults, for a work of this kind cannot necessarily be free from errors, either of judgment or wisdom, but it is to be hoped that the value of the work, as a vehicle of truth and information, may not materially be affected by reason of them.

THOMAS G. GENTRY.

PHILADELPHIA, June 1, 1892.

CONTENTS.

	PAGE
PREFACE	3
FROM THE IRISH	7
HISTORY—THE CELTS	9
LESSONS IN IRISH	13
NAMES—THEIR DERIVATION	18
FROM THE ANGLO-SAXON	51
HISTORY—JUTES, SAXONS, ANGLES	53
LESSONS IN ANGLO-SAXON	57
NAMES—THEIR DERIVATION	65
FROM THE ANGLO-NORMAN	171
HISTORY—NORMAN CONQUEST	173
ANGLO-NORMAN LANGUAGE	175
NAMES—THEIR DERIVATION	180
FROM THE SCOTCH	189
HISTORY—THE SCOT	191
SCOTCH—AS IT NOW EXISTS	195
NAMES—THEIR DERIVATION	197
ADDENDA ET CORRIGIENDA	208

From the Irish.

HISTORY—THE CELTS.

Careful study and research have enabled philologists to establish a system of linguistic classification. They have given us such families as the Chinese, the Polynesian, the Scythian, the Semitic, and others; and above them all the great Indo-European Family, which comprehends ten members—three Asiatic and seven European.

Seven of these ten families have long been recognized, namely: Iranian, or Ancient and Modern Persian; Indian, or Sanskrit, used in Hindostan; Hellenic—Ancient and Modern Greek; Italic, that is, the Latin and its descendants—Italian, Spanish, Portuguese, French, Provençal, Rheto-Romanic, and Wallachian; Slavonic, preëminently the Russian; Celtic, or Keltic, made up of the Cymric and the Gaelic; Teutonic, subdivided into Gothic, Scandinavian, High German, and Low German. Into the Low German the English falls. Recent scholars have added to these seven the Lithuanian, Armenian, and Albanian, making ten in all.

So unlike are these languages now, that it was not suspected until this century that they were once the same speech spoken by a people dwelling together long enough to build up a respectable vocabulary and a common language. The home of this mother-tribe is involved in obscurity. Conjecture, at one time, placed it upon the high table-land of Eastern Persia. Recent surmise, principally German, locates it in Germany, in Scandinavia, in Russia just north of the Caucasus mountains. When, and in what order, the migrations took place is also conjectural. That great migrations did occur, and that each migrating horde carried along with it the parent speech, is no longer questioned. Strong authorities make it credible that the Celtic tribes were the first to abandon the old homestead and seek their fortunes in new and strange lands.

Of this people, the Celts, when first they appear upon the historical horizon, some prefatory remarks are needed. They occupied the Spanish Peninsula, Gaul when conquered by Cæsar, and Britain, when visited by him in 55 and 54 B. C. In Britain, they were divided into many tribes, and were seldom known to unite in a common cause. They lived in houses hollowed out of the hills, built with low stone walls, thatched with reeds and straw, and lighted only by the door. Their dress consisted of the tunic and short trousers. Fruits, milk, flesh, and grain bruised and baked, constituted their food. They manufactured earthenware, war chariots, arrows, the sword, the spear, the battle-axe, and the shield, burned or buried their dead, tattooed their bodies, and were largely controlled by their priests. The latter — the *druids* — monopolized the learning, took to themselves supreme authority, settled all disputes, civil and criminal, and were exempt from taxation and all public duties.

No determined resistance was offered by the Celts to Roman occupancy of Britain, for, under Agricola, the Romans had by 84 A. D., conquered as far north as the Firth of Forth, which they joined to the river Clyde by the wall of Antoninus. Subsequently, they built as additional protection against the Picts, the noted wall of Severus, sometimes called Hadrian's wall, which united the Solway and the Týne. No attempt of a thorough conquest of the island was made by the Romans, but with their headquarters at Eboracum, now York, they held it by a chain of fortified posts, whose site is now mainly indicated by towns with names terminating in *chester, cester* or *caster*—modifications of the Latin *castra*, a camp. These posts the Romans connected by broad and straight military roads over which their legions could readily march.

Roman aggrandizement was of primary importance. Taxes were levied on arable land, on pasture land, and on fruits, and duties were exacted at the ports. Agriculture was fostered, and large quantities of grain exported to Rome. But the imperial city whose empire was so wide, and whose armies were mostly composed of conscripts from subjugated people, and lead by generals of their own blood, was threatened by invading hordes, and was compelled to withdraw her legions for home defense. By 420 the soldiers had all been withdrawn, and the Celts were themselves once more. But their freedom and rejoicing were of short continuance. A more formidable invasion than that of the Roman followed, and by the middle of the fifth century they were the slaves of the Angles, the Saxons, and the Jutes.

Upon the withdrawal of the Roman legions from Britain, the unsubdued Picts and Scots of the north attacked the Celts of the south, who had been subjects of Roman oppression. Whether the assailed Britons detached the Gothic tribes from an alliance with the Picts and Scots, and turned them against their former allies; whether, without having been in league with them, the strangers came from their home beyond the North Sea to help beat back the Picts and Scots; or whether, tempted by the fertile soil, they came on their own account, we may never know; but one thing is certain, that they came, and that they came never to go away. Their coming is of weighty significance, for they became the basis of the English nation, and their speech the parent of the English language.

The unconquered Celts of the west and north spoke their own tongue—the Celtic—while that of the conquered portion was overwhelmingly the language of the conquerors, and was called the Anglo-Saxon. It was not, however, entirely pure, for some few Celtic words had unavoidably entered it. The names for the rivers, lakes, hills and mountains, given by the Celts, clung pertinaciously to these objects, and are found with the English of the present day. Throughout the whole of England there is hardly a river-name that is not Celtic. *Avon*, Celtic for *water*, occurs as the name of fourteen English rivers upon our maps. *Esk*, of like meaning, designates more than twenty, and has also entered into the names of towns, as in *A*rminster, *E*xeter, *O*xford, and *U*xbridge. *Cam, Humber, Ouse, Thames*, and *Wye*, and many other river-names, are Celtic. *Pen*, or *Ben*, Celtic for *mountain*, is seen in the name for the range called *Pen*nine, in that of the hills called *Pen*tland, and in *Ben*-Nevis and *Ben*-Lomond. *Dun*, a hill-fortress, is found in *Dun*barton, *Dun*dee, *Dun*keld. Hundreds of other Celtic words can be observed on almost any map of England, and, indeed, on the maps of Spain, France, Italy, Switzerland, and Germany. The names of the rivers Rhine, Rhone, Garonne, and Seine are Celtic. Italy is Celtic for "beautiful region," and German for "rough man." Besides the numerous geographical names of Europe that are traceable to this language, such common names as *camel, clock, comma, fodder, gun, snake*, and *whiskey*, owe to it their origin, not to mention scores of well-known family names of every-day occurrence.

The remains of the Celtic language are still to be found in the Welsh, the Gaelic of the Scottish Highlands, the Erse or Irish, and the Manx of the Isle of Man.

LESSONS IN IRISH.

Irish Letters—Their Sounds.

There are seventeen letters in the Irish Alphabet, of which five are vowels, the remaining twelve being consonants. Their correspondents in English are *a, b, c, d, e, f, g, i, l, m, n, o, p, r, s, t,* and *u*.

The designation of the letters by their Irish names, *Ailm, Beith*, etc., which is only a convenient contrivance for distinguishing them from those of other languages, has been purposely omitted, partly because they are, at present, seldom or never called by their appellations, and partly because there is often danger in mistaking the names for the sounds of the letters.

Regarding the pronunciation of Irish letters, and of the Gaelic language generally, the fullest and most open enunciation is required. The vowels must be sounded as in Italian or French; the consonants, as in German or Spanish. This open, full sounding of the letters enables foreigners to learn to speak Irish more correctly and more readily than English-speaking people; for, of all spoken languages, the pronunciation of the English is the most opposite to that of Irish.

Sounds of the Consonants.

The letters *b, f, m, n, p,* and *r*, except when aspirated, are sounded like their English analogues. *C* is never at all pronounced like *s* or *ch* soft, but always hard like *k; d,* like *dh; g* hard, as in *get;* and *l*, generally, like the first *l* in *William*.

More variable, however, is *s*. Before or after the vowels *e* or *i*, it is most generally sounded like *sh*, there being but a single exception to the rule, and this occurs in the word *is*—the third person singular present indicative of the assertive form of the verb *to be*, which is pronounced *is*, and not *ish*. Before or after *a*, *o*, *u*, it takes simply the sound of *s* in *soon*, the demonstrative pronoun *so*, this, being in Connaught, where it is pronounced *sho*, the only exception.

Sounds of the Vowels.

A long, as in *wall*, has the broad sound as in English; *a* short, that of *a* in *bat*. There is a third sound, very common in the South and West of Ireland, corresponding to the sound of *a* in *what*.

E long is sounded as in *where*, *e* short, as in *when*; *i* long, as *ee* in *pique*, *i* short, as in *pick*; *o* long, as in *told*, *o* short as in *got*; *u* long, as in *rule*, *u* short, as in *full*.

Vowels are divided into *broad* and *slender*. The *broad* are *a*, *o*, *u*; the *slender* are *e*, *i*.

Union of Vowels, and their Sounds.

Two vowels coming together constitute a *diphthong*; three, a *triphthong*. In Irish there are *thirteen* diphthongs and *five* triphthongs. Of the former, *six* are always long, or naturally so, and the remainder naturally short, but becoming long when accented. The long diphthongs, as they are invariably long, require no accent. The *seven* short need the presence of this character to show that their sound is, in the case so designated, to be pronounced long.

The long diphthongs are:—*ae, ao, eo, eu, ia,* and *ua*.

Sounds of the Six Long Diphthongs.

Ae is sounded like *ae* in the Latin word *Musæ*; *ao*, usually like *ee* in *queer*, except in Munster where it has the sound of the first *e* in *there*; *eo*, like *eo* in the proper noun *Keon*; *eu*, long, like *ai* in *wail*; *ia*, like *ee* in *teem*; *ua*, like *ooe* in *wooer*.

Sounds of the Seven Short Diphthongs.

Ai, accented, is equivalent to the sound of *awi* in the English word *sawing*, being nothing more than the combined sounds *â* and *i*; *ai*, not accented, has the sound of *ai* in the French *taille*, cut, and is hard to be learned by an English-speaking student; *ea*, accented, is sounded like *ea* in *swear*, unaccented, like the same letters in *heart*; *ei*, accented, like *ei* in *deign*, unaccented, like *e* in *den*; *io*, accented, like *ee* in *green*, unaccented, like *i* in *grin*; *iu*, accented, like *iew* in *review*, unaccented, like *oo* in *blood*; *oi*, accented, like *oi* in *boil*, unaccented, like *u* in *shut*; *ui*, like *ui* in *fruit*, unaccented, like *ui* in *quiet*.

Triphthongs, and their Sounds.

All the triphthongs—*aoi, eoi, iai, iui, uai*—are pronounced long, and differ but little in their sounds from those of the long diphthongs from which they are formed. They differ mainly in two particulars—first, in a slight prolongation of the diphthongal sound; secondly, in imparting to the immediately succeeding consonant, on account of its nearness to the slender vowel *i*, a liquid, slender sound, which it would not otherwise receive. *Aoi* is sounded like *uee* in *Queen*; *iai*, like the diphthong *ia* (*ee*), except that the final *i* gives to the consonant that follows a slender or liquid sound; *iui*, like *ceyu*, sounds that cannot be represented in English, as heard in the Irish word *ciuin*, pronounced *keeyuin*, in one syllable.

Aspirated Consonants.

We come now to consider the twelve Irish consonants. Of these consonants—*l, n, r*—never alter their primitive or radical sounds. The remaining nine do change their radical sounds to those of cognate nature.

This change, arising from a rough breathing after the vowel sound, is properly called *aspiration*, as it merely modifies, rather than destroys, as is sometimes erroneously supposed, the sound of the consonant. The notation for the aspirate is indicated by an accent (´) or *h*.

P´(asp.) is equivalent to *ph* or *f*. *B́*, before or after *e* or *i*, to *v;* but before or after *a, o, u*, to *w*.

Ḿ, before or after *e* or *i*, to *v;* before or after *a, o, u,* to *w*, with a slightly nasal sound.

F́ is usually silent; in some words, however, it has the sound of *h*.

Ć, like *ch* in *och*, or the Greek letter *chee*. Before *a, o,* or *u* it has the former sound, which is that of the German *ch;* but before *e* or *i*, it invariably takes the latter sound.

Ǵ, in the beginning of a word, if before the vowels *a, o, u*, has the guttural sound *gh;* but before *e* or *i*, it is sounded like *y*. At the end, or in the middle of words, it has no other power than that of prolonging the sound of the preceding vowel.

D́ has a thick, guttural sound, very analogous to *g*. In the beginning of a word, before *e* or *i*, it has exactly the sound of *y;* but in the middle, or at the end, it has the force of *g*, that is, it merely lengthens the sound of the preceding vowel or diphthong.

T́ loses its power as a consonant, and has the force of *h*.

Ś has the sound of *k; s*, final, is never aspirated.

Derivative Nouns.

Derivative Nouns in Irish are *personal* or *abstract*.

Personal Nouns end in *ōir, aire, ai, aíd*, and are produced from primitive nouns, or past participles.

The terminations *ōir, aire*, are supposed to be broken forms of the word *fear*, pronounced *fär*, a man. If so, then *fear* must be considered as the root of the Latin ending *or*, and of the English suffix *er*.

Abstract Nouns terminate in *as* or *cas*, masculine; in *āct*, feminine; or in the genitive case singular feminine of adjectives.

Diminutives are formed from nouns and adjectives, and end in *an*, masculine; in *ín*, masculine or feminine; in *óg*, feminine.

Many words that are not diminutives end in *an*.

Other words terminating in *an*, from *tan*, time, or from *tain*, possessions, are of this class. *Iat*, a region, a territory, is, in its fragmentary form *ia*, the termination of almost all the Latin names of places that have that ending.

From the active signification of the ending *ac*, and from the meaning of the term *neac*, an individual, an agent, of which *ac* is apparently a mere fragment, adjectives with this suffix become personal nouns, and as such are expressive of office, action, or individuality.

Sounds of Certain Terminations.

In Connaught, final *cad* is pronounced like *oo* in English; in Munster, like *a*. As the final syllable of the imperfect tense of verbs, it is pronounced incorrectly in Munster, and in some districts in the southern parts of Connaught, like guttural *agh*.

Generally, *ad* final, in words of two or more syllables, is pronounced like *ead*; in Munster, like unaccented *a*; and, in Connaught and Ulster, like English *oo*. But in words of one syllable and their compounds, however, the Munster pronunciation is not only adopted in the South, but also in the West and North of Ireland.

In Kilkenny, Waterford, and Tipperary, the diphthongs *ea*, *io*, and sometimes *iu*, are incorrectly pronounced like *ow* on coming before *l*, *m*, and *n*.

In the words *bean*, a woman, *bard*, a poet, and *bord*, a table, the initial consonant *b*, when not preceded by the possessive pronouns singular, is not aspirated. Put, however, these pronouns, excepting the feminine, before the same words, and *b* immediately assumes the aspirate sound; that is, it is pronounced like *v*, if *e* or *i* follow, and like *w*, if *a*, *o*, or *u* follow.

NAMES—THEIR DERIVATION.

A.

Adaire. *A* for *an*, the; *dair*, oak. The oak; hence, strong, powerful, robust. *Adare*, from the same.

Aincy. *Ain*, a circle; *neac*, corrupted into *cy*, an individual, an agent.

Aitken. *Ait*, pleasure, fancifulness; *ceann*, head. Mental delight.

Alney. *Aluin*, beautiful; *neac*, an individual. A pleasing person.

Arran. *Ara*, kidney; *an* for *tan*, land, riches, possessions in land or stock. Land of the kidney.

Ardry. *Ard*, chief; *rig* (*ree*), king. Head king or ruler. *Awrdry*, of like derivation.

B.

Baine. *Baine*, milk, from the adjective *bán*, white. Milk. Bain, contracted from the original name.

Baile. *Báile*, a town, a village.

Bailey. *Báile*, a town; *lac*, a broken form of *luct*, folk, people. Resident of a town.

Baird. *Bârd*, genitive *baird*, a poet. Offspring of a Celtic minstrel.

Ball. *Báll*, a member; one of a community, society, or association. Baull has the same root.

Ballantyne. *Báile*, a town; *an*, of the; *tan* or *tain*, land, region. The town of the region.

Bannigan. *Baine*, milk; *gan*, offspring, descendant. One nourished from infancy upon milk.

Bannon. *Bân*, white; *on* for *an*, a termination indicative of personality. A pale-faced person.

Barmore. *Bârr*, top, summit, swelling tide, head; *muir*, the sea, genitive *mâra*, of the sea. Swelling tide of the sea.

Barney. *Bârr*, head; *neac*, an individual. A leader. Perhaps, the equivalent of *bairneac*, a limpet, because found on tops (*bârr*) of rocks when the tide has ebbed.

Barr. *Bârr*, top, summit, head.

Barret. *Bârr*, head; *aid*, a suffix expressive of a personal noun. Manager; superintendent; leader.

Barry. *Bârr*, top; *aid*, indicative of personality; originally, *barraid*. One at the summit; a man of eminence.

Baugh. Possibly a corruption of *beac*, pronounced *bäch*, a bee.

Beahney. *Beata*, life; *neac*, an agent. A living being.

Benaugh. *Biad*, food; *neac*, an individual. One who provides food; a victualler.

Benner. *Benn*, a mountain; *er*, a contraction for *fear*, a man. A mountaineer.

Binney. *Binn*, harmonious; *neac*, an individual. An agreeable person.

Bourke. Irish for Burke.

Bowan. Possibly from *buan*, lasting, enduring.

Bower. *Bodar*, pronounced *bower*, deaf.

Brattan. *Brat*, a cloak; *an*, expressing personality. A cloak-wearer; a clergyman.

Breen. *Braon*, pronounced *breen*, a drop.

Brennan. *Breun*, fetid; *an*, expressive of personality. An offensive person.

Britain. *Brith*, painted, speckled; *tain*, country. The country of the painted inhabitants.

Britt. *Brith*, painted. A painted person.

Brock. *Broc*, a badger.

Brodie. *Bröd*, pride, pleasure; *aid*, implying personality. An arrogant person; a voluptuary.

Brogan. *Bro*, a hand-mill; *gan*, offspring. Offspring of a hand-mill.

C.

Cabell. *Cab*, the mouth; *aille*, the genitive of *aill*, a cliff. The mouth of the cliff.

Cahal. In Irish *Catal*, from *cat*, pronounced *cah*, battle; *al*, support. Help in battle.

Caham. *Cat*, battle; *am*, time. Hour of battle.

Cahey. *Cat*, battle; *ac* for *neac*, a person; possibly, *catac*, in the original. A warrior.

Cahill. *Cat*, battle; *aill*, a cliff. A battle-cliff.

Callan. *Caillin*, a girl; or, perhaps, from *calla*, a hooded cloak; *an*, a personal suffix. The wearer of a hooded cloak; a nun. Sometimes written Callen.

Camm. *Cam*, crooked, bent, curved.

Cameron. *Cnimir*, a valley; *on* for *an*, small. A small valley.

Camsuile. *Cam*, bending; *suile*, genitive of *suil*, eye. Bending of eye.

Cangan. *Cean*, pronounced *cahn*, fondness; *gan*, offspring. Child of fondness.

Cann. *Cean*, fondness, affection, esteem, regard.

Cannon. *Cean*, affection; *on* for *an*, personal suffix. An affectionate person.

Cannavan. *Cean*, affection; *a bean*, of his woman. Fondness of his woman.

Caird. *Cara*, a friend, genitive *carad*, plural *cairde*, friends. Carde, only another form of the word.

Carey. *Car*, dear; *aid*, a personal suffix. One that is dear, or beloved.

Carlin. *Car*, dear; *lin*, a marsh; a swamp. A highly valuable bog.

Carlyle. *Car*, dear; *lile*, lily. Beloved lily.

Carmack. *Car*, dear; *mac*, son. Dear son.

Carmichael. *Car*, dear; Michael, a Hebrew word signifying "who is like God." Dear Michael. In Irish, Michael is written *Miccal*, the genitive of which is *Micil*.

Carney. *Carn*, a heap of stones; *neac*, personal suffix; originally written, doubtless, *Car-neac*. A quarryman.

Carrell. *Car*, dear; *aill*, a cliff. Beloved cliff. Carruill, the primitive form of the name.

Carrick. *Car*, dear; *rig*, a king. A dear king. Possibly, from *carraic*, a rock.

Carson. *Car*, dear; Anglo-Saxon *sun*, a son. A beloved son.

Carthy. *Car*, dear; *tir*, pronounced *teer*, a country; *ac* for *neac*, an individual; originally *Cartac*. A beloved countryman. Carty, corruption of the original.

Cciort. *Ccirt*, a question.

Claney. *Cli*, left-handed; *neac*, individual. Left-handed individual.

Cloonan. *Cluan*, a retreat; *an*, a person. One who lives in a retreat; a hermit; an anchorite. Clunen, of like derivation.

Cloonas. *Cluan*, a retreat, a cloister; Anglo-Saxon *sun*, a son. A monk; one who lives in a monastery.

Clough. *Cloc*, a stone. Cluff, Anglicised form of the name.

Clune. *Cluan*, a retreat. A sequestered spot.

Coile. *Coill*, wood. Coyle, a modified form of the name.

Colahan. *Col*, kindred; *leatan*, wide. Large kindred; wide circle of relations.

Colgan. *Col*, kin; *gan*, a descendant. Near relative.

Colman. *Colman*, a pigeon.

Conley. *Conn*, of heroes; *lac*, people. Nation of heroes.

Connell. *Conn*, of heroes; *aill*, a cliff. A rampart of brave men; a cliff of heroes.

Connaught. *Connact*, in the original, from *conn*, of heroes; *act* a termination, like *tas* in Latin, or *tion* in French or English. Having the quality of heroes.

Connor. *Conn*, of heroes; *cubar*, fond of. Fond of heroes.

Corbin. *Cor*, a knot, a union; *binn*, harmonious. A happy union; a joyous wedlock.

Corbitt. *Cor*, a knot; *bit*, life. Wedlock.

Corley. *Cor*, a knot; *lac*, people. United people.

Connell. *Conn*, of heroes; *aill*, a cliff, a wall. A close, compact body of heroes.

Cornell. *Corn*, horny; *uille*, an elbow. An elbow inflexible as horn.

Cornwall. *Corn*, a goblet, a drinking-cup, a tumbler, so called because in ancient times drinking-cups were commonly made of horn (*corn*); *aill*, a cliff. The horny cliff.

Cowel. *Cocal*, a hood, a cowel, a vestment. Or, perhaps, from *cuac*, hollow; *fal*, a cover. A hood, or hollow cover.

Cowgill. *Com*, together; *giolla*, a servant. Co-laborer.

Craig. *Cre*, creed; *ac*, an individual. A churchman; the possessor of a creed.

Cravin. *Craob*, a branch; *in*, denoting small. A branchlet; a twig.

Cree. *Cre*, creed, earth, the symbol of faith.

Creegan. *Cre*, creed; *gan*, offspring. An inheritor of a creed.

Creagh. *Cre*, creed, earth; *ac*, an agent. Teacher of a creed; cultivator of the earth.

Creen. *Crion*, pronounced *creen*, withered, palsied.

Creenan. *Crion*, withered; *an*, personal suffix. A palsied person.

Cromwell. *Crom*, crooked; *aill*, a cliff. A crooked cliff.

Cronin. *Coroin*, a crown; *in*, implying diminutiveness. A coronet; a small crown.

Crowley. *Croda*, pronounced *crowya*, brave; *lac*, people. Magnanimous people.

Crupp. *Crup*, a wrinkle, a contraction.

Currie. *Curam*, care (applied in Irish to all over whom one has charge); *lac*, an agent. A supervisor; a superintendent; a manager. Curry, the commoner form of the name.

D.

Dalcy. *Dall*, blind; *cac*, individual. Blind person.

Dall. *Dàll*, blind, sightless.

Dana. *Dana*, strong, powerful, mighty; bold, daring.

Darr. *Daor*, pronounced *deor*, dear, condemned.

Darra. *Daor*, dear; *a*, contraction of *neac*, an individual. A person of wealth.

Darragh. Same derivation as Darra. In certain parts of Ireland, *ac* is pronounced *agh*, or *ach*. Darrach is an apt illustration of the latter sound.

Dearr. *Daor*, dear. Perhaps in Darr, Darrach, etc., the *c*, in the course of time, has been dropped for the sake of brevity, or to satisfy the whims of the possessors of those names.

Deaver. Originally *Duibir*, from *dub*, black; *ir*, man. A dark-complexioned man.

Deegan. *De*, of God; *gan*, an offspring. Son of God. Degan has the same signification.

Deor. *Daor*, dear.

Dermod. Originally *Diarmoid*, from *Dia*, God; *armoid*, of arms. God of arms.

Dermott. See Dermod for derivation. So intimately related are the dentals *t* and *d*, that it is not at all unreasonable that they should be interchangeable.

Derr. *Dair*, an oak.

Devlin. *Dub*, black; *linn*, a marsh, a swamp.

Dill. *Dill*, fond, affectionate.

Dinnan. *Dion*, protection; *an*, implying a person. A protegé.

Donahugh. *Dona*, unhappy, bad, evil; *Hugh*, the Dutch for spirit. An evil spirit; an unhappy disposition.

Donegan. *Dona*, unhappy; *gan*, offspring. An unhappy child.

Donnell. *Domnac*, Sunday; *aille*, of beauty. The Sunday of beauty. Perhaps, Irish for Daniel.

Dooner. *Dun*, a fort, a stronghold; *er* for *fear*, a man. The defender of a fort.

Dooley. *Duil*, expectation; *eac*, an individual. A sanguine person.

Dornan. Dorn, a clenched fist; *an*, denoting personality. A pugilist.

Duff. Dub, pronounced *dubh* or *duv*, black.

Duffy. Dub, black; *cae*, an individual. A black person.

Dunbarton. Dun, a stronghold; *barton*, a corruption of *Britain*. A stronghold of the Britain.

Dunaghan. Dun, a stronghold; *a* for *an*, of the; *gean*, affection. A stronghold of the affection.

Duncan. Dun, a fort; *cean*, a head. The head of a fort; a chieftain.

Dungan. Contraction of *Dungannon*, which, in Irish, is *Dungeanain*. From *dun*, a stronghold; *gein*, affection; *ain*, a land. A stronghold of the land of affection.

Dunkin. Dun, stronghold; *cinn*, genitive of *ceann*, head. The stronghold of the head.

Dundore. Dun, stronghold, *de*, of; *oir*, gold. Stronghold of gold.

Dunmore. Dun, the fort; *an*, of the; *oir*, gold; originally, *Dun-an-oir*. The fort of the gold.

Dunmoulin. Dun, the fort; *muillin*, a mill. The fort of the mill.

Dunn. Dun, a fort, a stronghold, a castle, a hill, a mound.

Dunpatrick. Dun, stronghold; *Padruic*, Patrick. The stronghold of Patrick.

E.

Eagen. See Egan. *Gen* is probably a corruption of *gan*.

Eagin. See Egan. *Ginn* is the equivalent of *gan*.

Egan. Aod, pronounced *ey*, Hugh; *gan*, offspring. Descendant of Hugh. *Aodgan*, the original form. Eoghan, a corrupted phase of the word.

Eill. Eile, aile, oile, another.

Eire. Eire, Ireland. Eyre, a slightly altered form of the name.

Eirey. Eire, Ireland; *ac*, an individual. An Irishman; a native of Ireland.

Ennis. *Inis*, an island.

Erionnach. Originally, *Eireannac*, equivalent to *Eire*, Ireland; *an*, of; *nac*, an individual. Native of Ireland; an Irishman.

Ey. *Ad*, pronounced *ey*, luck, fortune, chance.

F.

Fadden. Corruption of *Padruic*, Patrick. Patrician; nobleman.

Fagan. *Fat*, cause, reason; *gan*, offspring. Result; effect; consequence.

Fahan. *Fat*, a plain, a field; *an*, indicative of a person. A farmer; a cultivator of the earth.

Fahy. *Fat*, reason; *ac*, an individual. A reasoner; a logician.

Farnell. *Fearn*, a shield; *aille*, beautiful. A beautiful shield.

Farnan. *Fearn*, a helmet; *an*, person. One who carries a helmet; a warrior. Sometimes written Farnon.

Farne. *Fearn*, a shield, genitive *fearne*. Belonging to a shield.

Farney. *Fearn*, a helmet; *eac*, an individual. A knight; a warrior.

Fearn. *Fearn*, a shield, a helmet.

Farr. *Fear*, pronounced *far*, a man.

Feenan. *Fion*, pronounced *feen*, wine; *an*, a person. Wine-merchant.

Feeney. *Fion*, wine; *eac*, an agent. Wine-dealer.

Fei. *Feit*, pronounced *fäh*, a sinew.

Feighan. *Feit*, a sinew; *an*, expressive of diminutiveness. A small sinew.

Fenton. *Fiontan*, perhaps, in the original, a vineyard; from *fion*, wine; *tan*, a land.

Fergus. Originally, *Feargus;* from *fear*, a man; *gus*, a suffix denoting towards. One tending towards manhood; a youth.

Fernley. *Fearn*, a helmet; *lac*, people. A warlike people. Fernly, a slightly abbreviated form of the same.

Filmore. *File*, a poet; *Muire*, Mary. A poet devoted to Mary; one that writes or sings of Mary.

Finbar. *Fionn*, pronounced *fin*, fair, white; *barr*, summit, head. A white summit.

Finnley. *Fionn*, fair; *lac*, people. Fair people.

Finne. *Fionn*, fair, white.

Flinn. *Fionn*, white; *linn*, a marsh, a swamp. In allusion, doubtless, to a summer array of white flowers. Flynn, the same word, in slightly altered garb.

Fow. *Fog*, reward, booty, spoil.

Fowne. *Fionn*, fair. In Tipperary, Waterford, and Kilkenny, *fionn* is pronounced *fown* and not *fin* as is the case generally in Ireland.

Fulmer. *Feolmar*, jealous, envious of another's fame, reputation, or glory.

G.

Gahn. *Gean*, pronounced *gahn*, affection, esteem.

Gall. *Gall*, a foreigner, an Englishman, a stranger.

Galligan. *Gall*, genitive *gaill*, stranger; *gan*, offspring. Descendant of the stranger.

Gallagher. *Geall*, promise; *geallac*, genitive *geallaig*, promise; *er*, person. A person of promise.

Gallen. *Geallan*, a linnet.

Galloway. Doubtless, same as Galway. In the original *Gaillim*, the town of the strangers.

Garrett. *Gearroid*, from *gearr*, short; *aod*, compounded of *aoi*, a being, and *De*, of God. An humble servant of God.

Garrity. *Gearroid*, Garrett; *eac*, an agent. A representative of Garrett.

Garvin. *Garb*, pronounced *garv*, rough, rude; *in*, indicative of personality. A rough, rude, or unlettered person.

Gaw. *Gab*, pronounced *gaw*, to conceive.

Gear. *Gearr*, short, not tall.

Gee. *Aod*, pronounced *cey*, Hugh.

Geir. *Gair*, gladness, merriment, rejoicing.

Geogh. *Ge*, a goose; *ac*, an agent. One that acts like a goose; a silly person. Geough, Gough, of kindred origin.

Geugan. *Geug*, a branch; *an*, a diminutive. A branchlet. Geugen, doubtless, earliest change from the ancient form.

Gilchrist. *Giolla*, a servant, one devoted to another; *Criosd*, Christ. A servant of Christ; one devoted to Christianity.

Gill. *Giolla*, a servant, one devoted to another's interests; a menial.

Gilmartin. *Giolla*, a servant; *martin*, Martin.

Gilmore. Originally, *giolla—Muire*; *giolla*, a servant; *Muire*, Mary. One devoted to Mary.

Ginn. *Ginn*, an offspring, a descendant.

Ginnelly. *Ginn*, offspring; *aille*, of a cliff, the genitive of *aill*. The fruit of a cliff.

Glass. *Glas*, green.

Glassy. *Glas*, green; *eac*, an individual. An inexperienced person.

Gleason. *Gle*, pure; *gleas*, purity; *on*, implying a person. A chaste person.

Glennessy. *Glinn*, clear; *eas*, denoting quality, equivalent to *ness*; *y* for *neac*, an individual. A clear-sighted person.

Glenny. *Glean*, a valley; *eac*, an individual. A dweller in a valley.

Glinn. *Glinn*, the bright heavens. Home of the Blessed. Glynn, of like significance.

Gorman. *Gorm*, blue; *an*, expressive of person. A blue-eyed person.

Grane. *Graine*, grain.

Greany. *Grian*, pronounced *green*, sun; *neac*, an agent. Sun-god.

Grogan. *Gruag*, hairy; *an*, denoting a person. A hairy person. Grugan, derivable from the same roots.

Guill. *Giolla*, a servant, a menial.

Guinan. *Guin,* wound, hurt, sting, from *ga,* an arrow, and *an,* a circle, an opening ; *an,* a personal suffix. A sufferer ; a wounded man.

Guinn. *Guin,* an opening, a wound.

Guiness. Irish for Æneas, a corruption of *Mac Anguis,* which latter being the genitive of *Aongus,* pronounced *eny-as,* the equivalent of Angus.

Guire. Contraction of Maguire, which is traceable to *mag,* plain ; *uire,* a contraction of *Muire,* Mary. Plain of Mary.

Gunn. *Guin,* a wound, by dropping *i,* and doubling its final consonant, becomes the word under consideration.

Gwin. Anglicised form of Guin. Gwinn, Gwynn, and Gynn are referable to the same word.

H.

Hallahan. *At,* a ford ; *leatan,* wide. In Irish, pure and simple, the vowels are never aspirated, but in certain parts of Ireland, as before stated, the English habit prevails, as is attested to by the word under notice.

Heany. Anglo-Saxon *hean,* humble ; *neac,* an individual. An humble person.

Hinch. *Leat-inse,* from *leat,* pronounced *leh,* half, and *inse,* pronounced *insh,* island, the final consonant of the first half of the word being carried over to the remaining portion : hence, Le Hinch, or the half-island.

Hugh. *Aod,* pronounced *eey,* is its Irish equivalent: in the Dutch, its parental language, it signifies mind, spirit.

I.

Innis. *Inis,* an island. Innis is only another phase of the same word.

Ireland. *Eire,* west, and *land.* West-land.

J

Jarlath. *Jarflait,* from *iar,* inferior; *flait,* a prince, a chief, one in rank next to a chieftain or prince. A feudatory prince.

Jarley. *Iar,* inferior; *lac,* people. Perhaps, derivable from *jarla,* an earl.

Jennings. Corruption of *Mac Eonin,* which is compounded of *mac,* son; *Eonin,* young Owen, or John. Son of John.

K

Kahn. *Cean,* pronounced *kahn,* fondness, regard. Kahne, referable to the same root.

Kame. *Ceim,* pronounced *kame,* step, grade, dignity.

Kane. *Cain,* reproach, chaste, undefiled.

Kean. *Ciuin,* pronounced *keeyuin,* calm, gentle.

Kearney. *Carn,* pronounced *karn,* a heap of stones; *cac,* an agent. So also Karney.

Keefe. *Caoim,* pronounced *kueev,* gentle.

Keegan. *Kee,* contraction of *Mac Aoid,* son of Hugh; *gan,* offspring. Descendant of the son of Hugh.

Keenys. *Ciuin,* gentle; *eas,* a termination expressive of quality. Gentleness.

Kelley. *Cailleac,* a woman in a hood. The *calla* was generally worn by the old, and hence the term *cailleac* came to signify an old woman, a hag.

Kenallay. *Cineal,* pronounced *knawl,* a race, clan; *ac,* an individual. A clansman; one who belongs to a clan.

Kennard. *Ceann,* pronounced *ken,* head; *ard,* top, summit. Top of the head.

Kenna. *Ceanna,* genitive of *ceann,* belonging to the head.

Kent. *Ceantir,* compounded of *ceann,* head; *tir,* country. Head of the country.

Kehoe. *Ceo*, pronounced *keogh*, darkness. Keogh, similarly derived.

Keohne. *Ceo*, darkness; *ain*, a circle, genitive *aine*, of a circle. Darkness of the circle.

Keonen. *Mac Eonin*, from *Mac*, son, and *Eonin*, young Owen. Son of young Owen.

Kevin. *Caoimgein*, from *caoim*, gentle, and *gein*, an offspring. A gentle child.

Kiernan. *Ciaran*, from *ciar*, black; *an*, expressing personality, and indicative of a noun derived from an adjective. A black person.

Kilgore. *Cill*, church; *gáir*, rejoicing, merriment.

Kilbritain. *Cill*, church; *Brith*, painted; *tain*, country. The church of the country of the painted inhabitants.

Kineal. *Cin*, of the head, source; *al*, offspring. Clan; class; race; progeny.

Kincaid. *Cionn*, affection, regard; *cead*, first. First love; earliest affection.

Kinkora. *Cionn*, love; *cora*, genitive of *coir*, justice. Love of justice.

Kinnear. *Cionn*, affection; *fear*, a man. An affectionate man.

Kinney. *Cionn*, pronounced *kin*, esteem, regard; *neac*, an individual. A person of esteem. Kinnie, of like derivation.

Kirin. *Ciaran*, from *ciar*, black; *an*, implying person. A black person.

Kirwin. *Ciarduban*, a swarthy, black-haired person.

Krean. *Crion*, pronounced *kreen*, withered, palsied.

Kueney. *Ciuin*, gentle, mild; *neac*, an individual. A mild person.

Kynett. *Cionn*, pronounced in certain parts *kynn*, affection; *aid*, sign of a personal noun. An affectionate person.

L.

Langdon. *Loing*, of ships; *dion*, a harbor. A harbor of ships.

Leahy. *Leatan*, pronounced *leahan*, wide; *an*, denoting personality. A large person.

Lillagan. *Lile*, genitive of *lil*, lily; *gan*, offspring. Descendant of a lily.

Limerick. *Luimneac*, from *luime*, or *loime*, bareness; *neac*, for *na eac*, of the horses. Bareness of the horses. The original possessor of this name was, doubtless, a native of the town of the same name, which was built on a peninsula made bare by the many horses sent thither to graze.

Linn. *Linn*, a marsh, a swamp.

Linnehan. *Linn*, a marsh; *leatan*, wide. A broad marsh. Linahan and Linehan are from the same roots.

Linch. *Leat-inse*, *leat*, half; *inse*, island. Half-island. Lynch has like derivation.

Linton. *Linn*, a marsh; *ton*, from *tun*, Anglo-Saxon for town. A town built on a marsh.

Loch. *Loc*, pronounced *loch*, *lokh*, *logh*, a lake.

Long. *Long*, a ship. Not to be mistaken for the Anglo-Saxon *long*, or *lang*, having length. The typical Longs were of Celtic origin.

Loughlin. *Loc*, lake; *linn*, a marsh. A lake within a marsh.

Loughry. *Loc*, lake; *rig*, pronounced *reegh*, or *reey*, king. The lake of the king. Lowry, an abbreviation of the name.

Lunn. *Luan*, the moon.

M.

McAdam. *Mac*, son; Hebrew word *Adam*, a red, or dark-brown man.

McAdoo. *Mac*, son; *Adam*, pronounced either *Adk-oo* or *Awoo*, Adam. Son of Adam.

MacAlister. Mac, son; *Alister*, Alexander. Son of Alexander. MacAllister, of the same parentage.

Mac Aller. Mac, son; *alla*, a cliff; *er*, a man. Son of a cliff-dweller.

McAlonan. Mac, son; *aluin*, beautiful; *an*, sign of personal noun. Son of a beautiful person.

McAlvin. Mac, son; *Alvin*, corruption of *Alban*, genitive case of Alba, Scotland. Son of Scotland.

McAnally. Mac, son; *anail*, genitive of *anal*, breath; *ac*, an individual. Son of the breath of a person. McNally, only an abbreviated form of the same.

McAndrew. Mac, son; *Andrew*, a Greek word meaning strong, manly. Son of the strong. MacAndrias is the Irish form, from which are obtainable Anderson and Andrews.

McArdle. Mac, son; *ard*, high; *le*, contraction of *aille*, genitive of *aill*, a cliff. Son of a high cliff.

McAran. Mac, son; *arain*, genitive of *aran*, bread. Son of bread.

McArty. Mac, son; *art*, pronounced *awrt*, a place; *eac*, an individual. Son of a man of the place.

McAteer. Mac, son; *an*, of the; *tir*, pronounced *teer*, country. Son of the country; a countryman.

McAva. Mac, son; *Eba*, pronounced *Awa*, which is corrupted into *Ava*. Son of Eve.

McAuley. Mac, son; *caille*, genitive of *caille*, fame; *eac*, an individual. Son of a famous person.

McBeth. Mac, son; *beith*, genitive of *beth*, a house. Son of the house. Macbeth is another form of the same name.

McBreen. Mac, son; *braone*, pronounced *breen*, genitive of *braon*, a drop. Son of a drop.

McBrian. Mac, son; *Brian*, corruption of Britain. Son of the country of the Brith, or painted people.

McBronn. Mac, son; *bronn*, genitive of *bruinn*, a womb. Son of a womb.

McBryde. Mac, son; Anglo-Saxon *bryd;* Irish genitive *bryde*, of bride. Son of a bride.

McBurney. Mac, son; *bur*, an inner chamber; *neac*, an individual. Son of the inner chamber of a person.

MacCabe. Mac, son; *cabe*, genitive of *cab*, a mouth. Son of a mouth.

MacCalla. Mac, son; *alla*, a cliff, the final *c* of *mac* being carried over to *alla*. Son of a cliff.

McCallan. Mac, son; *calla*, a hood, genitive same; *an*, indicative of personality. Son of the wearer of a hood; son of a nun.

McCambridge. Mac, son; *cam*, treacherous; Scottish *brig*, a bridge. Son of the keeper of a treacherous bridge.

McCammon. Mac, son; *camm* or *cam*, deceitful; *on* for *an*, denoting a person. Son of a deceitful person.

McCamy. Mac, son; *cam*, deceitful; *eac*, an individual. Son of a deceitful person.

McCardle. Mac, son; *ard*, high; *aille*, genitive of *aill*, a cliff. Son of a high cliff.

McCarne. Mac, son; *carn*, a heap of stones; *neac*, an individual. Son of a heap of stones.

McCarroll. Mac, son; *carruill*, from *car*, dear, beloved; *uille*, genitive of *uill* or *aill*, a cliff. Son of the beloved cliff.

McCaughan. Mac, son; *caig*, genitive of *cat*, a warrior; *an*, a diminutive. Son of a short warrior.

McCaull. Mac, son; *caille*, genitive of *caill*, fame. Son of fame. McCaulley, from the same.

McCaw. Mac, son; *cat*, pronounced *cah*, corrupted, doubtless, into *caw*, battle. Son of battle.

McCeever. Mac, son; *caoim*, gentle; *fear*, a man. Son of a gentle man.

MacClean. Mac, son; *lean*, pronounced *lane*, a marsh. Son of a marsh. MacClaon and MacClane, of similar origin.

McCleary. Mac, son; *cleircac*, pronounced *cleary*, a superannuated clergyman. Son of a superannuated clergyman.

McCleil. Mac, son; *lile*, genitive *lil*, a lily. Son of a lily.

McClow. Mac, son; *cloice*, pronounced *clokh*, genitive of *cloc*, a stone. Son of a stone.

McClune. *Mac*, son; *cluain*, genitive of *cluan*, a retreat. Son of a retreat. McCloon, corruption of same.

McColey. *Mac*, son; *col*, kindred; *eac*, an individual. Son of a relative.

McConkle. *Mac*, son; *conn*, of heroes; *caille*, genitive of *caill*, fame. Son of heroes of fame.

McConn. *Mac*, son; *conn*, of heroes. Son of heroes.

McConnolly. *Mac*, son; *conn*, of heroes; *aille*, genitive of *aill*, a cliff. Son of the heroes of a cliff.

McCool. *Mac*, son; *cuile*, pronounced *kool*, the genitive of *cul*, the hinder part. Son of the hinder part.

McCorkle. *Mac*, son; *Corcaig*, Cork; *aille*, genitive of *aill*, a hill. Son of a hill of Cork.

McCosh. *Mac*, son; *coise*, pronounced *coshe*, genitive of *cos*, a foot. Son of a foot.

McCotis. *Mac*, son; *cotis*, genitive case of the Latin *cos*, a grindstone. Son of a grindstone.

McCrea. *Mac*, son; *cre*, pronounced *cra*, of creed. Son of a creed. From the same roots is derived McCray.

McCreary. *Mac*, son; *cre*, of earth; *rige*, of king. Son of the King of the earth.

McCritt. *Mac*, son; *cruite*, genitive of *cruit*, a hump. Son of a hump.

McCrossin. *Mac*, son; *croise*, genitive of *cros*, a cross; *in*, diminutive. Son of a small cross.

McCrum. *Mac*, son; *croime*, crookedness, a noun derived from the adjective *crom*. Son of waywardness.

McCrunn. *Mac*, son; Scotch *croon*, a groan. Son of a groan.

McCrystal. *Mac*, son; *criostail*, genitive of *criostal*, a crystal. Son of a crystal.

McCully. *Mac*, son; *cuile*, genitive of *cul*, the hinder part; *eac*, an individual. Son of a person's hinder part.

McCullough. *Mac, son; cuile*, genitive of *cul*, the hinder part; *loice*, genitive of *loc*, a lake. Son of the lake of the hinder part.

McCummisky. *Mac*, son; *cuimin*, of valley; *uisge*, genitive of *uisge*, water. Son of the valley of water.

McCurdy. *Mac*, son; *coire*, pronounced *kūrh*, genitive of *coir*, crime, sin; *d*, of; *cac*, individual. Son of the original sin of man; son of Adam's fall.

McDavit. *Mac*, son; *Daibid*, pronounced occasionally *Daivit*, but more commonly *Dávee*, of David. Son of David. McDevitt, from same.

McDermott. *Mac*, son; *Diarmuid*, from *Dia*, God, *armuid*, of arms. Son of the God of arms.

McDiarmuid. *Mac*, son; *Diarmuid*, God of arms. Son of the God of arms.

McDill. *Mac*, son; *dille*, genitive of *dill*, fondness. Son of fondness.

Mac Donnell. *Mac Domnaill*, in the original, from *mac*, son; *Domnaill*, genitive of *Domnall*, Donnell. Son of Donnell; Son of the Sunday of Beauty; Son of the Resurrection; Son of God. See Donnell.

McDonough. *Mac*, son; *donaig*, genitive of *donac*, an unhappy person. Son of an unhappy person.

Mac Dowell. *Mac*, son; *doman*, the world, genitive *domain*, of the world; *aille*, of beauty. Son of the World of Beauty; Son of Heaven.

Mac Egan. *Mac*, son; *Aodgan*, pronounced *Eeygan*, of Egan, the Irish equivalent of Hugh. The son of Hugh.

McElway. *Mac*, son; *Elway*, a corruption of *Gaillim*, Galway. Son of Galway, the town of the strangers.

McEnnery. *Mac*, son; *Henri*, genitive of *Henri*, Henry. Son of Henry.

McFadden. *Mac*, son; *Fadden* is the same as *Padden*, which is a corruption of *Padruic*, Patrick, a Latin word for patrician. Son of Patrick. Fitzpatrick, so common in the Celtic, has the same signification.

McFarlan. *Mac*, son; *fara*, genitive of *fear*, a man; *lain*, of a castle, the nominative singular being *lan*. Son of the man of the castle.

McFaul. *Mac,* son; *faile,* genitive of *fail,* fate. Son of fate.

McFee. *Mac,* son; *favi,* genitive of *favi,* faith. Son of faith.

MacFeeley. *Mac,* son; *fialaig,* genitive of *fialac,* a generous person. Son of a generous person.

McFetridge. *Mac,* son; *Fetter-rice,* from Anglo-Saxon *fetor,* a chain for the feet, and *rice,* dominion. Son of a dominion in chains, or that is in bondage.

Mac Gahan. *Mac,* son; *geain,* genitive of *gean,* affection. Son of affection. McGahn, McGhan, are equivalents.

McGail. *Mac,* son; *gaille,* genitive of *gail,* steam. Son of steam.

McGarry. *Mac,* son; *gearraig,* genitive of *gearrac,* a short person. Son of a short person. McGarey, McGary, McGeary, are of similar origin.

McGarvey. *Mac,* son; *garbeaig,* pronounced *garvey,* genitive of *garbeac,* a rough person. Son of a rough person.

McGaver. *Mac,* son; *gabair,* of a goat. Son of a goat.

McGee. *Mac,* son; *Aod,* pronounced *cey,* Hugh. Son of Hugh.

McGill. *Mac,* son; *giolla,* genitive of *giolla,* a servant. Son of a servant.

McGlinn. *Mac,* son; *glinne,* genitive of *glinn,* the bright heavens. Son of the bright heavens. Sometimes spelt McGlynn.

McGloon. *Mac,* son; *gluin,* pronounced *gloon,* genitive of *glun,* the knee. Son of the knee. McGlone, McGlune, from the same.

McGlory. *Mac,* son; *gloireaig,* pronounced *gloircay,* genitive of *gloireac,* a glorified person, or saint. Son of a glorified person.

McGowan. *Mac,* son; *goban,* pronounced *gowan,* genitive of *goba,* a smith. Son of a smith.

McGrane. *Mac,* son; *grain,* genitive of *grân,* a grain. Son of a grain. McGran, McGrann, equivalents.

MacGrath. *Mac*, son; *graide*, genitive of *grad*, love. Son of love.

MacGraw. *Mac*, son; *graide*, pronounced *grath* or *graw*, love. Son of love.

McGrenery. *Mac*, son; *greine*, genitive of *grian*, sun; *rig*, pronounced *ry* or *ree*, king. Son of the sun-king.

McGuinn. *Mac*, son; *guine*, genitive of *guin*, a wound, an opening, a circle. Son of an opening.

McGuinness. Corruption of MacAnguis, the son of Anguis, Irish for Æneas.

McGuire. *Mac*, son; *Mag-Muire*, from *mag*, plain, *Muire*, of Mary. Son of the plain of Mary.

McGurk. *Mac*, son; *gurke*, German for cucumber. Son of a cucumber.

McHallahan. *Mac*, son; *Talla*, genitive, of hall; *leatan*, wide. Son of a wide hall.

MacHugh. *Mac*, son; *Aod*, Hugh. Son of Hugh. From this name have sprung M'Coy, M'Gee, M'Kay, M'Coy, and Magee. *Ua Aoid*, descendant of Hugh, has given us Hughson and Hughes.

MacHulay. *Mac*, son; *Aoid*, of Hugh; *lac*, people. Son of Hugh's people.

McInnis. *Mac*, son; *inis*, an island. Son of an island.

McInteer. *Mac*, son; *in* for *an*, of the; *tir*, pronounced *teer*, country. Son of the country. McIntyre, the usual spelling, is from the same roots.

McKaig. *Mac*, son; *coige*, genitive of *coig*, war. Son of war.

McKane. *Mac*, son; *caine*, genitive of *cain*, the undefiled. Son of the undefiled.

McKeefy. *Mac*, son; *caoimeaig*, genitive of *caoimcac*, a gentle person. Son of a gentle person.

McKeene. *Mac*, son; *ciuine*, of silence. Son of silence.

MacKeever. *Mac*, son; *caoim*, gentle; *er* for *fear*, a man. Son of a gentle man.

MacKiernan. *Mac*, son; *ciarain*, genitive of *ciaran*, a dusky person. Son of a dusky person.

McKieman. *Mac*, son; *caoim*, gentle; *an*, implying person. Son of a gentle person.

McKim. *Mac*, son; *caoim*, gentle. Perhaps, a contraction of McKieman.

McKinney. *Mac*, son; *Kinney*, from *cionn*, pronounced *kin*, affection, esteem; *eac*, an individual. Son of Kinney.

McKnight. *Mac*, son; *cniocta*, genitive of *cnioct*, a knight. Son of a knight.

MacKeon. *Mac*, son; *Eoin*, genitive of *Eon*, Owen or Eugene. Son of Owen or Eugene. MacKoun, Keon, Coyne, Owens, and Owenson, are all from the same roots.

McLain. *Mac*, son; *leune*, pronounced *laine*, genitive of *leun*, misfortune, misery. Son of misfortune.

McLuth. *Mac*, son; *luait*, genitive of *luai*, swiftness. Son of swiftness.

McMain. *Mac*, son; *miain*, genitive of *mian*, desire. Son of desire.

McMam. *Mac*, son; *maim*, genitive of *mam*, a mother. Son of a mother.

McMillin. *Mac*, son; *muillin*, of a mill. Son of a mill. McMullin, from the same.

McMinn. *Mac*, son; *min*, genitive of *min*, pronounced *min*, meal. Son of meal.

McMurrich. *Mac*, son; *murraig*, genitive of *murrac*, a man of the sea. Son of a seafaring man.

McNarr. *Mac*, son; *nairr*, Irish genitive of the German *narr*, a fool. Son of a fool.

McNamara. *Mac*, son; *na*, of the; *mara*, genitive of *muir*, the sea. Son of the sea.

McNamee. *Mac*, son; *anaim*, genitive of *anam*, a soul; *ee* for *eac*, an individual. Son of a person of soul; a generous person.

McPadruic. *Mac*, son; *Padruic*, Patrick. Son of Patrick. Fitzpatrick has the same significance, *fitz* being the Scotch for son.

McPayne. *Mac*, son; *payne*, from old English *payne*, pain. Son of pain.

McPhail. *Mac*, son; *fâile*, genitive of *fâil*, fate. Son of fate.

McQuade. *Mac*, son; Dutch *kwade*, genitive *kwaide*, evil. Son of evil.

MacQueen. *Mac*, son; Anglo-Saxon *quean*, a woman, allied to Irish *gein*, an offspring. Son of the Queen.

McQuigan. *Mac*, son; *caoi*, pronounced *kwee*, wailing; *gan*, offspring. Son of lamentation.

McQuillan. *Mac*, son; *cuilleain*, genitive of *cuillean*, a cur. Son of a cur. Quillen, Quillan and Quilkin, of like derivation.

McRae. *Mac*, son; *rae*, pronounced like *ray*, genitive of *rae*, the moon. Son of the moon; one influenced by the moon; a lunatic.

McShain. *Mac*, son; *Seagâin*, pronounced *Shawn*, genitive of *Seagan*, John. Son of John. McShane, McShawn, McShaughn, of like significance.

McShimon. *Mac*, son; *Shimoin*, Simon. Son of Simon. Fitzsimon, a kindred form.

McSorley. *Mac*, son; *Somairle*, of Sorley, or Charles. Son of Charles.

McSwain. *Mac*, son; Scotch *swayn*, genitive *swayne*, a lover. Son of a lover.

McSweegan. *Mac*, son; *saoi*, pronounced *swee*, a sage, a philosopher; *gan*, offspring. Son of the descendant of a philosopher.

McTague. *Mac*, son; *Tadg*, pronounced *Taig*, genitive *Taidg*, of Thaig. Son of Thaig.

McTamanney. *Mac*, son; *tam*, still, sluggish, placid; *ncac*, an individual; originally, doubtless, *tamnac*, genitive *tamnaig*. Son of a quiet person. Tamany, Tamney, slightly modified forms of the same.

McTancy. *Mac,* son; *Tancy,* from *tcann,* pronounced *tāne,* stiff, straight, independent, stubborn, hopeful, strong, reliant; *cy* for *cac,* an individual. Son of Tancy; son of an independent person.

McTask. *Mac,* son; *taisg,* genitive of *tasg,* task, labor. Son of labor.

McTeer. *Mac,* son; *tir,* pronounced *teer,* country. Son of the country. Corruption of McIntire.

McThomas. *Mac,* son; *Tomais,* genitive of *Tomas,* Thomas. Son of Thomas. Thompson, from the same, is an analogous, but inverted, form.

McTighe. *Mac,* son; *tige,* pronounced *tighe,* genitive of *teac,* a house. Son of a house.

McTurk. *Mac,* son; *tuirc,* genitive of *torc,* a boar, a hog. Son of a boar.

McVan. *Mac-a-bean,* from *mac,* son; *a,* of his; *bean,* pronounced *van,* woman. Son of his woman.

Mackin. *Mac,* son; *cionn,* of fondness. Son of fondness.

Macoun. *Mac Eoin,* from *mac,* son; *Eoin,* of Owen. Son of Owen. Mackuen, of similar origin.

Magagal. *Mag-a-geall,* from *mag,* plain; *a,* of the; *gall,* stranger. The plain of the stranger.

Magher. *Mag,* pronounced *māgh,* a plain, genitive *maig,* of plain; *er,* a man. A man of the plain.

Maguire. *Mag,* a plain; *uire,* contraction of *Muire,* of Mary. The plain of Mary.

Main. *Mein,* mind.

Malone. *Mag,* plain; *luain,* genitive of *luan,* pronounced *loon,* the moon. The plain, or face of the moon.

Maloney. *Mag,* plain; *luain,* of the moon; *neac,* individual. The man in the face of the moon.

Martin. *Martan,* from *mart,* an ox; *an,* denoting diminutiveness. A young ox.

Marvin. *Marb,* pronounced *marv,* dead; *in,* implying personality. A dead person.

Maury. *Màiri*, of the Mauri; *rig*, king. The king of the Mauri.

Moyall. *Mag*, pronounced, occasionally, *moy*, a plain, a level country; *aille*, of the cliff. The plain of the cliff. Sometimes written Moyal.

Meehan. *Mian*, pronounced *mee-an*, desire, the *h* being ornamental rather than useful.

Meenan. *Mion*, pronounced *meen*, small; *an*, suffix expressive of littleness. A small person.

Menough. *Maon*, pronounced *meen*, wealth; *cac*, an individual. A person of wealth.

Milnamow. *Muillin-na-mag*, from *muillin*, a mill; *na*, of the; *mag*, pronounced *mow*, plain. The mill of the plain.

Mishney. *Misncac*, pronounced *mish-neay*, or *mishneach*, courage.

Miskey. *Meisge*, pronounced *misge*, or *miske*, drunkenness.

Moll. *Mol*, active verb imperative, signifying "praise thou."

Molloy. *Mol-ad*, pronounced *moloo*, "let him praise."

Morgan. *Muir*, the sea, genitive *mara*, of the sea; *gan*, offspring. A descendant of the sea; a mariner.

Mowbray. *Mag*, pronounced *mow*, a plain, a level country; *braig*, pronounced *bragh*, or *bray*, genitive of *brac*, malt. The level country of the malt.

Mowrey. *Mag*, plain; *rig*, of king. The plain of the king. Mowry, the same.

Moy. *Mag*, sometimes pronounced *moy*, a level country.

Moyer. *Mag*, the level country; *er* for *fear*, a man. A man of the level country.

Muir. *Muir*, the sea. Other forms, Muire, Muhr, Moor, Moore, Murr.

Muirhead. *Muir*, the sea; Anglo-Saxon *head*. Head of the sea.

Muirney. *Muir*, the sea; *neac*, an individual. One that follows the sea; a mariner. Murney, from the same roots.

Mulcahey. Originally *Mulcataig,* genitive of *Mulcatcac,* from *mul,* mound, *cataig,* of warrior. Mound of a warrior. Mulcahy, another form of spelling.

Mulcrone. *Mul,* axle; *cruine,* pronounced *croon,* of the world. The axle of the world.

Muldoon. *Mul,* a mound, a knoll; *dun,* stronghold, castle. The mound on which the castle stands.

Mullin. *Muillin,* a mill. Mullen betrays like origin.

Mullock. *Muillin,* a mill; *loice,* genitive of *loc,* lake. The mill of the lake.

Murdock. *Muir,* the sea; Gothic *dok,* an inlet, a gulf. Sea-harbor.

Murlin. *Muir,* the sea; *linn,* a marsh. A marsh by the sea.

Murray. *Murrac,* Murragh, from *muir,* the sea, and *ac,* an individual. A navigator; a sailor.

Murtagh. *Muir,* the sea; *teac,* sometimes incorrectly pronounced *teagh,* a house. A house by the sea; a light-house. Murtagh, Murtaugh, indicate their kinship.

N.

Neachtan. *Neac,* a man; *tain,* of the country. A man of the country; a countryman; a farmer. Naughten, corrupted form of the name.

Nee. *Ni,* or *nig,* pronounced *nee, neegh, ncey,* a daughter.

Neeley. *Niall,* Neill, genitive *Neill,* of Neill; *y* for *ncac,* an individual. Child of Neill. Sometimes written Neely.

Neilan. *Neill,* of Neill; *an,* denoting personality. One of the family of Neill. Neelan and Neelen are the same. Neelans, the son of Neelan, the final *s* being a contraction of *sun,* Anglo-Saxon of son.

Neill. *Niall,* from *ni,* a daughter; *aille,* genitive of *aill,* a cliff. Daughter of the cliff. Neill, Neille, Niell, Nille, Neal, Neel, Newill, Nihill, a few of the many forms of the name.

Neilson. *Neill,* of Neill; Anglo-Saxon *sun,* son. The son of Neill. Nelson, of like derivation and import.

Nesbit. *Nees*, son of Nee; *bit*, life. Life of Nees; life of the son of Nee; life of the son of a daughter. Sometimes written Nesbitt.

Ney. *Neac*, pronounced *neay*, a man. More probably from *nig*, a daughter.

Nicoll. *Neac*, occasionally pronounced *neach*, a man; *aille*, genitive of *all*, a cliff. The man of the cliff. Nicol is similarly derived.

Noell. *Neul*, pronounced *na-il*, a cloud. Noel, Nowel, Newell, cognate forms.

Nolan. *Noell*, from *neul*, a cloud, and *an*, implying person. Son of Noell; son of the cloud. Nolen, a less common form of the name.

Noon. *Noin*, pronounced like *oi* in *toil*, noon. Noone, Nune, are forms of the same.

Noonan. *Noinean*, a daisy, from *noin*, day, noon. Like the Saxon term daisy—day's eye—derived from day.

O.

O'Beirne. *O*, for *ua*, a grandson, a descendant; *beirne*, genitive of *beirn*, a child. Grandson of a child.

O'Brien. *O*, descendant; *Brien*, corruption of *Britain*. Grandson of a Briton. O'Bryan, of similar signification.

O'Connell. *Ua Connaill*, from *ua*, grandson; *Connaill* from *conn*, of heroes, and *aille*, of a cliff. Descendant of Connell; grandson of heroes of the cliff.

O'Connor. *O*, descendant; *Connor*, from *conn*, of heroes, *cubar*, fond of. Grandson of Connor; descendant of those fond of heroes. O'Conner, slightly modified form.

O'Daley. *O*, grandson; *dalaig*, genitive of *dalac*, a blind fellow. Descendant of a blind man.

O'Dare. *O*, descendant; *dara*, genitive of *dair*, the oak. Grandson of Dare.

O'Dea. *O*, descendant; *Dea*, of God. Descendant of God. O'Day, an obscure form of the name.

O'Donovan. *O'Don-a-bean,* from *o,* grandson ; *dona,* unfortunate ; *a,* of; *bean,* woman. Descendant of an unfortunate woman. O'Donovan, of like significance.

O'Donnell. *Ua Domnaill,* from *ua,* descendant ; *Domnaill,* of Donnell. Grandson of Donnell ; a descendant of Christ. O'Donal, an abbreviated form of the name. See McDonnell.

O'Farra. *O,* descendant ; *fara,* genitive of *fear,* a man. Grandson of man.

O'Farrell. *O,* grandson; ; *fara,* of man ; *aille,* of cliff. A descendant of the man of the cliff.

O'Gara. *O,* descendant ; *gara,* genitive of *gearr,* a noun derived from an adjective of the same name, meaning shortness. Grandson of a short person.

O'Gorman. *O,* grandson ; *Gorman,* a blue-eyed person. Descendant of a blue-eyed person.

O'Grady. *O,* descendant ; *graide,* genitive of *grad,* affection; *y* for *eac,* an individual. Grandson of Grady ; descendant of an affectionate person.

O'Hara. *O,* grandson ; *hara,* Irish genitive of the Anglo-Saxon noun *hara,* a hare. Descendant of a hare.

O'Kee. *O,* descendant ; *Kee,* corruption of *Mac Aoid,* pronounced *Mac Ecy,* son of Hugh. Grandson of the son of Hugh.

O'Keef. *O,* offspring ; *caoim,* gentle. Descendant of the gentle. O'Keef, O'Keeffe, analogous words.

O'Kelley. *O,* descendant ; *Kelley,* from *caillaig,* genitive of *cailleac,* an old woman, a hag. Grandson of an old woman.

O'Leary. *O,* grandson ; Anglo-Saxon *lær,* learning ; Irish *y* for *eac,* an individual. Descendant of an educated person.

O'Lone *O,* descendant ; *luain,* genitive of *luan,* a warrior. Grandson of a warrior.

O'Lochlin. *O,* grandson ; *loice,* genitive of *loc,* pronounced *loch,* a lake ; *linn,* a swamp. Descendant of Lochlin. O'Loughlin, O'Laughlin, cognate terms.

O'Malachlyn. *O'McLochlin,* from *o,* descendant ; *McLochlin,* son of Lochlin. Descendant of McLochlin.

O'Mara. *O*, descendant; *mara*, genitive of *muir*, the sea. Offspring of the sea. O'Meara, most generally in use.

O'Millin. *O*, offspring; *muillin*, of the mill. Descendant of the mill. O'Mullen, O'Mullane, derivable from the same roots.

O'Neill. *Ua Neill*, from *ua*, grandson; *Neill*, genitive of *Niall*, Neill. Descendant of Neill. O'Neil, O'Neal, quite commonly occur, and are similarly derived.

Oram. *Or*, gold; *am*, time. Time is gold; precious opportunity.

Ord. *Ord*, order, arrangement.

O'Regan. *O*, descendant; *Regan*, from *rig*, a king; *an* for *tan*, place, region. Descendant of Regan.

O'Reilly. *Ua Ragallac*, from *ua*, grandson, *riagail*, a rule; *ac*, an individual. Descendant of a ruler; grandson of a king.

O'Rourk. *Ua Ruarcac*, from *ua*, descendant; *radarc*, pronounced in Connaught *rooarc*, sight, and *ac*, an individual. Grandson of Rourk; descendant of a man of judgment. O'Rourke, O'Rorke, kindred names.

Orr. *Or*, gold, wealth, riches. In a secondary sense, precious, valuable.

O'Shaughnessy. *O*, descendant; *Seagan*, pronounced *Shaughn*, or *Shawn*, genitive *Seagain*, John; *nees*, *ni*, daughter, and Anglo-Saxon *s* for *sun*, son; *y* for *eac*, an individual. Grandson of a person belonging to the son of the daughter of John. O'Shannessy, of like derivation.

O'Shanter. *O*, descendant; *Seagain*, John's; *ter*, from *tir*, country. A descendant of John's country.

Ossian. *Osna*, a sigh; *n* for *an*, denoting a personal noun. One who sighs; a mourner.

O'Sullivan. *O*, descendant; *suile*, pronounced *soo-il*, genitive of *suil*, the eye; *i* for *a*, his; *bean*, woman.

O'Toole. *O*, descendant; genitive *tuile*, pronounced *too-il*, of flood. Descendant of a flood.

Owen. Eon, perhaps from *uan*, pronounced *oo-an*, a lamb. From *Mac Eoin*, son of Owen, have arisen MacKeon, Keon, Coyne, Owens, and Owenson.

Owenson. Owen, and *sun*, the Anglo-Saxon of son. Son of Owen. Owens is the same name curtailed of the last two letters.

O'Weir. O, descendant; Anglo-Saxon *wer*, a man, Irish genitive *weir*. Descendant of man.

P.

Padden, corruption of *Padruic*, Irish for Patrick. A patrician; a nobleman. Paddin is another spelling of the name.

Pearson. Pearsan, genitive of *pearsa*. A person.

Pollard. Poll, a hole, a pit; *ard*, high, chief, supreme. A high hole; a deep pit.

Q.

Quillin. Cuillean, a cur. Quillen, a slightly changed, and Quill, a largely abbreviated form of the same word.

Quin. Caoin, pronounced *kween*, weeping, wailing. Quinn, of like derivation.

Quinlivan. Caoin, weeping; *luib*, pronounced *liv*, genitive *luibe*, grass, weed; *an* for *tan*, garden. A garden of weeping grass.

Quinney. Caoin, weeping; *ney* from *neac*, an individual. A mourner.

R.

Rainear. Rainn, genitive of *rann*, song, poem, stanza; *ear* for *fear*, a man. A singer; a minstrel; a poet. Rainier, a name farthest removed from the primitive form, but the one that is most generally used.

Rainey. Rainn, genitive of *rann*, song, poem; *eac*, an individual. A writer of songs; a poet. Raney, Reaney, cognate names.

Redfearn. Anglo-Saxon *read*, red; Irish *fearn*, pronounced *färn*, alder-tree. The red alder-tree.

Regan. *Rig*, king; *an* for *tan*, possessions, country. A kingdom. Reagan, Ragan, and, perhaps, Rogan, of like import.

Reilly. *Ragallac*, from *riagail*, a rule; *ac*, an agent. A ruler; a king. Reilley, Reily, Rielly, Riley, cognate forms.

Richardson. *Mac Risdeard*, son of Richard. Richards, Dicson, Dixon, have the same signification, Richard, in Old German, meaning rich-hearted, powerful.

Rock. *Roc*, pronounced *rokh*, rock, a large stone.

Rourk. *Ruarcac*, from *radarc*, pronounced *rooarc*, sight, and *ac*, an individual. An observant person; a man of judgment. Rourke, Rorke, Rork, Riark, referable to the same roots.

Rox. *Rocks*, from *roc*, a rock, and Anglo-Saxon *sun*, son. Son of Rock.

Ruan. *Run*, pronounced *roon*, secret, dear, beloved. Ruane, Ruene, analogous words.

Runey. *Run*, secret, beloved; *ney* for *neac*, an individual, an agent. One that is beloved. Rooney, Roney, common spellings of the name.

Ryan. *Rigin*, pronounced *ry-an*, slow.

S.

Searle. *Somairle*, pronounced *Sowarley*, Sorley, or Charles. Shorley is from the same root, only the initial consonant has its characteristic force before the slender vowel *e*.

Sewell. *Suil*, pronounced *soo-ill*, the eye. Sewall, a slightly modified form of the name.

Shane. *Sean*, pronounced *shane*, old. Shan, Shean, Sheain, Sheahan, Sheehan, of similar derivation.

Shannon. *Sean*, old; *aman*, pronounced *awan*, river. An ancient river.

Shaughney. *Seagain,* pronounced *Shawn,* genitive of *Seagan,* John; *neac,* an individual, an agent. The helpmeet of John.

Sheely. *Sile,* pronounced *Shee-le,* Celia.

Shinn. *Sinn,* pronounced *shinn,* we, us. Sinn, the same, only the *s* has not taken its accustomed sound of *sh* before the slender vowel *i.*

Sinnott. *Sinn,* we, us; *aid,* or *aoid,* a person. One who uses the pronoun *we*; an editor; a reviewer; a governor. Sinett, Synott, Shenett, Sennett, equivalent names.

Smiggins. *Smiggin,* from *smigin,* the chin; *s,* contraction of *sun,* Anglo-Saxon for son. Son of Smiggin; son of the chin.

Stephenson. *Mac Stepain,* from *mac,* son, and *Stepain,* genitive of *Stepan,* Stephen. Son of Stephen. Fitzstephen has the same signification.

Sullivan. *Sul-a-bean,* from *sul,* the eye; *a,* of; *bean,* woman. The eye of woman.

Sully. *Sul,* the eye; genitive *suile,* pronounced *soo-il-le,* belonging to the eye.

Sweegan. *Saoi,* pronounced *swee,* a philosopher, a man of letters; *gan,* descendant. The offspring of a philosopher.

Sweeney. *Saoi,* a gentleman, a hero; *neac,* an individual, an agent. A valet; an aid-de-camp.

T.

Taine. *Teine,* pronounced *tain,* fire. Toyne, greatly modified form of the original.

Tammaney. *Tam,* still, sluggish, placid; *neac,* an individual, an agent. A cool, calm, deliberate person.

Taney. *Teine,* fire; *neac,* an agent, an individual. An ardent, zealous man.

Tenney. *Teann*, pronounced *tane*, straight, independent, stubborn, hopeful, strong, reliant ; *eac* for *neac*, an individual. A strong, hopeful, reliant person. Tenny, Teeney, Teeny, of similar import.

Terrell. *Tir*, pronounced *teer*, a country ; *ell* for *aill*, a cliff. The cliff-country. Tirrill, Tyrell, familiar forms of the same name.

Terry. *Tir*, country ; *rig*, the king. The king's country.

Thoreau. *Torad*, pronounced *thoroo*, produce, fruit, fruitfulness.

Tierney. *Tir*, country ; *neac*, an individual. A countryman ; a farmer.

Tighe. *Tige*, pronounced *tighe*, genitive of *teac*, a house. Belonging to a house.

Toole. *Tuile*, pronounced *too-il-e*, a flood. Tool, Tull, Tully, cognate names.

Torrey. *Torac*, pronounced *torach*, thunder.

Trall. *Traill*, pronounced *trawll*, a slave, a bastard.

Trombar. *Trom*, heavy ; *barr*, top, summit. Top-heavy. Trumbar, similarly derived.

V.

Van Barr. *Van*, Dutch for son, doubtless from Irish *bean*, woman ; *barr*, summit, top. Son of Barr ; son of a man of eminence.

Vannaman. *Van-na-mann*, from *van*, son ; *na*, of the ; *mann*, man. Son of the man. Names commencing with *van* are considered by writers of philology as Dutch, but in many such terms the student readily perceives an Irish origin. *Van*, without doubt, is nothing but *bean*, the Irish for woman, with its initial consonant aspirated.

W.

Williamson. *Mac Uilleam*, from *mac*, son ; *Uilleam*, genitive of *Uilliam*, William. Son of William. Fitzwilliam, Williams and MacWilliam are forms of the word, the last being the Irish name assumed by the Bourkes of Connaught on the death of their chief, William De Bourg, third earl of Ulster.

Y.

Yarnall. *Eireann*, genitive of *Eire*, Ireland ; *aill*, a cliff. A cliff of Ireland.

Yarrick. *Eire*, Ireland ; *caċ* for *neaċ*, an individual. An Irishman.

Yarrow. *Iar*, western ; *aċ*, fragmentary form of *neaċ*, pronounced *ach*, or *agh*, an individual. A western man ; a native of Ireland.

From the Anglo-Saxon.

HISTORY—JUTES, SAXONS, ANGLES.

Every Englishman—and we apply the term in a comprehensive sense—who would clearly understand the force of his mother-tongue, should study Anglo-Saxon, as it is the direct and copious source of his own beloved language. Out of the many thousand words in use in English, more than five-eighths are of Anglo-Saxon origin. These, not only in number, but in their peculiar character and significance, as well as in their influence on grammatical forms, give to our language, it is universally admitted, its chief vigor. In short, they constitute its bone and sinew. Volumes may be written in words of Anglo-Saxon parentage alone, but it would be impossible to express the simplest thought in language of Latin derivation. Words expressive of the dearest relations, the strongest and most powerful feelings of nature, the language of every-day life, as of duty, business, pleasure, etc., find in the Anglo-Saxon their deepest, sincerest, and most energetic portrayals. Every speaker or writer, if he would convince the understanding and reach the heart, must shun Latinized expressions, and use the Anglo-Saxon, for the one awakens vivid, soul-stirring thoughts, and the other thoughts that are cool and unimpassioned.

With this view of Anglo-Saxon's importance to every Englishman, a brief account of the origin of the present inhabitants of England will show that we owe to the Gothic tribes—the Jutes, the Saxons and the Angles—our physical vigor, yea, our very existence, as well as our highly expressive language. Like all the Teutonic tribes, the Saxons were of Oriental origin. They derived, most probably, their appellation from the Sacæ, who doubtless gave the name of Sakasina to a part of Armenia. In Ptolemy's time, A. D. 90, they were as far westward as the Elbe, and, consequently, were among the first of the Teutonic tribes that visited Europe. Their location, between the Elbe and the Eyder in the south of Denmark, strengthens the belief that they were the vanguard of Germanic emigration. The Jutes, the Saxons and the Angles, which were the only tribes that successively made settlements in Britain, are therefore deemed of sufficient interest to claim especial attention.

The first to obtain possession were the Jutes. Two brothers, Hengist and Horsa, from Jutland, in Denmark, arrived in three small ships at Ebbs-fleet, in the Isle of Thanet, in 449. This island was assigned to them by the Britons for their assistance against the Picts and Scots. Subsequently, they became possessors of Kent, the Isle of Wight, and part of Hampshire.

Forty-two years later, 491, the Saxons entered Britain. Their first kingdom was established by Ella, under the name of South-Saxons, including what is now known as Sussex, together with a part of Surrey. In 494 another powerful colony, under Cerdic, arrived. Being west of the other, it took the name West-Saxons. They occupied Hants, Berks, Wilts, Dorset, Somerset, Devon, and part of Cornwall. A third Saxon kingdom, in 527, was planted in Essex, Middlesex and the south of Hertfordshire, under the name of East-Saxons (East-Seaxe).

The Angles (Engle), from Anglen, the country between Flensburg and the Schley in the southeast of Sleswick in Denmark, settled about 527 in East Anglia, and exercised control over what now embraces Norfolk, Suffolk, Cambridge, and part of Bedfordshire. Ida, in 547, began to establish himself in Bernicia, comprehending Northumberland and the south of Scotland, between the Tweed and Firth of Forth. About 559 Ella conquered Deira, a tract of country between the Humber and the Tweed, embracing the counties of York, Durham, Northumberland, Cumberland, Westmoreland, and Lancashire. Mercia, bounded by the Thames, Humber and Severn, and comprehending the counties of Chester, Derby, Huntingdon, Lincoln, Northampton, Nottingham, Rutland, the north of Beds, Bucks, Hertford, Warwick, Oxon, Worcester, Hereford, Gloucester, Stafford and Salop, was formed by Crida, about 586, into an independent state.

From the foregoing remarks it appears that one Jute, three Saxon, and four Angle, altogether eight kingdoms, were established in Britain by the year 586, and that the Angles and Saxons were the leading spirits in the expeditions. They, therefore, when settled in this country, were collectively called Anglo-Saxons. From the Angles (Engle), who were the most numerous and predominant, the land was named Engla land, the Engle's or Angle's land—an appellation which was afterwards contracted into England.

Anglo-Saxon, that is, Angle-, Engle-, or English-Saxon, is the language of the Platt, Low, Flat, or North part of Germany, introduced into England by the Jutes, the Angles, and the Saxons, and modified, spoken, and written by Englishmen. The less daring and enterprising of these peoples who remained in their continental home bore the name of Old-Saxons, and their language Old-Saxon, but their brethren who settled in Britain were fitly designated Anglo-Saxons, and their language, perfected in England, was denominated Anglo-Saxon. To King Alfred, and the many writings of Alfric, we are indebted for the finest specimens of Anglo-Saxon spoken and written in England in their days.

Persons who are desirous of tracing the origin of Anglo-Saxon, or of comparing it with kindred dialects, must first go to the Old-Saxon, the Low-German spoken by those who remained in the old home of the Jutes, the Angles, and the Saxons. No written specimen of the language spoken by these Old-Saxons is extant, but there is, in a collateral dialect, a very fine poem, written in the ninth century, which is entitled

Heliand, Healer or Saviour. While some of the Low-German race migrated to England, others passed to the lower Rhine and settled there. This poem being written in the dialect of these Rhenish Old-Saxons, and the latter being akin to the Anglo-Saxon, there can be no question as to its vast importance in the study of the language which is the foundation of our own. Recourse may then be had to other works in Low-German. High-German, Icelandic, Danish, Norwegian and Swedish may then be consulted, and carried back to their Oriental source. None of the German or Scandinavian dialects have writings antedating those of the Anglo-Saxons, except the Germanic in the Moeso-Gothic Gospels of Ulphilas, published in 370, and some Icelandic. A zealous attempt, tracing the origin of the English, Germanic, and Scandinavian languages and nations, with a sketch of their early literature, and short chronological specimens of Anglo-Saxon, Friesic, Flemish, Dutch, German, from the Moeso-Goths to the present time, Icelandic, Norwegian and Swedish, and tracing the progress of these languages and their connection with the modern English, was made by Rev. Joseph Bosworth, in 1848. All interested in such knowledge will find themselves abundantly repaid by an examination of this learned scholar's investigations, as shown in the work to which reference has just been made.

LESSONS IN ANGLO-SAXON.

Anglo-Saxon Letters—Their Names.

The Anglo-Saxon alphabet has twenty-four letters, namely, *a, æ, b, c, d, dh, e, f, g, h, i, l, m, n, o, p, r, s, t, th, u, w (vv), x* and *y*. All but three, *dh, th, w*, are Roman characters, the variations from the common form being cacographic fancies.

No difficulty is experienced by German-speaking students in calling the letters by their proper appellations as their resemblance to the German names, excepting in three instances, is very intimate and striking. *Ah, ä, bay, cay, day, edh, ay, ef, gay, hah, ee, el, em, en, o, pay, er, es, tay, thorn, oo, wên, ex, ypsilon*, express very accurately their syllabic representation.

An accent is found in Anglo-Saxon manuscripts, but in none so regularly used as to become an objective feature of Anglo-Saxon text. It is found oftenest over a long vowel; sometimes over a vowel of peculiar sound, not long; seldom, except over syllables requiring a stress of voice. There are times, it seems, when nothing but stress is indicated. English editors represent it mostly by an acute accent, but the Germans generally print Anglo-Saxon with a circumflex over all single long sounds in the root of words, and an acute over the diphthongs; as *brôder, freónd*. In this book, an acute accent is used over all long vowels and diphthongs.

Sounds of Vowels.

A short or unaccented is sounded like *a* in *man*. It is often found in the final syllables of inflections, and generally appears in the radix before a doubled consonant, or two different consonants.

The radical short *a* can only stand before a single consonant, and *st, sc,* when this single consonant and these double letters are followed in the inflections by *a, o, u* in nouns; *a, o, u, e* in adjectives; and *a, o, u,* and *ia* in verbs.

Specially important are the remarks contained in the last paragraph in the declension of words, for, monosyllables, ending in a single consonant, in *st,* or *sc,* reject the *e* from the short *æ,* and leave the short *a* alone, whenever, in declining, the consonant or consonants happen to be followed by *a, o, u* in nouns, and *a, o, u, e* in adjectives.

It must be remembered, then, that a short *a* cannot stand in a word. 1. When it ends in a single consonant, that is, when no inflection of *a, o, u* in nouns follow, as in *stæf.* 2. When in nouns a single consonant is followed by *e,* as in *wæter.* 3. When the word has any other double consonants than *st, sc,* even though followed by *a, o, u,* as in *cræft.* 4. In contracted words, when *æ* is not in the last syllable, as in *æcer.*

When the *á* is accented it is then long, and words containing this long or accented *á* are now represented by English terms with the vowel sounded like *o* in *no* and in *bone.* Hám *home,* bán, *bone,* án, *one,* stán, *stone,* have either the same or an analogous meaning in English and Anglo-Saxon. Sometimes the accented or long *á* is represented in English by *oa,* as ác, *an oak,* gád, *a goad,* lám, *lome.* Occasionally, *á* becomes *oe* in English, as dá, *a doe,* fá, *a foe,* rá, *a roe,* but the *oe* in these words has the sound of *o* in *no.* The same may be said of *oa* in *boar.* Hence, it appears that the Anglo-Saxon *á* is represented by the modern English *o, oa,* and *oe,* which have the sound of *o* in *no,* or *bone.* The long *á* is often changed into *æ,* as *lár,* lore, *læran,* to teach.

-*A,* added to words, denotes *a person, an agent, an actor,* hence,—All names ending in *a* are masculine, and make the genitive in *an,* as from *cum,* come (thou), *cuma,* a person who comes, or a guest, is derived. Some words, denoting inanimate things, terminate in *a,* and these words, having the same declension as those which signify *persons* or *actors,* are also masculine. *A-* is an inseparable prefix, denoting negation, determination or opposition, as *from, out, away*. *A-* does not always appear to alter the signification, but generally, however, it adds some little force or intensity to the original meaning of the word to which it is joined.

Anglo-Saxon words, containing the short or unaccented vowel *e*, are often represented by modern English words of the same meaning, having the sound of *e* in *fed*, as *nett, bedd, webb*. Before a double consonant, two different consonants, or one or two consonants when followed by a long or final vowel, the short *e* is most generally used.

Words containing the long or accented *é* are very frequently represented by English terms of the same meaning, and have the sound of *e* in *meet*. Long *é* is used, as in *thé*, at the end of words, and before the consonants *l, m, n, r, s, t, d, dh, c, g* and *f*.

-*E*, in the ending of nouns, denotes a person, as *hyrde*, a shepherd, from *hyrdan*, to guard. It is also used to form nouns denoting inanimate objects, as *cyle*, cold, but these are mostly derived from verbs, and hence are masculine; but, when they come from adjectives, they are feminine. Final *e* is the termination of derivative adjectives, and is also the usual letter by which adjectives ending in a consonant become adverbs.

Unaccented *i* has the sound of *i* in *fin*, as is evidenced by the following Anglo-Saxon words which have the same meaning in English as in Saxon:—*tin, dim, scip, wit, ribb, milc*, etc.

I long has the sound of *i* in *fine*, as in the cognate words, *tine, win, dic, hwil*.

The verbal termination *ian*, or with a consonant before the *i*—*cian, gian, nian, sian*—is the most simple and universal. It is joined to various parts of speech, but especially to nouns and pronouns. These verbs almost always make the perfect tense in *ode*, and the perfect participle in *od*. Verbs thus formed from adjectives are generally neuter, but they become active by prefixing *ge*, as *lytl*, little, *lytlian*, to become little, *gelytlian*, to diminish.

I and *ie* are often used for *g*, *ge*, *y*, and *e*.

Short *o*, in Anglo-Saxon, has probably the sound of *o* in *for*, as *corn, horn, loc*.

O, accented, was sounded in Saxon as *oo* in *cook*, as proved by the cognate words *cóc, bóc, gód, cól, fót*, etc.

Final *o* is chiefly used to form the names of qualities from adjectives, as *menigeo*, the many, multitude. Nouns ending in *o* are feminine and indeclinable, but they often end in *u*, and in that case have a regular feminine declension.

A few nouns in final *o* are neuter, and make the genitive in *ewes*, as *ealo*, ale, genitive *ealewes*.

The unaccented *u* in Anglo-Saxon had most probably the sound of *u* in *fun*, as testified to by *butt, dun, munc, up*, etc., which have the same meaning in English as in Saxon.

Long *ú* had the sound of *ou*, or *ow*, in *about, foul, house, town*, as *fúl, hú, mús, nú, úre*, Saxon words which have the same signification, as their English representatives most plainly show.

Eo are sometimes used for *u*, as *sweord, swurd*, and *y* for *ú*, as *swytol, swútol*. In later times, *u* was employed for *f* and *v*, as *lune, lufe, Dauid, David*.

Some few names ending in *u* are masculine or neuter, but they are mostly feminine, and form the names of qualities from adjectives.

Short *u* or accented Anglo-Saxon *y* had the *y* sounded as in *mystery, duty*, as *tynder, hyp, syn, mynster*, which are represented by modern English words of like signification.

The long or accented *y* had the sound of *y* in *type, sky*, as will be evident from the following cognate words: *lýs, fýr, hýd, brýd*, and *lýf*.

Unaccented *i* is often used for *y*, and long *i* for *y*; as *listan, litel, minster* for *lystan, lytel, mynster*, and *fir, brid, lif*, for *fýr, brýd, lýf*.

SOUNDS OF CONSONANTS.

The consonants have their common English sounds: *c*, like *k*, always; *ch*, like *kh*, in *work-house;* *cw*, like *qu;* *dh*, like English *th* in a similar word, as *ódher*, other, *dódh*, doth; *g*, like *g* in *go*, always; *h*, very distinct; *hw*, like *wh* in New England; *i* (=*j*), before a vowel, like *y;* *s*, like *s* in *so;* *t*, like *t* in *to;* *th*, like *th* in *thin;* *w*, like *w;* *wl*, *wr*, and final *w* nearly close the lips; *x*, like *ks*.

ACCENT—ITS USE.

The primary accent is on the first syllable of every word: as, *bród'-her*, brother; *un'-cúdh*, uncouth.

Proper prefixes in verbs and participles take no primary accent; such are *á, an, and, æt, be, bi, ed, far, ful, ge, geord, in, mis, ódh, of, ofer, on, or, tó, thurh, un, under, widh, widher, ymb, ymbe: an-gin'-nan*, begin; *on-geán'*, again. The syllable after the prefix assumes the accent.

Derivatives from nouns, pronouns, or adjectives, retain their accent. Such are all verbs in *and-, ed-, or-*, found in Anglo-Saxon poetry, and many adverbs in *un-*, etc.

Compounds, formed of adverbs and verbs, retain their accent. Such are these with *æfter, bi, big, efen, eft, fore, ford, from, fram, hider, mid, midher, gegn, geán, gén, tó, up, út, wel*.

The inseparable prefixes *á-, be-* (*bi-*), *for-, ge-*, are unaccented; as, *á-lýs'-ing*, redemption.

A secondary accent may fall in the tone syllable of the lighter part of a compound or on a suffix; as, *ó-fer-cum'-an*, overcome.

EUPHONIC CHANGES.

Gemination is the doubling of a letter. When final, or next to a consonant, it is simplified, *mm* changing to *mb, nn* to *nd, ss* to *st, ii* to *ig, nn* to *up:* as, *timbr* for *timmr*, timber; *spindl* for *spinnl*, spindle; *lufast* for *lufass*, lovest; *lufige* for *lufie*, love; *bearupes* for *bearuues*, grove. Double *g* is written *cg*, and double *f*, *bb*.

Umlaut is the assimilation of a vowel by the vowel of the succeeding syllable: *a-umlaut* changes *i* to *e* (*eo*), *u* to *o*; *i-umlaut, a* to *e, u* to *y, ea* to *y, eo* to *y, á* to *ǽ, ó* to *é, ú* to *ý, eá* to *ý, eó* to *ý; u-umlaut, a* to *ea* (*o*), i to *eo*. The *i* which produces *i-umlaut* is often changed to *e* or dropped: as, *man,* plural *men,* from *meni; fót,* plural *fét,* feet, from *féti.*

Breaking is the change of one vowel to two by a consonant. *G, c,* and *ac* may break a following *a* to *ea, o* to *eo, i* to *ie, á* to *eá, ó* to *eó; l, r* and *h* may break a preceding *a* to *ea, i* to *eo* (*io*), *ie*: as, *geaf,* gave; *sceó,* shoe; *sealm,* psalm; *hleator,* laughter; *meolc,* milk.

Shifting is the weakening of a letter not produced by other letters: *a* to *æ, ǽ* to *é, eá* and *eó* to *é,* etc.; *dæg,*from *dag,* day.

NOUNS—THEIR DECLENSION.

There are two classes of declensions of Anglo-Saxon nouns:—*Strong,* those which have sprung from vowel stems, and *weak,* that which has sprung from stems in *an.* Of the four declensions, the first, second and third are distinguished by the genitive singular ending in *es, e,* and *a,* respectively, and the fourth by its termination in *an.*

Strong nouns have all masculines of the first or third declension; all feminines of the second or third, and all neuters of the first.

Abstract nouns have their gender controlled by the terminations. In derivatives, the feminine gender prevails, while compound nouns follow the gender of the last part.

Names of males, of the moon, and of many weeds, flowers, winds, are *masculine.* Nouns representing names of females, of the sun, and of many trees, rivers, and soft and low musical instruments, are *feminine. Neuter* nouns are names of wife, child, as well as diminutives, many general names, and words made an object of thought.

Epicene nouns have one grammatical gender, but are used for both sexes. Names of mammalia, except a few little timid ones, are masculine. Large and fierce birds are masculine; others, especially singing-birds, are feminine; large fishes are masculine, small, feminine; insects are feminine.

While in English there are but three cases, in Anglo-Saxon there are six. The nominative and vocative are always alike; the nominative, accusative, and vocative are alike in all plurals, and in the singular of all neuters and strong masculines. The genitive plural ends always in *á* or *ená*, and the dative and instrumental always in *um* (*on*).

Names of women in *u* or a consonant are strong, those in *e* or *a* are weak; while those of men in *u*, *e* or a consonant are strong, and those in *a* are weak.

Adjectives.—Their Degrees.

Adjectives, in Anglo-Saxon, have one set of strong and one set of weak endings for each gender. The latter are used when the adjective is preceded by the definite article or some word analogous thereto. Hence, there are two declensions: the *definite* and the *indefinite*.

Degrees of quantity or quality in adjectives are shown by comparison. They are regularly compared by suffixing to the theme of the primitive *ir*, *er* or *or* for the theme of the comparative, and *ist*, *est* or *ost* for that of the superlative.

Verbs.—Their Attributes.

Verbs have two voices. The *active* represents the subject as acting, the *passive* as affected by the action. The *active* has inflective endings for many forms, the *passive* only for a participle. Other passive forms help this participle with the auxiliary verbs *eom* (*am*), *beón*, *wesan*, *weordhan*. There is, however, a middle voice, which represents the subject as affected by its own action; but, as this is expressed in Anglo-Saxon by adding pronouns, no paradigms are necessary.

There are six moods. The *indicative* states or asks about a fact; the *subjunctive* a possibility; the *imperative* commands or entreats; the *infinitives* (and *gerunds*) are substantives, and the *participles* adjectives. Certain forms of possibility are expressed by auxiliary modal verbs with the infinitive, and these are conveniently called a *potential* mode.

Five tenses, *present, imperfect, future, perfect* and *pluperfect*, are found in the language. The present and imperfect have tense stems; the future is expressed by the present, or by the aid of *sceal* (shall) or *wille* (will); the perfect by help of the present of *habban* (have) or, with some intransitives, *béon* (be), *wesan* or *weordhan* (be); the pluperfect by the aid of the imperfect of *habban, béon, wesan*, or *weordhan*.

Verbs are classified for conjugation by the stems of the imperfect tense. *Strong verbs* express tense by varying the root vowel; *weak verbs* by composition. Strong verbs in the imperfect indicative singular first person have the root vowel *unchanged*, or changed by accent, which is called *progression*, or by *contraction* with old reduplication. There are six conjugations. No change is manifest in the root vowel in the first conjugation; the second, third and fourth are varied by accent or progression; the fifth by contraction, and the sixth by composition.

Since all the names derivable from verbs, with which we have to deal in the present work, are concerned with the present infinitive, present indicative of the first person, and perfect participle, it is unnecessary to enter into any elaboration of the verbal inflections. What is needful to be said will appear in its proper place in the derivations.

NAMES—THEIR DERIVATION.

A.

Abbott. *Abbud*, an abbot, chief governor, father, or superior of an abbey, convent, or monastery.

Adkin. *Eard*, earth; *cyn*, kin, kind. Earth-relative. Akin, contraction of the name.

Albert. *Eal*, all; *beorht*, bright. All bright; illustrious.

Alder. *Aldor*, life.

Alice. *Ætheling*, corrupted into Adeline, thence into Alice. A princess.

Alison. *Alice*, a princess; *sun*, a son. Son of Alice; son of a princess.

All. *Eal*, all, every, whole.

Allingham. *Alling-hám*, from *All;* *ing*, descendant; *hám*, home. Home of Alling; home of the offspring of All.

Apgar. *Abgar*, Irish *ab*, a father; *gár*, a spear, a dart. Defender of the father.

Appleton. *Æppel-tún*, from *æppel*, an apple; *tún*, town. An apple garden; an orchard.

Askin. *Æscwine*, from *æsc*, an ash-tree, ash, ash-spear, a ship, a man; *wine*, a friend. Boats were made of ash, hence a small ship, a skiff. Among the northern nations it was supposed that the first man was made out of ash: hence the word came to signify a man, the chief of men, a leader. Æsc, the name of Hengist's son, was a leader.

Ashton. *Æsc*, Æsc; *tún*, town. The town of Æsc.

Asquith. *Æsc*, Æsc; *cyth*, home. The home of Æsc; the home of the ash.

B.

Bancroft. *Bán*, pronounced *bawn*, bone; *croft*, a level tract of country, an enclosed field. A graveyard.

Bald. *Báld,* bold, courageous, honorable.

Baldwin. *Báld,* pronounced *bawld,* bold; *win,* a contest, battle. Bold in battle. Baldewin, Boldwin, less ancient forms of the name.

Banham. *Bán,* bone; *hám,* home. The bone-home; the grave.

Barton. *Bere,* corn; *tún,* town. A corn-farm; a corn-village; a grange.

Beal. *Beal,* evil. Beale, identical in derivation.

Beda. *Beada,* counsellor, persuader, exhorter.

Bedell. *Bædel,* a beadle. A messenger belonging to a court, or public body; a petty officer in a church.

Beck. *Béc,* or *bóc,* a book. Beck, Bock, Bok, analogous names.

Beckingham. *Beck,* Beck; *ing,* a son; *hám,* home. The home of the son of Beck.

Bishop. *Bisccop,* a bishop, a high-priest, a prelate.

Blake. *Blæc,* black. Black, of like parentage.

Boardman. *Bórd,* a shield; *man,* a man. A warrior; a knight.

Brice. *Brice,* fragment, rupture, violation, use, service. Bryce, only another spelling of the same.

Brock. *Bróc,* a brook, a rivulet. Brook, Brooke, from the same root.

Brooks. *Brook,* Brook; *s* for *sun,* son. Son of Brook.

Bronson. *Brown,* from *brún,* brown, and *sun,* son. Son of Brown.

Bront. *Bront,* raging, streaming. Brunt, doubtless, from the same source. Some, perhaps, would consider it a corruption of *burnt,* made brown.

Browning. *Brown,* Brown; *ing,* a descendant. Descendant of Brown.

Burn. *Byrne,* burning, a coat of mail, a corselet.

Burr. *Búr,* a chamber, a bower. Perhaps, from *beorg,* or *beorh,* a hill.

Burwick. *Búr,* a chamber; *wic,* a dwelling, village, camp. The guest-chamber.

C.

Caster. *Ceaster* (Latin *castra,* a camp), a city. Chester, from the same derivation.

Caton. Anglo-Saxon for Cato, the Greek for downwards.

Chapman. *Cépman,* a merchant, a trader. Ceapman, in Chaucer's day.

Chichester. Originally, *Cicester,* the equivalent of *cyren-ceaster,* or *cyrn-ceaster;* from *cyren,* new wine; *ceaster,* a city, fort, castle, town. Castle of new wine.

Clark. *Clerc,* Latin *clericus,* a clerk. Clarke, similarly derived.

Cliffe. *Clif,* a crag, an overhanging rock. Cliff, another form of the name.

Clifford. *Cliffe,* Cliffe; *ford,* a stream, a current. Cliffe's ford.

Codman. *Codd,* scrip, satchel, small bag; *man,* a man. A cashier; a banker.

Coke. *Cóc,* a cook. Cook, Cooke, analogous forms.

Compton. *Comp* for *comb,* a valley; *tún,* town. A valley-town.

Cope. *Cop,* a cap, hood, or cloak.

Copp. *Copp,* the head, top, apex, a cup.

Coulter. *Colter,* a colter, a knife, a dagger. Colter, the commoner form of the name.

Cox. *Cokes,* from *cóc,* cook; *sun,* son. The son of Coke, or Cooke. Coxe, of kindred significance.

Cumberland. *Combra,* of valleys; *land,* land, ground, earth, field, region, country. A region of valleys.

Cunningham. *Cunning,* experience; *hám,* home. A home of art and letters.

Cunnington. *Cunning,* experience; *tún,* town. A cunning town; an enterprising town.

Cuthbert. *Cúth,* known, certain, familiar, domestic; *beorht,* brightness, a glistening, light, sight, glance. Known brightness; familiar glance.

D.

Dade. *Dǽd*, deed, exploit, achievement.

Dadaker. *Dead*, dead; *æcer*, acre. An acre set apart for the dead. Dedaker, of analogous derivation.

Dager. *Dagor*, day.

Dalton. *Dál*, a dale, a small valley; *tún*, a town. A valley-town.

Dalrymple. *Dál*, a vale; *hrympelle*, a wrinkle, a ripple, a fold. An undulating vale.

Davies. *Davie*, diminutive for David; *sun*, son. Son of Davie. Davis, abbreviation of the same.

Dodd. *Dead*, dead.

Dunham. *Dunholm*, from *dún*, mountain; *holm*, an island. A mountainous island.

Durham. *Deór*, beast; *hám*, home, dwelling. A park; a dwelling for wild animals. Dercham, an earlier form of the name.

Dyer. *Dýre*, dear, costly, precious.

E.

Earl. *Earl*, noble, earl, man. Earle, of similar significance.

Edgar. *Eard*, earth; *gár*, dart, spear. Earth-dart; defender of the earth.

Edmund. *Eard*, earth; *mund*, hand. Earth-hand; tiller of the soil.

Edmunds. *Edmund*, Edmund; *s* for *sun*, son. Son of Edmund. Edmundson, Edmondson, lengthened forms of the same name.

Edson. *Eard*, earth; *sun*, son. Son of earth. Edison, the same word, but of more euphonious pronunciation.

Edward. *Eard*, earth; *weard*, guardian, watchman. An earth-protector.

Edwards. *Edward*, Edward; *sun*, son. Son of Edward.

Egbert. *Ecg*, edge; *beorht*, glance. Side-glance.

Eldrick. *Eal*, all; *rice*, rich, powerful. All-powerful. Eldridge, doubtless, from the same roots.

Elmer. *Ethelmer*, from *éthel*, a home; *mǽre*, illustrious. An illustrious home.

Ely. *E'lig*, from *él*, eel; *ig*, an island. Eel-island.

Emery. *Earm*, arm; *rice*, powerful. Mighty in battle. Emmery, Emory, cognate forms.

Emerson. *Emery*, Emery; *sun*, son. Son of Emmery.

Engle. *Engel*, an angel. Ingle, a slightly modified phase of the name.

Englebert. *Engel*, an angel; *beorht*, brightness. An angel of brightness.

Erwin. *Eard*, earth; *wine*, friend. Earth-friend. Ervin, Ervine, names of similar import.

Eton. *Eten*, a giant. Eaton, the accepted spelling.

F.

Fager. *Fæger*, beauty, fair, beautiful.

Farnham. *Fearn*, a fern; *hám*, habitation. Habitation of the fern.

Farr. *Farr*, a wild boar.

Farrington. *Farringdún*, from *fearn*, a fern; *g*, for the sake of euphony; *dún*, a hill. A hill of fern.

Fell. *Fell*, gall, anger, death, a skin, cruel, severe.

Field. *Feald*, a field, a fold.

Fielding. *Field*, Field; *ing*, descendant. Descendant of Field.

Finch. *Finc*, a small bird. Fink, Finck, Fenke, kindred forms.

Firman. *Fir*, the living, chief of living beings, man; *man*, man. The living man.

Fisk. *Fisc*, a fish. Fiske, the more common name.

Fleming. *Fleming*, a runaway, a banished man. Flemming, another spelling.

Fletcher. *Flett*, house, chamber, bed, hall, palace; *cher* for *er*, a personal suffix. A companion; a bed-fellow; a prince.

Fogg. *Fog*, agreement, compact.

Foote. *Fót,* a foot.

Forsyth. *Forthsith,* death. Forsythe, another spelling of the name.

Fotheringham. *Fother,* a load, a burden; *ing,* son; *hám,* dwelling. The home of the son of burden.

Foulk. *Folc,* folk, people. Foulke, an equivalent.

Frederick. *Freá,* a lord; *ricc,* rich, powerful. A mighty lord.

Frick. Possibly a corruption of *Frig,* pronounced *Freeg,* the goddess of love, the Saxon Venus, and wife of Odin.

G.

Gall. Irish *gaill,* genitive of *gall,* stranger; *tún,* town. Town of the stranger. Gault, of similar derivation.

Galvin. Irish *gaill,* of the stranger; *vin* for *wine,* friend. Friend of the Gall, the stranger.

Gate. *Geát,* a gate.

Gates. *Gate,* Gate; *s* for *sun,* son. Son of Gate.

Giddings. *Gidding,* from *gidd,* song, divination; *ing,* descendant; *s* for *sun,* son. Son of a descendant of song.

Gilbert. Irish *giolla,* a servant; *beorht,* bright. A witty servant.

Gilling. *Gill,* Gill; *ing,* son. Son of Gill; son of a servant.

Gillingham. *Gilling,* Gilling; *hám,* home. The home of Gilling; the home of the son of Gill.

Gipson. *Gilp,* glory; *sun,* son. The son of glory. Gibson, of like derivation.

Gladwin. *Glæd,* pleased; *wine,* a friend. A happy friend.

Glenning. *Glen,* a valley; *ing,* descendant. Son of Glenn; son of a valley.

Godfrey. *Gód,* good; *freá,* lord. A beneficent master.

Goodacre. *Gód,* God; *æcer,* acre. God's acre.

Goodwin. *Gód,* good; *wine,* a friend, a benefactor. Godwin, of similar signification.

Gould. *Gold,* a precious metal.

Graff. *Græf*, a grave. A ditch; a moat; a fosse. Groff, of like derivation.

Graham. *Græg*, gray ; *hám*, home. A weather-beaten home. Gramm, most probably a corruption of the same.

Grave. *Græf*, a grave.

Graves. *Grave*, Grave ; *sun*, son. Son of Grave. Greaves, Greves, Grieves, modifications of the name.

Gregg. *Græg*, gray. Grigg, corruption of the name.

Gregson. *Græg*, gray ; *sun*, son. Son of Gregg. Grayson, the same in another form.

Grindler. *Grindel*, a clog ; *er* for Irish *fear*, a man. The wearer of a wooden shoe.

Grindrod. *Grund*, ground ; *rod*, a rod. Divining-rod.

Grund. *Grund*, ground.

Grunder. *Grund*, ground ; *er* for *fear*, man. A farmer.

Guilford. *Gild*, tribute ; *ford*, a stream. Stream-tribute ; ferry-toll.

Gummery. *Guma*, man ; *rice*, kingdom. Kingdom of man.

Guthrie. *Gúth*, fight, war ; *rice*, kingdom. Kingdom of sin.

H.

Haeseler. *Hæsel*, a hat ; *er*, a personal suffix. A hatter.

Hamill. *Hám*, home ; *il*, a hedgehog. Home of the hedgehog.

Hamilton. *Hamill*, Hamill ; *tún*, farm. Farm of Hamill.

Hamlet. *Hám*, home ; *let*, implying diminutiveness. An humble home.

Hammond. *Hám*, house ; *mund*, hand. A house-hand ; a servant.

Hampshire. *Hám*, or *hamp*, home ; *scire*, shire, district, county, stewardship, charge, business. Home-district. Hampsher, corruption of the name.

Hampton. *Ham*, or *hamp*, home ; *tún*, town. Hometown.

Hampstead. *Hám-stede*, from *hám*, home, and *stede*, place. Homestead.

Henric. Hám, home; *ric,* rule, kingdom. Home-rule. Hamrick, from the same roots.

Hanrack. Hean, poor, needy, humble, worthless, despised; *ric,* a cook. A needy cook.

Hard. Heard, hard, stubborn, unsubmissive.

Harding. Hard, Hard; *ing,* son. Descendant of Hard.

Harold. Har, hoar, gray with age; *eald,* old. A veteran chief.

Harper. Hearpere, a harper.

Hart. Heort, a hart, a stag.

Hartford. Heort, a hart; *ford,* a ford, a stream, a current. The hart's ford, or the place of its crossing the stream.

Hatfield. Heat-feld, from *hæt,* heat; *feld,* a field, a plain. An open, sun-scorched plain.

Hebel. Hebel, thread of the shuttle.

Heber. Heber, a goat.

Hebener. Heben, heaven; *er,* indicative of a personal suffix. An inhabitant of heaven.

Helmbald. Helm, helmet, cover, protector; *bald,* bold, stout. A stout protector.

Herbert. Here, a host; *beorht,* bright, shining. An illustrious host.

Hild. Hild, battle.

Hildebrand. Hild, battle; *brand,* a brand, a torch. A battle-torch.

Hildeburn. Hild, battle; *bryne,* a burning, scorching, heat, fire. Battle-heat.

Hoar. Hár, hoar, white, or gray with age.

Holdcraft. Hold, kind, devoted, faithful, friendly; *craft,* craft, contrivance, skill, employment, strength, power, talent, ability, excellence, virtue. Faithful employment; friendly power.

Holme. Holm, a sea, a billow.

Holmes. Holme, Holme; *s* for *son,* son. Son of Holme.

Holt. Holt, a grove, a forest.

Hope. Hopa, hope.

Hopkin. *Hopa*, hope; *cyn*, kind, kin. A relative of Hope.

Hopkinson. *Hopkin*, Hopkin; *sun*, son. Son of Hopkin. Hopkins, an abbreviation of the name.

Humphrey. *Hám*, home; *freá*, lord, protector. Defender of home.

Humphreys. *Humphrey*, Humphrey; *s* for *sun*, son. Son of Humphrey. Humphries, Humphriss, Humphrys, kindred names.

Huntting. *Hunt*, Hunt; *ing*, a descendant. Son of Hunt.

Hurlock. *Hár*, hoary; *loc*, lock of hair. A hoary lock of hair. Harlock, a less common name, but one more closely related to the parent words.

Husband. *Hús*, house; *bond*, bound, tied. House-bound; house-tied: hence, one that is bound to the house.

Hustin. *Hústing*, a place of council.

Huston. *Hús*, house; *tún*, a farm. House-farm; kitchen-garden.

Huxley. *Huxlic*, from *hucs*, *hucx*, or *husc*, irony, slight, contempt, reproach, and *lic*, like. Ironical-like; disgraceful; contemptuous; vile.

I.

Idell. *I'del*, idle, vain, empty, useless.

Inskip. *In*, an inn, a dwelling; *scipe*, denoting form, condition, state, office, dignity. An innkeeper; a landlord. Inskeep, a kindred name.

Irwin. *Eard*, earth; *wine*, friend. Earth-friend. Irvin, Irvine, from the same roots.

Irving. *Irvin*, Irvin; *ing*, a descendant. Son of Irvin.

Isdell. *I's*, ice; *dǽl*, a dale, a small valley. Ice-dale.

Isenberg. *I'sen*, iron; *beorg*, mountain. Iron-mountain.

Isenberry. *I'sen*, iron; *berry*, corruption of *beorg*, or *beorh*, mountain. Iron-mountain.

Isham. *I's*, ice; *hám*, house, dwelling. Ice-house.

J.

Jackson. *Jack*, nickname for John; *sun*, son. Son of Jack. Jacques, French for James, is the most probable derivation of Jack.

Jameson. *Jame*, James; *sun*, son. Son of James.

Jamieson. *Jamie*, James; *sun*, son. Son of Jamie; son of James. Jamison, Jemison, Jimison, kindred terms, founded upon nicknames common to James in parts of Scotland and Ireland.

Jenkin. *Jen*, abbreviation for Jennie, Jane, John; *cyn*, kin, kind. Related to Jennie, Jane, John.

Jenkinson. *Jenkin*, Jenkin; *sun*, son. Son of Jenkin. Jenkins, abbreviated form of same.

Jenks. *Jen*, Jennie; *k* for *cyn*, kin; *s* for *sun*, son. Son of a relative of Jennie.

Johnson. *John*, Hebrew word signifying "gracious gift of God;" Anglo-Saxon *sun*, son. Son of John.

Jonson. *Jon*, contraction of *John*, John; *sun*, son. Son of John.

Jones. *Jon*, John; *s* for *sun*, son. Son of John.

K.

Keith. *Cith*, pronounced *keeth*, a germ, sprig, blade.

Kemp. *Cempa*, a young soldier, a warrior, champion, novice.

Kendall. *Cyn*, kin, kindred, race, tribe, nation, kind; *dæl*, dale, valley. Valley-kindred. Kindell, derivable from the same roots.

Kenworthy. *Cyn*, kindred; *weorthe*, worthy, honorable. Worthy kindred.

Kenyon. *Cyn*, nation, people; *ycong*, young. Young nation.

Kertell. *Kertl*, a woman's garment, a vest, mantle, kirtle.

Keyser. *Káser*, an emperor. Keiser, of similar origin.

Kim. *Cim*, feet, or bases of a pillar.

Kimball. *Cimbal,* cymbal. Kemble, Kimble, Kimple, analogous names.

Kissel. *Cystel,* a chestnut.

Kisterbock. *Cist,* choice; *bóc,* a volume, a book. A choice volume.

Kitt. *Kitte,* a vessel, a bottle.

Kitson. *Kitt,* Kitt; *sun,* son. Son of Kitt. Kitts, abbreviation of the same.

L.

Lambeth. *Lamb-hyth,* from *lamb,* lamb, and *hyth,* measure, gain, profit. Lamb's measure.

Lambert. *Lamb,* Lamb; *beorht,* brightness. The Lamb of Glory.

Lancaster. *Land,* ground, earth, field; *ceaster,* a camp, a castle, city, fort. An earth-fort.

Landreth. *Land,* field; *rithe,* a well, a fountain, a river. A field-well; a spring.

Lever. *Leófra, lever,* comparatives of *leóf, leef,* dear, agreeable. More agreeable; more pleasing.

Levering. *Lever,* Lever; *ing,* offspring. Son of Lever.

Lea. *Liga,* a flame.

Lester. *Lædhceaster,* from *lædhe,* hateful, unpleasant, loathsome, and *ceaster,* a city. A loathsome city. Leister, of like derivation.

Limbert. *Lim,* limb, member; *beorht,* brightness. Limb-brightness.

Liming. *Lim-ing,* from *lim,* limb; *ing,* implying action, originating from. Limning; painting.

Lind. *Lind,* linden, or lime-tree; also, what was made of lime-wood—shield, buckler, banner.

Linden. *Linden,* made of lime-tree.

Lindsey. *Lindes-ig,* from *lindes,* genitive of *lind,* lime-tree, and *ig,* an island. The island of the lime-tree. Lindsay, another form of spelling.

Lipp. *Lippe*, lip.

Lipkiss. *Lippe*, lip; *cyss*, kiss. Lip-kiss.

Lippincott. *Lippe*, lip, genitive *lippan*, of lip; *coth*, disease, malady. Lip disease.

Lipson. *Lippe*, Lipp; *sun*, son. Son of Lipp.

Lipton. *Lipp*, Lipp; *tún*, home. Home of Lipp.

Litchfield. *Licced-feld*, from *licced*, licked, lapped, and *feld*, a field, a plain. A licked plain; a pasture-field.

Lonsdale. *Londes-dǽl*, from *londes*, genitive of *lond*, land; *dǽl*, dale, valley. Land's-dale.

Loth. *Loth*, a band.

Lothrop. *Loth*, band; *thorpe*, a village.

Lyster. *Lyster*, a favorer. Lister, of like origin.

Lytle. *Lytle*, little, small, slender.

M

Manchester. *Manig-ceaster*, from *manig*, many, much; *ceaster*, city, fort, castle, town. Many castles.

Manning. *Mann*, Mann; *ing*, offspring. Son of Mann.

Marx. *Marcs*, from *marc*, a mark; *s* for *sun*, a son. Son of Marc.

Mase. *Mase*, a whirlpool, a gulf.

Maslin. *Mǽslen*, or *maslin*, brass.

Max. *Max*, noose, mesh, net, snare.

Maxfield. *Max*, Max; *feld*, a field. Max's field.

Maxwell. *Max*, Max; *wæl*, a well. Max's well.

Meadowcroft. *Mǽdewe*, a meadow; *croft*, a small enclosed field. A meadow-field.

Mearns. *Mearn*, mourned; *s* for *sun*, son. A mourned son.

Mear. *Mere*, lake, pool, sea.

Mears. *Mear*, Mear; *s* for *sun*, son. Son of Mear.

Medlar. *Mēd*, meed, merit, reward, recompense; *lǽr*, doctrine. Reward of doctrine.

Medway. *Mǽd,* meed, meadow, trunk of a tree; *wǽg,* a wave. Meadow-wave; a river.

Meredith. *Mere,* lake, sea; *diht,* ordering, direction, predicting, foretelling. Sea-predicting.

Merscher. *Mersc-ware,* from *mersc,* marsh, fen, and *ware,* used only as a termination, denoting inhabitants, dwellers. Marshmen; fenmen.

Merton. *Meretún,* from *mere,* lake, sea; *tún,* town. Seaport; lake-port.

Metsinger. *Metssunge,* from *mettsung,* messing, food, meat; *ere,* indicating a person. A victualler; a provider. Messinger, another form of the name.

Michener. Perhaps *Micg-aern,* from *micg-an,* to water; *ærn,* a place, a secret place, a closet, a habitation, a house. An urinary; a drain.

Midding. *Midding,* a dunghill.

Middlesex. *Middel,* middle; *Sexe,* Saxons. The Middle Saxons.

Middleton. *Middel,* middle; *tún,* town. The middle town.

Mitchell. *Mycg,* a midge, a gnat; *el,* a termination denoting a person. A dwarf; a pigmy.

Monteith. *Mon,* man; *téth,* teeth. Human teeth.

Montgomery. *Munt-guman-ric,* from *munt,* mountain; *guman,* of man, genitive of *guma ; ric,* pronounced *ree,* a postfix denoting dominion, power. Mountain of man's power; acme of human greatness.

Muckle. *Mucxle,* a muscle, a shell-fish.

Mumford. *Mund-ford,* from *mund,* a contraction of *munden,* remembered, and *ford,* ford. A remembered ford.

Munce. *Munc,* a monk. Munch, Munk, of similar derivation.

Murberry. *Murberie,* possibly from *múr,* a wall, from the resemblance of the fruit in roughness to a wall, and *berie,* a berry. *Mur* itself signifies a mulberry.

Murdock. *Mere,* a sea; *docce,* a dock. A naval dock.

N.

Nabes. *Na'bb*, a face; *s* for *sun*, sun. The sun's face.

Nachtigall. *Naetegale*, nightingale, from *nuecte*, night, and *gale*, a singer. A night-singer.

Nachod. *Na'cud*, naked, uncovered.

Nadely. *Na'dl*, a needle, *lic*, like. Needle-like.

Nagele. *Na'gel*, a nail, a pin, a nail of the hand. Nagel, Nagele, Naglee, other forms of the name.

Nebeker. *Neb*, face, countenance, mouth, neb, nib, nose; *weer*, field, land, anything sown, sown corn, an acre. Face-pimples.

Nebel. *Neb*, face, countenance; *el*, termination denoting a person. Human face.

Nebhut. *Neb*, face, head, mouth; *huth*, spoil, booty, prey. Blotched countenance.

Nedel. *Nedl*, a needle.

Needham. *Nead*, need, necessity, infirmity; *häm*, home, house, dwelling, village, farm. An almshouse; an infirmary.

Neef. *Nefe*, a niece, a granddaughter. Neff, from the same root.

Nesenger. *Nesse*, a headland; *ing*, originating from; *er*, a personal suffix. One raised upon a headland.

Ness. *Nesse*, a cape. Nesz, another form of the name.

Neswanger. *Nesse*, or *næs*, a rock, support, headland, ness, cape, promontory; *wang*, a plain, field, wong, land; *er*, a personal suffix. Possessor of a rock-plain.

Neswenger. *Nesse*, rock; *wengere*, a pillow, bolster. Rock-pillow.

Nester. *Nest*, support, food, wages; *er*, a personal suffix. A supporter; a wage-earner. Nester, a kindred name.

Neth. *Neth*, wickedness, malice, cunning, hatred, strife, zeal, punishment, slaughter.

Nething. *Neth*, Neth; *ing*, offspring, descendant. Son of Neth.

Nette. *Nett*, a net.

Netterville. *Nett,* a net; *er,* a personal suffix; French *ville,* a villa, a town. A fishing-place.

Nettinger. *Nett,* a net; *ing,* expressive of action; *er,* a personal termination. A seiner; a fisherman.

Nettleton. *Netele,* a nettle; *tún,* a farm. A nettle-farm.

Newbold. *Newe,* new, late, young; *báld,* bold, courageous, honorable. Lately honorable.

Newcomb. *Newe,* new; *comb,* a valley. New valley.

Newcomet. *Newe,* new; *cometa,* a comet. A new comet.

Newell. *Ncowel,* prone, prostrate, depressed, profound, deep. Newhall, perhaps, from the same root.

Nipe. *Nip,* darkness.

Nippes. *Nipp,* Nipe; *s* for *sun,* son. Son of Nipe.

Norman. *Nor,* contraction of *north,* north; *man,* a man. North-man.

Northrop. *Nor,* north; *thorpe,* town. North town.

Norwood. *Nor,* north; *wud,* wood. Northwood.

Nye. *Nyc,* a nye, a nest.

Nyholm. *Nye,* a nest; *holm,* the deep sea, an abyss, the ocean, a river island. Nest-water; nest-island.

Nyman. *Nye,* a nest; *man,* man, or woman. Nest-woman.

Nystrom. *Nye,* a nest; *streom,* a stream. Nest-stream.

O.

Obdyke. *Ob,* off; *dic,* bank, mound. Off the bank. Opdyke, from the same roots.

Oberdick. *O'ber,* over, above; *dic,* dyke, ditch, trench, moat. Overflowing ditch.

Oberholt. *O'ber,* above; *holt,* a forest. Mountain-forest.

Ofar. *O'fer,* a margin, brink, bank, shore.

Orcutt. *Or,* free from; *coth,* disease. Free from disease.

Ord. *O'rd,* beginning, origin, author, edge, sword, battle-array.

Ordmann. O'rd, the front of an army; *mann*, man. A general; a commander.

Orfe. Orfe, cattle. Orf, Orff, of similar derivation.

Orgill. Orgel, pride, arrogance.

Orgs. Org, pride; *s* for *sun*, son. Son of pride.

Orme. Or, free from; *me*, me. Free me from.

Ormerod. Or, free from; *me*, me; *rod*, rod. Free me from the rod. Ormrod, of like import.

Ormond. Or, free from; *mond*, care, protection. Free from care; without protection.

Ormsby. Orm, Orme; *s*, sign of genitive; *b̄y*, a termination denoting habitation, dwelling. Habitation of Orme.

Ormston. Orm, genitive *Ormes*, Orme; *tūn*, house. Home of Orme.

Orth. O'rth, breathing.

Orthwein. O'rth, breathing; *wine*, a man. A living man.

Orton. Or, free from; *tūn*, house, farm, village, town. Free from the cares of home, or of the town.

Orwig. Or, free from; *wig*, warfare, battle, strife. Free from warfare.

Osbeck. O's, a hero; *bec*, a book, a volume, a writing. Hero-book; a novel.

Osborne. O's, a hero; *beorn*, chief, general, prince, king. Hero-king. Osborn, Osbourn, Osbourne, kindred names.

Osler. O's, hero; *lær*, lore, learning. Hero-lore.

Osmond. O's, hero; *mond*, hand, defence, protection, security. Hero-protection.

Osmun. O's, hero; *mund*, a hand. Heroic hand.

Osmus. O's, hero; *mūs*, mouse, flesh, muscle,. Heroic muscle.

Osner. O's, hero; *nere*, refuge, safety, preservation. Heroic preservation.

Oswald. O's, hero; *wald*, ruler, governor, lord. Heroic ruler.

Ost. Ost, East. Also, a knot, a scale.

Oster. Oster, Easter.

Overholt. *Ouer*, over; *holt*, a forest. Hill-forest.

Oxenford. *Oxen*, from *oxan*, genitive of *oxa*, an ox; *ford*, a ford. The ford of the ox. Oxford, abbreviation of same.

P.

Palen. *Pællen*, purple.

Pennington. *Pening*, a penny; *tún*, dwelling, house. A mint; a bank.

Pepper. *Peppor*, or *peopor*, pepper.

Peppercorn. *Peppor*, pepper; *corn*, corn. A peppercorn.

Pile. *Pil*, a pile, dart, pole, stake.

Pilking. *Pil*, a pile, dart; *cyng*, a king, ruler, prince. Pile-king; warrior-king.

Pilkington. *Pilking*, Pilking; *tún*, house. Home of Pilking.

Pitt. *Pitt*, a well, a hole.

Pitfield. *Pitt*, a well; *feld*, a field, pasture, plain. A plain full of excavations.

Pitkin. *Pitt*, Pitt; *cyn*, kindred, posterity, nation. Pitt's posterity.

Pitts. *Pitt*, Pitt; *s* for *sun*, son. Pitt's son; son of Pitt.

Pitman. *Pitt*, a pit, a hole, a well; *man*, a man. A man who works in a pit; a pitman.

Pittenger. *Pitt*, Pitt; *eng* for *ing*, descendant; *er*, a personal suffix. Descendant of Pitt.

Plag. *Plæga*, play, sport, pastime, wager.

Plagman. *Plæga*, play, pastime, wager; *man*, a man. Man of pleasure. Plagemann, a cognate form.

Plumly. *Plume*, a plum; *lic*, form, shape, substance. Plum-shape.

Porter. *Port*, port, haven, town, city, gate of a town; *er*, a personal suffix. A gate-keeper.

Portman. *Port*, a city; *man*, a man. A citizen.

Preston. *Preost*, a priest, presbyter, clergyman; *tún*, a house. A parsonage.

Prevost. *Præfost*, prevost, president.

Priestly. *Preost,* a priest; *lic,* like. Priest-like.
Pund. *Púnd,* a pound, a fold.
Punger. *Pung,* a purse; *er,* a personal termination. A purser.
Punt. *Punt,* a boat.
Pusey. *Púse,* a purse, a bag.
Poole. *Púl,* pronounced *pool,* a pool.
Pyle. *Pyle,* a pillow, a cushion. Pywell, perhaps, from the same root.
Pyne. *Pin,* a pine.
Pyott. *Pytt,* a pit, a well. *Piatt,* a kindred name.

Q.

Quain. *Queán,* a barren cow.
Queen. *Quén,* a wife. Quen, Quein, of similar derivation.
Quick. *Cwic,* quick, living, active.
Quicksell. *Cwic,* active; *sel,* a companion. An active companion. Quicksall, a slightly modified term.

R

Raake. *Ræce,* a rach, a setting dog.
Rackham. *Ræce,* Raake; *hám,* house. Home of Raake.
Radcliff. *Rád,* that on which one rides, a road; *clyf,* a rock, a steep descent. A road-cliff. Radcliffe, another spelling.
Raddington. *Ræding,* Reading; *tún,* town. Town of Reading.
Raddish. *Rædic,* from *ræd,* red, and *isc,* an adjective termination denoting like. Red-like; a radish. Radisch, Radish, of similar origin.
Rader. *Rád,* traveling, journeying; *er,* a personal suffix. A traveler.
Radeker. *Rǽd,* red; *æcer,* acre, field, land. A red field.
Radfield. *Rǽd,* red; *feld,* a plain. A red plain.
Radford. *Rǽd,* red; *förd,* a ford, a stream. A red ford.

Radley. *Ræd*, red; *lic*, like. Red-like.
Rae. *Rá*, a roebuck, a hart.
Raeder. *Rá-deór*, a roebuck.
Rafferty. *Ræfter*, a rafter, a perch. Doubtless, a corruption of *ræfter*, produced by removing *t*, and placing it at the end of the word.
Rahill. *Rá*, a roe, a hart; *hill*, a hill. Roe-hill.
Rahm. *Ram*, or *ramm*, a ram. Rahme, of like significance.
Rahn. *Rán*, a whale.
Rahner. *Rán*, a whale; *er*, a personal suffix. A whaler.
Raith. *Ræth*, quick. Rath, of like import.
Ramm. *Ramm*, a ram, a male sheep.
Rammage. *Ram*, a ram; *mæg*, female. The female of the ram; an ewe.
Ramsey. *Rammes-ig*, from *rammes*, genitive of *ramm*, ram; *ig*, an island. Isle of Ram. Ramsay, from the same roots.
Ramson. *Ram*, Ramm; *sun*, son. Son of Ramm.
Ranck. *Ranc*, proud, haughty, rebellious, rank, fruitful. Rancke, slightly altered form.
Rand. *Rand*, a border, rim, edge, a shield, a bosc.
Randall. *Ran*, a deer; *dál*, or *dǽl*, a dale, a valley. Deer-valley. Randell, Randle, of like parentage.
Randolph. *Ran*, plunder, *dælf*, a delving, a digging. Plunder-delving.
Rankin. *Ran*, a deer; *cyn*, kin, race, tribe, kind. Deer-tribe.
Rankins. *Rankin*, Rankin; *s* for *sun*, son. Son of Rankin. Ranken, from the same.
Ranks, *Rank*, Rank, from *ranc*, pride, and *s* for *sun*, son. Son of Rank; son of pride.
Rapp. *Ráp*, a rope, a cord.
Rapson. *Ráp*, Rapp; *sun*, son. Son of Rapp.
Rasbold. *Ræs*, a rush, an onset, an attack; *báld*, bold, audacious, courageous, honorable. A courageous attack.
Rasch. *Ræs*, a rush, an onset, an attack.

Ratcliff. *Ræt,* a rat; *clyf,* a nest. Rat-nest.

Rathfon. *Rathe,* swift, nimble, ready; *fon,* a fan. A nimble fan.

Rau. *Rawe,* head of hair.

Rauch. *Reác,* smoke, reek, vapor.

Raucher. *Reác,* smoke; *er,* a personal suffix. A smoker.

Rauchfuss. *Reác,* smoke; *fús,* ready. Smoke ready. Ready for smoke.

Rawle. *Ræw,* a corpse; *el,* denoting a person. Human corpse. Rawley, of like derivation.

Rawlings. *Rawl,* Rawl; *ingas,* sons of. Sons of Rawl, or Rawle. Rawlins, contraction of the same.

Rea. *Rea,* a padder, a highwayman, an assailant, a stroller.

Reabey. *Rea,* a highwayman; *by,* a habitation. Dwelling of a highwayman.

Reabon. *Rea,* an assailant; *bon,* fatal. A deadly assailant.

Reach. *Reác,* smoke, reek, vapor.

Read. *Read,* red. Reade, Reed, from the same root.

Reading. *Read,* Read; *ing,* offspring. Son of Read. Redding, of like origin.

Reardon. *Reardian,* to speak, converse, read.

Reaser. *Reás,* rushed; *er,* a personal suffix. A hurried person.

Reath. *Réthe,* savage, fierce, hard, severe, austere.

Reck. *Rec,* an interpreter, explainer. Recke, another spelling.

Reckefuss. *Rec,* an interpreter; *fús,* ready. A ready interpreter.

Reckless. *Recce-leas,* from *recc,* care; *leas,* free from. Free from care; careless; reckless.

Reddick. *Rædic,* a radish.

Reddington. *Redding,* Redding; *tún,* house. Home of Redding.

Redmond. *Réd,* ready; *mond,* hand. Ready hand.

Redner. *Réd,* ready; *nere,* a refuge. A ready refuge.

Reece. *Resce,* a rush.   Rees, Reese, more modernized forms of the name.

Reeh. *Reh,* a deluge.

Reehm. *Hream,* a shout.

Reel. *Reol,* a reel.

Reen. *Rén,* robbery. Perhaps, from *rén,* rain.

Reenan. *Rinan,* pronounced *reenan,* to rain.

Regelmann. *Regel,* a rule, a law, a canon; *mann,* man. A ruler; a lawyer.

Rehfuss. *Reh,* a deluge; *fús,* prompt, quick, ready. A ready deluge.

Rehm. *Rem,* cream.

Rein. *Rein,* pure, sincere, chaste.

Reinhart. *Rein,* sincere, pure, clean, chaste; *heart,* or *heort,* a heart. A pure heart.

Reining. *Rein,* Rein; *ing,* an offspring, a descendant. Son of Rein.

Reinking. *Rein,* sincere, honest; *cyng,* a king. An honest king.

Reme. *Rem,* cream.

Remington. *Rem,* Reme; *ing,* offspring; *tún,* town, dwelling. House of the son of Reme.

Rench. *Renc,* pride, arrogance.

Rendell. *Rene,* a water-course; *dál,* a dale, a valley. A valley stream.

Renecker. *Reonig,* tired, weary, sad; *er,* a personal termination.   A tired person; a mourner.

Renne. *Rene,* a course, race, life, a water-course. Sometimes written Renn.

Rennick. *Rénig,* showery, having watery eyes, blear-eyed.

Resch. *Resce,* a rush.

Ressler. *Resele,* a riddle.

Retter. *Rét,* cheerful; *er,* denoting personality. A cheerful person.

Rhawn. *Hrán,* Anglicised form would be *rhán,* a whale.

Rhea. *Ræh,* a doe, a roe.

Rheem. Hream, a shout, clamor, a crying out, wailing, hue and cry.

Rice. Rice, power, dominion, greatness, kingdom, region.

Riceman. Rice, power, greatness; *man*, a man. A man of power; a person of influence.

Richard. Rice, or *riche*, rich, powerful, mighty; *ard*, implying an ensign of office. A mighty ruler.

Richardson. Richard, Richard; *sun*, son. Son of Richard. Richards, contraction for the same.

Richmond. Riche, mighty, powerful; *mond*, a hand. A mighty hand.

Ridd. Ridda, a knight, a rider.

Rider. Rid-ere, from *ridan*, to ride, sit or rest upon, press;. *ere*, implying person. A rider; a knight. Ryder, from the same roots.

Ridge. Ricg, a stack, a back.

Ridings. Rid, Ridd; *ings*, descendants of. Sons of Ridd.

Riegel. Rige, rye; *el*, a termination denoting a person. A rye-man; a cultivator of rye; baker of rye-bread.

Riegg. Rige, rye, by transposing the positions of *g* and *e*, becomes Rieg, and this differs from the name under consideration only in the absence of the additional *g*. ·Rigg, of similar import.

Riehl. Rihel, doubtless the original, is from *rih*, hairy, rough, and *el*, denoting personality. A hairy man; a rough person. Riehle, Rile, Riley, of analogous derivation.

Riff. Rif, a womb. Rife, perhaps, from the same root.

Riffert. Rifter, a sickle, a reaper.

Rigby. Rig, Rigg; *by*, habitation. Dwelling of Rigg.

Rigger. Rigg, Rigg; *er*, implying person. One who is a Rigg.

Riggin. Rigg, Rigg; *in*, an inn, a dwelling. Rigg's inn.

Riggins. Riggin, Riggin; *s* for *sun*, son. Son of Riggin.

Riggs. Rigg, Rigg; *s* for *sun*, son. Son of Rigg.

Righter. Riht-ere, from *riht*, right, justice, law, true, just; *ere*, denoting a person. A governor; a ruler.

Rightley. *Riht-lice*, from *riht*, right, just; *lice*, like, ly. Right-like; rightly; justly.

Riling. *Ril*, Ril, Riehl; *ing*, offspring. Descendant of Riehl. Rilling, of similar significance.

Rimby. *Rim*, a number, reckoning, computation, calendar; *by*, a habitation. Home of an arithmetician.

Rimer. *Rim*, number, reckoning, calendar; *er*, a personal suffix. An arithmetician; a reckoner; an astronomer. Rimmer, derivable from the same roots.

Rind. *Rind*, the rind, bark; *fús*, ready. Prepared bark.

Rindge. *Hrincg*, or *ringe*, a ring.

Rinear. *Rin*, course, course of years, life; *ear*, ocean, sea. Life-sea; sea of life.

Rinehart. *Rin*, race, course: *heort*, the heart. Race-heart; rapid heart-action.

Ringe. *Ringe*, a ring. Ring, an abbreviated form of the name.

Ringeisen. *Ringe*, a ring; *isen*, made of iron. An iron ring.

Ringer. *Ringe*, a ring; *er*, denoting a person. Ring-maker.

Ringgold. *Ringe*, a ring; *gold*, gold. A gold ring. Ring-gold, of like derivation.

Ringle. *Ringe*, a ring; *el*, a termination denoting a person. Ring-wearer; betrothed lady.

Ringley. *Ringe*, a ring; *lice*, like, ley, ly. Ring-like.

Rink. *Rinc*, a soldier, warrior, hero, a valiant or honorable man, a man. Rinick, doubtless, a corruption of the same.

Rinker. *Rinc*, a warrior, a valiant man; *ere*, an agent. A warrior.

Rinne. *Rine*, a race, course, life.

Ripley. *Rip*, harvest, reaping; *ley*, a song. A harvest-song.

Ripp. *Rip*, harvest, reaping.

Rippel. *Rip*, harvest, reaping; *el*, denoting a person. A reaper; a harvester.

Ripperger. *Rip*, harvest; *carg*, weak, evil, wretched, idle; *ere*, a person. An idle harvester.

Rishel. *Risel*, a handle. Rishell, Rissell, other spellings.

Risdon. *Riseudan*, a jangling fellow.

Risk. *Risce*, a rush.

Risley. *Risel*, doubtless, first changed to *risle*, a handle.

Ristine. *Rist*, Rist; *ine* for *in*, an inn, a dwelling. Rist's inn.

Ritner. *Rit*, ears of corn, a heap of fruit, corn, or grain; *nere*, support, protect, refuge. Corn-support.

Ritter. *Rit*, rides; *ere*, a person. A rider.

Ritterson. *Ritter*, Ritter; *sun*, son. Son of Ritter.

Roach. *Reohche*, a roach, a thornback. Roache, Roche, Roatch, Roesch, Roetsck, cognate forms.

Roat. *Rôt*, cheerful, rejoicing, splendid, adorned.

Roat. *Roat*, Roat; *s* for *sun*, son. Son of Roat. Roetz, possibly, from the same.

Rodbard. *Reod*, red; *beard*, beard. Red beard. Robert is, in Anglo-Saxon, Rod-beard, and doubtless comes from the same roots.

Rodd. *Reod*, red.

Rodden. *Reod*, red; *ian*, indicative of a verb. Redden; make red.

Roddy. *Reod*, red; *ig*, an adjective termination. Ruddy; florid.

Rode. *Reód*, a reed.

Rodearmel. *Reod*, red; *earm*, arm; *el*, indicating a person. A red-armed person.

Rodebaugh. *Reod*, red; *bæc*, back. Red back. Rodenbaugh, of like derivation.

Rodel. *Reod*, red; *el*, a personal suffix. A person of ruddy complexion.

Rodgers. *Rodger*, from *reod*, red; *ierre*, anger, indignation, fury; and *s* for *sun*, son. Son of Rodger; son of red-visaged anger. Rodgerson is an unabbreviated form of the name, and Rogers a slight modification thereof.

Rodig. Reod, red; *ig*, an adjective termination. Ruddy.

Rodiger. Rodig, ruddy; *er*, a person. A ruddy person.

Rodine. Rod, Rode; *inne*, an inn. Rode's inn.

Rodisch. Reod, red; *isc*, an adjective termination denoting the external quality of a subject. Reddish.

Rodman. Reod, red; *mann*, man. A ruddy man; a red-complexioned person.

Rodner. Reod, red; *nere*, support, protection. A zealous support. Perhaps, from *rǽdanere*, a reader, an interpreter.

Rodney. Rǽdne, law, counsel, control, condition.

Rodrick. Roder, firmament, sky, heavens; *rice*, power, dominion, greatness, kingdom. Heavenly power. Roderick, a more closely related form.

Roe. Rá, pronounced *rō*, a roe, a doe.

Roebuck. Rá, a roe; *buc*, a buck. A roebuck.

Roeck. Roec, smoke.

Roecker. Roec, smoke; *er*, a person. A smoker.

Roeckle. Roec, smoke; *le* for *el*, denoting a person. A reeking, steaming person.

Roedel. Rá, a roe; *dǽl*, a dale, a valley. The vale of the roe. Roedell, of like significance.

Roeder. Rá-deór, a roebuck.

Roeger. Rǽge, pronounced *ro-ge*, a roe, a doe; *ere*, an agent. A roe-hunter.

Roegler. Rǽge, a roe; *lǽr*, learning. Roe-knowledge.

Roehl. Hreol, a reel. Roell, of kindred meaning.

Roehler. Hreol, a reel; *ere*, an agent. A spinster; a dancer. Roeller, from the same roots.

Roehm. Rá, roe; *hm* for *hám*, home, dwelling, habitation. Home of the roe.

Roellig. Hreol, a reel; *ig*, an adjective ending. Reeling; whirling.

Roeper. Reapere, pronounced *roepere*, a seizer, spoiler, robber.

Roerich. *Rá*, roe; *rice*, a region, a country. The region of the roebuck.

Roese. *Rose*, a rose.

Roeser. *Rose*, a rose; *ere*, an agent. A rose-grower.

Roessing. *Roess*, Roese; *ing*, offspring. Son of Roese.

Roessler. *Rose*, a rose; *lär*, lore, learning. Rose-knowledge.

Roff. *Róf*, famous, renowned, illustrious, brave.

Roffel. *Róf*, famous, illustrious; *el*, denoting a person. A famous person. Roffle, of kindred signification.

Rogge. *Räge*, pronounced *röge*, a roe, a doe.

Rohde. *Ród*, pronounced *rohd*, genitive *rohde*, rood, cross. Belonging to the cross.

Rohe. *Reoh*, rough, fierce, stormy, cruel.

Rohlfing. *Hreol*, a reel; *fing*, doubtless, a contraction of *finger*, a finger. The reel-finger. Perhaps the name is derivable from *hreol*, a reel, and *fiong*, hatred. Hatred of the reel.

Rohm. *Róm*, pronounced *Rohm*, Rome.

Rohman. *Róman*, pronounced *Rohman*, genitive of *Róm*. Belonging to Rome.

Roland. *Row*, sweet, quiet; *land*, land, ground, earth, field, region, country. Sweet land; quiet country. Rolan, Rowland, kindred terms.

Rolen. *Row*, sweet; *leán*, reward, price. Sweet reward.

Rolf. *Row*, quiet, restful; *lf* for *lif*, life. A quiet life. Roloff, Rolph, cognate terms.

Rolfing. *Rolf*, Rolf; *ing*, offspring, descendant. Son of Rolf.

Romberg. *Róm*, Rome; *beorg*, a hill fortification, citadel, defence, refuge. Citadel of Rome.

Romberger. *Róm*, Rome; *beorg-ere*, defender of a citadel. Defender of the citadel of Rome.

Rombold. *Róm*, Rome; *báld*, bold, courageous. Courageous Rome.

Romel. *Róm*, Rome; *el*, denoting a person. Citizen of Rome. Rommel, Rommell, of like origin.

Romig. *Reómig*, tired, weary.

Rommelman. *Rommel*, Romel; *man*, a servant. The servant of Romel.

Romoser. *Róm*, Rome; *O'ster*, Easter. Roman Easter.

Ronald. *Rún*, pronounced *rown*, a letter, magical character, mystery, council, meditation, conversation; *ald*, an age. An age of mystery.

Ronaldson. *Ronald*, Ronald; *sun*, son. Son of Ronald.

Ronan. *Rúnan*, pronounced *rownan*, a whisperer, a sorcerer.

Rone. *Rún*, a letter, a mystery, a council; *e*, indicating person. A man of mysteries; a sage. Roney, Rooney, from the same roots.

Rood. *Ród*, pronounced *rood*, rood, cross.

Roof. *Róf*, pronounced *roof*, top, the highest part of a house or chamber.

Roohr. *Rure*, pronounced *ruher*, a noise.

Rook. *Róc*, pronounced *rook*, a rook. Rooke, Ruch, Ruck, other spellings.

Rooks. *Rook*, Rook: *s* for *sun*, son. Son of Rook.

Rookstool. *Rook*, Rook; *stól*, pronounced *stool*, seat, chair, throne. Rook's chair or throne.

Room. *Rúm*, pronounced *rowm*, room, space, place, wide, open, spacious, ample, of good cheer or heart, august, fortunate. Roome, of like import.

Roomes. *Roome*, Room; *s* for *sun*, son. Son of Room.

Roop. *Roop, rop*, a distaff.

Root. *Rúte*, pronounced originally *rowte*, rue, a plant.

Roots. *Root*, Root; *s* for *sun*, son. Son of Root.

Roper. *Rop*, a distaff; *er*, a person. The woman who twirls the distaff.

Roppel. *Rop*, a distaff; *el*, a personal ending. A distaff.

Roray. *Rure*, pronounced *ruhr-e*, a noise, the final *e* taking the French sound of *a*.

Rorer. *Rure*, a noise; *ere*, an agent. One who makes a noise; a babbler; a prattler.

Rose. *Rose*, pronounced *raws*, a rose. Ross, Rosse, Roos, analogous forms.

Roseberry. *Rose*, a rose; *berige*, a berry. The fruit of the rose.

Roseman. *Rose*, Rose; *man*, a servant. A servant of Rose. Rosemann, of like derivation.

Rosen. *Rose*, Rose; *en*, resembling. Resembling Rose; rosy; blooming.

Rosenacker. *Rosen*, Rosen; *æcer*, acre. Rosen's acre; ground belonging to Rosen.

Rosenfeld. *Rosen*, Rosen; *feld*, field, pasture, plain. Rosen's field; a blooming pasture. Rosenfelt, from the same roots.

Rosensky. *Rosen*, rosy, flushed; Danish *sky*, a cloud. A crimson cloud.

Rosewarne. *Rose*, a rose; *wearn*, a hindrance, obstacle, resistance, denial. Rose-obstacle.

Rosewig. *Rose*, a rose; *wig*, war, warfare, battle. Rose-warfare.

Roskeep. *Rose*, a rose; *ceáp*, a bargain, sale, business, chattel. Rose-sale.

Rosney. *Rose*, a rose; *ney*, from the Irish, an individual, an agent. Rose-dealer.

Rost. *Ræst*, pronounced *rost*, rest, repose, a place of rest, a bed.

Rowan. *Rówan*, pronounced *roow-an*, to row, to sail. Rowand, Roan, from the same root.

Rowe. *Reowe*, an Irish mantle or rug, soldier's cloak, a frieze cassock, a priest's garment. Row, of like significance.

Rowson. *Row*, Rowe; *sun*, son. Son of Rowe.

Rox. *Rocks*, from *Rock*, Rock; *s* for *sun*. Son of Rock. Rock is from the Irish *roc*, pronounced *rokh*, a rock.

Roxberry. *Roxbury*, from *Rox*, Rox, and *byrig*, a town, a city. Town of Rox.

Roxbrough. *Roxborough*, from *Rox*, Rox, and *burh*, a town, a city. Town of Rox.

Rucher. *Róc,* a rook; *cr,* indicative of a person. One who acts like a rook; a croaker. In the South of Germany *ruch,* a rook, is the form of the word, and this agrees much better with the name under consideration.

Ruckman. *Ruck,* Ruck; *man,* a servant. Ruck's servant.

Rucks. *Ruck,* Ruck; *s* for *sun,* son. Son of Ruck.

Rudd. *Rud,* red, ruddy. Later *rud,* became a noun, and signified redness, blush, ruddle, red ochre, and a river-fish. The last-named, from its red eyes, was called the rudd, or red-eye.

Rudden. *Rud,* red, ruddy; *en,* a termination of adjectives and participles. Make red; ruddy.

Rudduck. *Rudduc,* robin-red-breast. Ruddick, Ruddach, Ruddock, kindred names.

Ruddiman. *Rud,* ruddy; *ig,* an adjective ending; *man,* a man. A ruddy man. Rudman, Rudmann, of like significance.

Ruddy. *Rud,* ruddy; *ig,* implying an adjective. Ruddy. Rudy, of same derivation.

Ruder. *Rud,* ruddy; *er,* a person. A ruddy person.

Rudge. *Rud,* red; *ige,* an island. Red island.

Rudhart. *Rud,* red, ruddy; *heort,* a hart. A ruddy stag.

Rudling. *Rud,* ruddy; *ling,* denoting state or condition of a person, an image, an example. Healthy condition; picture of health.

Rudloff. *Rud,* redness, blush; *lóf,* praise. Blush-praise.

Rudolph. *Rud,* red ochre, red iron-ore; *dælf,* pronounced *dolf,* a delving, a digging. Iron-digging.

Ruf. *Hróf,* or *róf,* a roof, a raised part. Perhaps, from *róf,* famous, renowned, illustrious. Rufe, Ruff, Ruoff, of kindred signification.

Ruffell. *Hróf,* a roof, a raised part; *el,* denoting a person. A roof-rearer; a ruff-wearer.

Rumbol. *Rúm,* room, space, place; *bol,* a sleeping-room.

Rumboltz. *Rúm*, a room; *boltes*, genitive of *bolt*, a house. Room of a dwelling.

Rumel. *Rúm*, a room; *el*, indicative of a person. A room-mate. Rummel, Rummell, from the same.

Rumford. *Rúm*, wide, spacious, ample; *ford*, a ford. A spacious ford.

Rumig *Rúm*, a room; *ig*, an adjective ending. Roomy; spacious; ample.

Rumsey. *Rúm*, room, space, place; *rumes*, genitive of space; *ig*, an island. A spacious island.

Runner. *Rún*, pronounced *roon*, mystery; *ere*, a person. A dealer in mysteries; a sorcerer.

Runser. *Rún-seó-ere*, from *rún*, a secret; *seó*, I see; *ere*, a person. A foreteller of secrets.

Runyon. *Rún-ian*, to whisper, to speak mysteriously, from *rún*, a mystery, and *ian*, a verbal ending.

Rusch. *Risce*, pronounced *reesche*, a rush. Rush, Rusk, from the same.

Rusher. *Rush*, Rush; *er*, a person. One who is a Rush; son of Rush; one who uses the rush.

Rushman. *Rush*, Rush; *man*, a servant. A servant of Rush; a rush-collector.

Rushmire. *Risce*, rush; *mere*, a mere, lake, pool. A rush-pool.

Rushton. *Rush*, Rush; *tún*, town, house. Home of Rush; habitation of the rush.

Rushworth. *Rush*, Rush; *weordh*, worth, worthy, honorable. An estimable Rush; value of rushes.

Rust. *Rust*, rust, rustiness.

Ruth. *Rúte*, rue, a bitter herb. From the bitter property of the rue, we have *ruth*, expressive of pity, sorrow, tenderness for the misery of another, mercy. Rutt, more closely related to derivation.

Rutnard. *Ruth*, rue, pity, sorrow; *ard*, an ensign of office, such as a pole, staff, etc. A physician; a clergyman; a consoler.

Rutherford. *Ruther,* Rutter; *ford,* a ford. Rutter's ford.

Ruths. *Ruth,* Ruth; *s* for *sun,* son. Son of Ruth.

Rutledge. *Rúte,* rue; *leger,* place for laying or lying, as bed, couch, grave, churchyard. Rue-bed; a bed of rue.

Rutter. *Rutt,* Rutt, or Ruth; *ere,* a person. A descendant of Rutt.

Ruttley. *Rutt,* Rutt; *ley* for *lic,* having the form of. Resembling Rutt.

Ruttman. *Rutt,* Rutt; *man,* a servant. Rutt's servant.

Rutty. *Rúte,* rue; *ig,* an adjective termination. Like rue. Or, *Rutt,* Rutt; *ig,* expressing the quality of. Having the character of Rutt.

Rutz. *Rutts,* from *Rutt,* Rutt; *s* for *sun,* son. Son of Rutt.

Ruwell. *Ruw,* rough, hairy; *el,* denoting a person. A rough, or hairy person.

Ruxton. *Rucks,* Rucks; *tún,* town, habitation. Home of Rucks.

Ryer. *Rye,* hairy; *ere,* a person. A hairy person.

Ryerson. *Ryer,* Ryer; *sun,* son. Son of Ryer.

Ryers. *Ryer,* Ryer; *s* for *sun,* son. Son of Ryer.

Ryland. *Rye,* hairy, rough; *land,* ground, earth, region, country. A rough country.

S.

Saake. *Sæc,* pronounced *sahke,* war, battle.

Saal. *Sæl,* pronounced *sahal,* a hall.

Saam. *Sæme,* pronounced *sā-am,* weak, slow, lazy, bad.

Sabin. *Sǣ,* the sea; *bin,* a crib, a manger, a bin, a hatch. Sea-crib. Sabine, of like import.

Sabins. *Sabin,* Sabin; *s* for *sun,* son. Son of Sabin.

Sabold. *Sǣ,* the sea; *bold,* a house. A sea-house; a ship.

Sabot. *Sǣ,* the sea; *bāt,* boat. A sea-boat; a ship.

Sacal. *Sacol,* from *sǣ,* the sea; *cól,* coal. Sea-coal.

Sach. *Sæc*, pronounced *sāc*, a sack, a bag. Sack, of like derivation.

Sachs. *Sach*, Sach; *s* for *sun*, son. Son of Sach. Saches, Sachse, Sacks, from the same roots.

Sackwright. *Sæc*, a sack; *wyrhta*, a workman, artificer, wright, maker. A sack-maker.

Saddington. *Sæd*, pronounced *sad*, satisfied, sated; *dineg*, broken or fallow ground; *tūn*, a farm. A farm of sated, fallow ground.

Sadler. *Sadel*, a saddle; *ere*, an agent. A saddle-maker. Sadleir, Saddler, cognate terms.

Sæger. *Sæ*, the sea; *ger*, a year. Sea-year.

Saffer. *Sæfn*, pronounced *safn*, a dream; *er*, an agent. A dreamer.

Saffin. *Sæfn*, pronounced *safin*, a dream.

Safford. *Sæfn*, a dream; *ōrd*, author. Dream-author.

Sage. *Sage*, a sage, a wise man.

Sagee. *Sage*, a sage; *e*, denoting a derivative adjective. Wise; philosophical.

Sagehorn. *Sage*, a sage; *horn*, a pinnacle, a trumpet. A sage's trumpet.

Sager. *Sage*, a sage; *ere*, a person. A man of wisdom.

Sagers. *Sager*, Sager; *s* for *sun*, son. Son of Sager.

Saget. *Sage*, a sage; *æt*, meat, food. The food of a sage.

Sague. *Sag*, pronounced *săg*, a sack.

Saiger. *Sag*, a sack; *er*, an agent. A sack-maker.

Sainsbury. *Sanctes*, genitive of *sanct*, a saint; *bury*, from *beorh*, a place of burial. Saint's burying-place.

Sale. *Sæl*, pronounced *sā-el*, a cord, a strap. Saile, from the same root.

Saler. *Sæl*, a cord; *er*, an agent. A cord-maker.

Sales. *Sale*, Sale; *s* for *sun*, son. Son of Sale.

Salfinger. *Sæl*, a cord; *finger*, a finger. Cord-finger.

Salin. *Sale*, Sale; *in*, a habitation. Sale's dwelling.

Saling. *Sale*, Sale; *ing*, offspring. Descendant of Sale.

Salinger. *Saling,* Saling ; *er,* an agent. A servant of Saling.

Salisbury. *Salis,* Sale's ; *beorh,* a burrow, or barrow. Sale's barrow.

Saalmann. *Sæl,* pronounced *sa-al,* a hall ; *mann,* a man. Hall-man.

Salt. *Salt,* salt.

Salter. *Salt,* salt ; *ere,* an agent. A manufacturer of salt. Also, from *saltere,* a psaltery, a dulcimer.

Salters. *Salter,* Salter ; *s* for *sun,* son. Son of Salter.

Sanborn. *Sand,* earth ; *born,* born. Earth-born.

Sand. *Sand,* sand, earth.

Sandberg. *Sand,* sand ; *berg,* a hill. A sand-hill.

Sandberger. *Sandberg,* a sand-hill ; *er,* an agent. A sand-hill dweller.

Sander. *Sand,* sand, earth ; *er,* an agent, or doer. A sand-digger. Saner, a contraction of the same.

Sanders. *Sander,* Sander ; *s* for *sun,* son. Son of Sander. Saunders, of like derivation.

Sanderson. *Sander,* Sander ; *sun,* son. Son of Sander. Saunderson, similarly derived.

Sandford. *Sand,* sand ; *ford,* a ford. A sandy ford. Sanford, an abbreviation of the name.

Sandgran. *Sand,* sand ; Latin *granum,* a grain. A grain of sand.

Sandgren. *Sand,* sand ; *grene,* green. Green sand.

Sands. *Sand,* Sand ; *s* for *sun,* son. Son of Sand.

Sandy. *Sand-ig,* from *sand,* sand, and *ig,* an adjective ending. Sandy.

Sangborne. *Sang,* song ; *born,* born. Song-born.

Sanger. *Sang,* a song ; *ere,* an agent. A singer.

Sangers. *Sanger,* a singer ; *s* for *sun,* son. Son of Sanger ; son of a singer.

Sank. *Sanc,* a song.

Sapp. *Sæpp,* pronounced *sapp,* sap, juice.

Sappel. *Sæpp,* sap, juice ; *el,* an agent. A sapper.

Sapper. *Sæpp,* sap; *ere,* an agent. A sapper.

Sappington. *Sæpp,* sap; *ing,* denoting action; *tún,* town, village. A sapping town.

Sarfert. *Sár,* wound, sore, pain, grief; *ferht,* fright, fear. Pain-fear.

Saring. *Sár,* a wound; *ing,* expressive of action. Wound-producing.

Sattler. *Sætel,* pronounced *sahtel,* a seat; *ere,* an agent. A settler.

Saul. *Sáwl,* pronounced *sáw-el,* a soul. Saull, of like import.

Saulnier. *Sául,* a soul; *nere,* refuge, preservation. Soul-refuge.

Saulsberry. *Sáules,* genitive of *sául,* a soul; *berry,* from *byrig,* a city. Saul's city; city of the soul.

Saulsburg. *Saul's,* genitive of Saul; *burg,* a city. Saul's city.

Sawyer. *Sáwere,* pronounced *saw-yere,* a sower.

Sawyers. *Sawyer,* Sawyer; *s* for *sun,* son. Son of Sawyer.

Sax. Sachs, from *Sach,* Sach, and *s* for *sun,* son. Son of Sach. *Saxe,* of kindred meaning.

Saxer. *Sax,* Sax; *ere,* an agent. A servant of Sax.

Saxton. *Sax,* Sax; *tún,* town, house. Home of Sax.

Saybolt. *Sǽ,* the sea; *bolt,* a house, a dwelling. A sea-house; a ship.

Sayer. *Sǽ,* the sea; *ere,* an agent. A navigator. Sayre, from the same roots.

Sayers. *Sayer,* Sayer; *s* for *sun,* son. Son of Sayer. Sayres, a cognate form.

Saylor. *Sǽ,* the sea; *lǽr,* pronounced *lore,* doctrine. Sea-knowledge.

Scank. *Scanca,* the hollow bone of the leg, the shank.

Scanlan. *Scand,* shame, modesty, disgrace; *land,* land, earth, region, country. Disgraced region. Scanlin, Scanlon of like significance.

Scannell. *Scand,* shame, disgrace; *el,* a personal suffix. A person in disgrace.

Scarborough. *Scear,* an estate, landed property; *burh,* a town, a city. The landed property of a town.

Scattergood. *Sceat-wer,* a shooter; *gud,* good. A good shooter.

Schaab. *Sceabb,* or *scæb,* a scab.

Schaaf. *Sceaf,* pronounced *skaaf,* a sheaf, a bundle of corn.

Schaal. *Sceale,* pronounced *skaal,* a school. Schall, of like significance.

Schaar. *Scear,* pronounced *skaar,* a share, a fortune, an estate.

Schaker. *Sceacere,* pronounced *skaker,* a thief.

Schaler. *Sceale,* a school; *ere,* an agent. A scholar. Schaller, a kindred name.

Schallinger. *Sceale,* a school; *ing,* expressive of action; *ere,* an agent. One who is acquiring his schooling; a scholar.

Scham. *Scame,* pronounced *skam,* shame, disgrace, nakedness.

Schamel. *Sceamel,* a stool, footstool, bench, form, desk.

Schell. *Scell,* a shell, a rind, a cavity.

Scobel. *Scobl,* a shovel.

Scofield. *Sceawe,* shoe; *feld,* a field, a plain. A shoe-field.

Scollean. *Scól-lean,* from *scólu,* a school, and *lean,* reward. A school-reward. Scollan, from the same roots.

Scollay. *Scól-ley,* from *scólu,* a school, and *ley,* a song. A school-song.

Scollin. *Scól-in,* from *scólu,* a school, and *in,* a habitation. A school-house.

Scollon. *Scól-lond,* from *scólu,* a school, and *lond,* land. School-land.

Scorr. *Score,* the shore.

Scotland. *Scot,* shot, payment; *land,* land. Payment-land.

Scotney. *Scot,* shot, payment; *ney,* from the Irish, implying an agent. A paymaster.

Scott. *Scot,* shot, payment.

Scouler. *Scolere,* a scholar.

Scovel. *Scofl,* a shovel.

Scudder. *Sculder,* a shoulder.

Seabert. *Sǣ,* the sea; *beorht,* bright. Sea-bright.

Seabold. *Sǣ,* the sea; *bóld,* a house. A sea-house; a ship.

Seabourne. *Sǣ,* the sea; *burne,* a stream. A sea-current.

Seabrook. *Sǣ,* the sea; *bróc,* a brook. A sea-brook; a rivulet that empties into the sea.

Seagrove. *Sǣ,* the sea; *græf,* a grove. A sea-grove; a grove near the sea.

Seafert. *Sǣ,* the sea; *ferdh,* a spirit. A sea-sprite.

Seal. *Seal,* a willow, a sallow. Seel, an analogous name. Perhaps, from *seal,* a seal.

Sealey. *Seal,* a willow; *ig,* an adjective termination. Willowy; abounding with willows. Scaly, Seely, Seeley, similarly derived.

Seals. *Seal,* Seal; *s* for *sun,* son. Son of Seal.

Seaman. *Sǣ-mann,* a sea-man. Seeman, Seemann, kindred names.

Seamans. *Seaman,* Seaman; *s* for *sun,* son. Son of Seaman.

Seamen. *Sǣ,* the sea; *men,* plural of *man.* Sea-men.

Seamens. *Seamen,* Seamen; *s* for *sun,* son. Son of Seamen.

Seamon. *Sǣ,* the sea; *mon,* man. A sea-man.

Seanor. *Sǣ,* the sea; *nor,* for north. North Sea.

Search. *Serce,* a shirt.

Searchfield. *Search,* Search; *feld,* a field, a plain. Search's field.

Sear. *Sear,* from *scarian,* to sear, to dry up. Dry; withered.

Searing. *Sear,* Sear; *ing,* offspring. Son of Sear.

Searle. *Sear-el,* from *sear,* sear, and *el,* denoting a personal noun. A withered person; an aged person. Searl, from the same roots.

Searles. *Searle,* Searle ; *s* for *sun,* son. Son of Searle.

Sears. *Sear,* Sear ; *s* for *sun,* son. Son of Sear.

Seary. *Sear,* dry, withered; *ig,* denoting an adjective. Withered. Seeary, an analogous term.

Seaton. *Sǣ,* the sea; *tún,* a town. A sea-town; a seaport.

Sebald. *Sé,* pronounced *se,* the sea; *báld,* bold, audacious. Sea-daring.

Seckel. *Sec,* battle ; *el,* indicative of a person. A warrior.

Seckinger. *Sec,* war, battle ; *cyng,* a king, ruler, prince ; *ere,* an agent. A warrior-king.

Seddinger. Perhaps, from *Sedling,* an Ethiopian, and *ere,* an agent. A slave-trader. Sedenger, a corruption of the same.

Sedgwick. *Secg,* warrior, soldier ; *wic,* a camp, a station. A military camp.

See. *Sé,* pronounced *sē,* the sea.

Seebach. *Sé,* the sea ; *bæc,* pronounced *bāc,* back. An ebbing sea.

Seeber. *Sé,* the sea; *bere,* a bear. A sea-bear.

Seeberger. *Sé,* the sea ; *berg,* a mountain, a hill ; *ere,* an agent. One that occupies a sea-mountain ; a mermaid. Seeburger, of like significance.

Seebeth. *Sé,* the sea ; Irish *beth,* a house. A sea-house ; a bath-house.

Seed. *Sēd,* pronounced *sēd,* seed.

Seeds. *Seed,* Seed ; *s* for *sun,* son. Son of Seed.

Seefelder. *Sé,* the sea ; *feld,* a field, a plain ; *ere,* an agent. A follower of the sea-plain ; a seafaring man.

Seegrist. *Sé,* the sea ; *grist,* grist, a grinding. Sea-grist ; sea-grinding. Segrest, of like import.

Sechofer. *Sé,* the sea ; *hofer,* a humpback. The sea-humpback.

Seelaus. *Sé*, the sea; *lus*, German *laus*, a louse. A sea-louse.

Seeler. *Seal*, a seal; *ere*, an agent. A seal-fisher.

Seehorst. *Sé*, the sea; *horst*, watching. Sea-watching.

Seelig. *Sé*, the sea; *lig*, a flame. A sea-flame. Selig, an analogous name.

Seelos. *Sé*, the sea; *los*, loss, losing, destruction. Sea-loss.

Seery. *Sé*, the sea; *ric*, pronounced *rē*, power, dominion. Sea-power.

Sees. *See*, See; *s* for *sun*, son. Son of See. Seese, Seez, cognate names.

Sefer. *Sé*, the sea; *fer*, a journey. A sea-journey.

Sefton. *Seft*, soft, mild, quiet; *tún*, a town, a house. A quiet home.

Segall. *Sé*, the sea; *gál*, pronounced *gaul*, lightness, folly. Sea-folly.

Segner. *Segne*, a net; *ere*, an agent. A seiner.

Seher. *Sé*, the sea, *here*, an army, a host, a legion. A sea-army; a naval expedition.

Sehers. *Seher*, Seher; *s* for *sun*, son. Son of Seher.

Selbert. *Sel*, a dwelling, a palace, a hall; *beorht*, brightness. Hall-brightness.

Selby. *Sel*, a hall, a palace; *by*, a habitation. A palatial dwelling.

Selden. *Seld*, a royal seat, a throne, a palace; *en*, an adjective ending. Palatial.

Selfridge. *Self*, same, self-same; *ricg*, a back, a ridge, a roof. Self-same ridge.

Seligman. *Selig*, Selig; *man*, a servant. Selig's servant.

Sell. *Sel*, a dwelling, a mansion, a palace, a hall.

Seller. *Sel*, a palace; *ere*, an agent. A king; a prince.

Sellers. *Seller*, Seller; *s* for *sun*, son. Son of Seller.

Sellick. *Sel*, a companion; *lic*, like. Companion-like.

Sells. *Sell*, Sell; *s* for *sun*, son. Son of Sell.

Selman. *Sell*, Sell; *man*, a servant. Servant of Sell; servant of a palace.

Selner. *Sel,* a palace ; *nere,* refuge, protection. Palace-refuge ; protection of the king.

Selover. *Sé,* the sea ; *lóf-ere,* a lover. A sea-lover.

Selser. *Sells-ere,* from *Sells,* son of Sell, and *ere,* an agent. A servant of Sell's son. Selser, perhaps, from the same roots.

Semebroth. *Sæme,* weak ; *bróth,* broth. Weak broth.

Semisch. *Sem,* a seam, a bag ; *isc,* like. Like a bag.

Semler. *Sem,* a bag ; *lǽr,* doctrine, knowledge. Bag-knowledge.

Senat. *Senat,* a senate. Senate, from the same root.

Senatz. *Senats,* from *Senat,* Senat, and *s* for *sun,* son. Son of Senat.

Senn. *Sen,* sin.

Senneff. *Senn,* Senn ; *nefe,* a niece. Niece of Senn.

Senner. *Senn,* Senn ; *ere,* an agent. Senn's servant.

Setner. *Setnere,* a seditious person, a revolter.

Settel. *Setel,* a settle, a seat, a bench, a stool. Settle, of similar derivation.

Setter. *Settere,* a thief.

Seubel. *Séw,* the sea ; *bel,* a bell. A sea-bell.

Scubert. *Séw,* the sea ; *beorht,* brightness. Sea-glistening.

Sharp. *Scearp,* sharp. Sharpe, another spelling.

Sharpless. *Scearp,* sharp ; *læs,* less, comparative of *lytel.* Less sharp. Sharples, of similar meaning.

Sharpley. *Scearp,* sharp ; *lic,* like. Sharp-like.

Sharps. *Sharp,* Sharp ; *s* for *sun,* son. Son of Sharp.

Sharr. *Scear,* a ploughshare. Also, *scear,* a division.

Sharsig. *Sceares,* genitive of *scear,* Sharr's, and *ig,* an island. Sharr's island.

Sharswood. *Sharr's,* Sharr's ; *wud,* wood. Sharr's wood. Sharwood, an abbreviated form of the name.

Shaw. *Sceawe,* a show.

Sheaff. *Sceaf,* a sheaf, a bundle of corn.

Shealer. *Sceale,* a scale, a balance ; *ere,* an agent. A weigher.

Shean. Sceán, shone. Sheen, from the same root.

Shear. Scear, sheared. Sheer, of like derivation.

Sheard. Sceard, a sheard, a division, a remnant.

Sheardown. Scear, sheared; *dún,* a mountain, hill, downs. A sheared mountain; a shaven hill.

Shearer. Sceare-ere, from *sceare,* shears, scissors, and *ere,* an agent. One who uses the shears.

Shearf. Scearfan, to carve in pieces; *scearfe,* a fragment.

Shearman. Sceare, sheers; *man,* a man. A shearer; a reaper.

Shears. Shear, Shear; *s* for *sun,* son. Son of Shear.

Shearwood. Scear, sheared; *wud,* a wood. A cleared wood. Sherwood, from the same.

Sheble. Sceabb, a scab; *el,* denoting a person. A shabby fellow.

Sheck. Sceac, slow, sluggish, lazy, benumbed, costive, bound.

Shecklin. Sceac-line, a line which fastens the bottom of a sail.

Shedaker. Sceáde, genitive of *sceádo,* shadow; *æcer,* a field. A field of shadow; a shaded field.

Shedden. Sceáden, shaded, shadowed, overwhelmed, oppressed.

Sheddy. Sceáde, genitive of *sceádo,* belonging to shade. Shady; shadowy.

Shedinger. Sceádan, to shade, to overwhelm, to oppress; *ing,* expressive of action; *ere,* an agent. A person that overshadows another; an oppressor.

Shedwick. Sceáde, genitive of *sceádo,* a shadow, a shade; *wic,* a habitation, a village, a convent. A habitation of shade; a shaded village.

Sheedy. Sceáde, of shadow; *ig,* an island. An island of shadow; a shaded island.

Sheeler. Sceale, a scale, a balance; *ere,* an agent. A weigher; a balancer.

Sheen. Scén, pronounced *skĕne,* sheen.

Sheering. *Scir,* shire; *ing,* offspring, descendant. Son of the shire.

Sheldon. *Scel,* a shell; *dún,* a mountain, a hill. A shell-hill.

Shell. *Scell,* a shell.

Shellenberger. *Scellenâ,* of shells; *berg,* a hill, a mountain; *ere,* an agent. A dweller of a shell-hill. Shelberger, of similar derivation.

Sheller. *Scell,* a shell; *ere,* an agent. A dealer in shells.

Shelley. *Scell,* a shell; *ig,* an adjective termination. Shelly. Shelly, from the same roots.

Shelling. *Scelling,* a shilling. Or, *Shell,* Shell; *ing,* an offspring. A descendant of Shell.

Shellinger. *Shelling,* Shelling; *ere,* an agent. A servant of Shelling.

Shelmerdine. *Scel,* a shell; *mere,* a mere, a lake, a sea; *dinne,* stormy. A tempestuous shell-lake.

Shelton. *Shell,* Shell; *tún,* town, house. Home of Shell.

Sheneman. *Sheen,* Sheen; *man,* a servant. A servant of Sheen.

Shenton. *Scén,* beautiful; *tún,* a house, a habitation. A beautiful house.

Shepherd. *Sceáp-hyrde,* from *sceáp,* sheep, and *hyrde,* a keeper of sheep; a shepherd. Shepard, Shephard, Sheppard, analogous names.

Shepherdson. *Shepherd,* Shepherd; *sun,* son. Son of Shepherd. Shepperson, of like significance.

Shepler. *Sceáp,* sheep; *lær,* doctrine. Sheep-knowledge.

Shepley. *Sceáp,* sheep; *ley,* a lay, a song. A sheep-lay.

Sheran. *Scéran,* to shear, to shave, to cut off, to share, to divide, to grant.

Sherer. *Sccare,* shears; *ere,* an agent. A shearer. Sherar, from the same roots.

Sherick. *Scer-icge,* an actress. Sherk, Shirk, possibly, from the same derivation.

Sheridan. *Scérian,* to divide, to rive, to part.

Sheriff. *Scir-gerefa,* from *scir,* a shire, and *gerefa,* a steward, a bailiff, a governor. A governor of a shire; a shire-reeve; a sheriff.

Sherlock. *Scir,* white, bright, glorious; *locc,* a lock, hair. A lock of white hair. Shirelock, of similar meaning.

Sherlow. *Scir,* a county, province, district; *low,* a grave, a barrow, a small hillock, a tract of country gently rising, a low. A district-low. Shirlow, from the same roots.

Sherman. *Scir-mann,* from *scir,* a share, shire, county, district; *mann,* a man. A man who superintends; a shire-man; an overseer; a governor, a provost. Shearman, Shireman, of kindred derivation.

Shermer. *Scir,* a district, province; *mere,* a mere, a lake, a pool, the sea. A sea-district; a lake-province.

Sherr. *Scir,* a district, a province. Shire, of kindred significance.

Sherrard. *Scir,* superintendence, stewardship; *ard,* an ensign of office. A badge of stewardship. Sherrerd, of like import.

Sherrat. *Scir,* shire, district, county; *ath,* an oath. An oath required by a shire from one in power.

Sherrell. *Scir,* a shire, a district; *el,* indicative of a person. A resident of a shire.

Sherrer. *Scir,* care, charge; *ere,* an agent. A superintendent; an overseer.

Sherrie. *Sherr,* Sherr; *ig,* an island. Sherr's island. Sherry, from the same roots.

Sherwin. *Scir,* a shire; *win,* a friend. A friend of the shire; one devoted to the shire.

Sherwood. *Scir,* glorious; *wude,* a forest. A glorious forest. Or, from *scir,* a district; *wud,* a wood. A district wood.

Shetzline. *Scetes,* genitive of *scete,* a sheet, a sail; *line,* a line. The lower sail line.

Shew. *Sceawe,* a show.

Shewell. *Sceawe,* a show; *el,* indicative of a person. A show-man.

Shiel. *Sciell,* a scale, a shell.

Shield. *Scield,* a shield, a refuge.

Shields. *Shield,* Shield; *s* for *sun,* son. Son of Shield.

Shill. *Scill,* a shilling, a piece of uncoined silver, which, when coined, would make five pennies, each of which was 2½ pence.

Shillady. *Shill,* Shill; *hlǣfdie,* a mistress, a lady. Shill's mistress.

Shilling. *Scilling,* a shilling. Or, from *Shill,* Shill, and *ing,* an offspring. A son of Shill.

Shillingford. *Shilling,* Shilling; *ford,* a ford. Shilling's ford. Shillingsford, from the same roots.

Shillingsburg. *Shillinges,* Shilling's; *beorg,* a hill. Shilling's hill.

Shimer. *Scima,* a brightness, splendor, glittering; *ere,* an agent. A wit; a humorist; a scholar.

Shinn. *Scinne,* beauty, splendor.

Shinneberry. *Shinn,* Shinn; *byrie,* a burial-place. The burial-place of Shinn.

Shipley. *Scip,* a ship, a boat; *ley,* a lay, a song. A boat song.

Shipman. *Scip-mann,* a ship-man, a sailor.

Shippen. *Scyppend,* a former, a creator.

Shipper. *Scip-ere,* a sailor.

Shipps. *Scipes,* genitive of *scip,* a ship. Belonging to a ship.

Shirley. *Scire,* a shire; *lic,* like. Resembling a shire.

Shoe. *Scoe,* or *sceó,* a shoe.

Shoell. *Scoe,* a shoe; *el,* denoting a person. A shoe-maker.

Shoemaker. *Scoe,* a shoe; *mace,* make; *ere,* an agent. A maker of shoes.

Shoneman. *Scóne,* beautiful; *mann,* a man. A beautiful man.
Shook. *Sccóc,* shook.
Shoop. *Scóp,* a farmer, a maker, a poet, a minstrel.
Shore. *Score,* the shore.
Short. *Sccort,* short.
Shortell. *Sccort,* short; *el,* indicative of a person. A short person.
Shorten. *Sccort-ain,* from *sccort,* short; *ain,* to make. To make short.
Shortley. *Short,* Short; *lic,* like. Resembling Short. Or, from *sccort-lic,* short, momentary.
Shorts. *Short,* Short; *s* for *sun,* son. Son of Short. Shortts, from the same roots.
Shoser. *Scós,* shoes; *erc,* an agent. A shoemaker.
Shott. *Scot,* shot, payment.
Showaker. *Sceawe,* a show; *æcer,* a field. A show-field. Showeker, from the same roots.
Showalter. *Sceawe,* a show; *alter,* an altar. A show-altar.
Showell. *Sceawe,* a show; *el,* indicative of a person. A showman.
Shower. *Sceawere,* a beholder, spectator, spy, a railer, a scoffer.
Showers. *Shower,* Shower; *s* for *sun,* son. Son of Shower.
Showman. *Sceawe,* a show; *mann,* a man. A showman.
Shreeve. *Scréf,* a den, a cave, a layer. Shreve, of like derivation.
Shreeves. *Shreeve,* Shreeve; *s* for *sun,* son. Son of Shreeve. Shrieves, a kindred name.
Shrigley. *Scric,* a thrush, a throstle; *ley,* a song. Thrush song.
Shriner. *Scrin,* a shrine, casket, chest; *erc,* an agent. A maker of shrines, caskets.

Shriver. *Scrifan,* to shrive, to receive confession ; *ere,* an agent. One who receives confessions ; a shriver.

Shroder. *Scrúd,* a garment, clothing, shroud ; *ere,* an agent. A tailor ; a shroud-maker.

Shronk. *Scruncen,* shrunk, withered.

Schropshire. *Scrob,* a shrub ; *scír,* a shire, county, district. A shrub-shire ; a shrubby district.

Shubert. *Scúa,* a shade, a shadow ; *beorht,* bright, lucid, clear. A lucid shadow.

Shuck. *Scucca,* Satan, the devil.

Shuff. *Scúfan,* to shove, to thrust, to cast down ; *sceáf,* cast down, removed ; *sceaf,* that which is cast down, as a sheaf.

Shugard. *Scúa,* a shade ; *geard,* a hedge, enclosure, garden. A shaded garden. Shugardt, Shugart, of like parentage.

Shuler. *Scúl,* a scowl ; *ere,* an agent. One who scowls.

Shull. *Scúl,* a scowl, a frown.

Shumaker. *Sceó,* a shoe ; *macian,* to make ; *ere,* one who. A shoe-maker.

Shuman. *Sceó,* a shoe ; *mann,* a man. A shoe-man ; a dealer in shoes.

Shumate. *Sceó,* a shoe ; Dutch *maat,* a husband, a wife, a companion. A shoe-companion.

Shumway. *Sceome,* of shame, genitive of *sceamu* ; *wæg,* way. The way of shame.

Shupard. *Scóp,* a poet, minstrel ; *ard,* a badge of office. A minstrel's staff. Shuperd, slightly altered form of the word.

Shupe. *Scóp,* a poet, a minstrel. Shupp, an analogous name.

Shur. *Scúr,* a shower of rain, a storm, tempest, a shower of arrows, battle, fight. Shurr, from the same root.

Shute. *Scute,* given, expended, transferred, rushed, shot. Shutt, of kindred meaning.

Shuttleworth. *Scuttel*, a scuttle, platter, charger, moment; *weordh*, worth, price, value. A moment's value.

Shutts. *Shutt*, Shutt; *s* for *sun*, son. Son of Shutt. Shutz, similarly derived.

Shyer. *Scyan*, to suggest, excite, prompt, persuade; *ere*, an agent. A prompter; a pleader.

Sibbet. *Sibbian*, to pacify, to compose; past participle *sibbod*, pacified, composed. Sibbitt, from the same root.

Sibbits. *Sibbit*, Sibbit; *s* for *sun*, son. Son of Sibbit.

Sibel. *Sib*, peace, adoption, companionship; *el*, indicative of personality. A companionable person. Sibole of like import.

Siber. *Sib*, peace, agreement, alliance; *ere*, an agent. An ally; an abettor.

Sibert. *Sib*, peace; *beorht*, famous, illustrious. A famous peace.

Sibley. *Sib*, concord, agreement; *ley*, a song. A melody.

Sibson. *Sib*, peace, adoption; *sun*, son. Son of adoption. Sibbs, an abbreviated form of the same.

Sick. *Sic*, sick.

Sickel. *Sicel*, pronounced *sickel*, a sickle. Sickle, Sickel, from the same root.

Sickels. *Sickel*, Sickel; *s* for *sun*, son. Son of Sickel. Sickles, a cognate term.

Sicker. *Sic*, sick; *ere*, an agent. A sick person.

Sickler. *Sicel*, a sickle; *ere*, an agent. One who uses a sickle.

Siddall. *Sid*, ample, spacious, broad, vast; *dál*, a valley. A broad valley. Siddell, Sidel, Sidle, alike in derivation.

Siddon. *Sid*, spacious, vast; *dún*, a mountain, a hill. A spacious hill.

Siddins. *Siddin*, Siddon; *s* for *sun*, son. Son of Siddon.

Side. *Sid*, ample, broad, various, diverse. Or, from *side*, silk.

Sidebotham. *Sid,* ample, full, vast; *bôt,* atonement, indemnity, redress, cure; *hám,* house, dwelling. The home of full atonement.

Sidebottom. *Sid,* broad; *botm,* bottom. Broad bottom.

Sidenburg. *Siden,* silken, made of silk; *burg,* a fort, a castle, a house. A house made of silk.

Sides. *Side,* Side; *s* for *sun,* son. Son of Side.

Sidleman. *Sidle,* Sidle; *man,* a servant. Sidle's servant.

Sidley. *Sidle,* Sidle; *lic,* like. Resembling Sidle.

Sidney. *Siden,* silken, made of silk.

Siebel. *Sie,* victory, triumph, crown; *bel,* a bell. A peal of triumph.

Siebeling. *Siebel,* Siebel; *ing,* offspring. Descendant of Siebel.

Sieber. *Sie,* a crown; *bere,* barley. A crown of barley.

Siebert. *Sie-beorht,* triumphantly, or gloriously bright.

Siebott. *Sie,* victory; *bôt,* atonement. A victorious atonement.

Siebrecht. *Sie,* crown; *brecht,* conquered. Crown conquered.

Siebrist. *Sie,* victory; *brist,* bearest. Victory bearest.

Siedenback. *Siden,* silken; *bæc,* back. A silken back.

Siedler. *Side,* silk; *lǽr,* doctrine. Silk-knowledge.

Siefert. *Sie,* triumph; *fert,* spirit. A spirit of triumph.

Siefken. *Sielf-cyn,* from *sielf,* a salve, and *cyn,* kind. A kind of herb salve.

Siegel. *Sigel,* the sun, a jewel. Siegle, from the same root.

Siegler. *Sigel,* a jewel; *ere,* an agent. A jeweller.

Siegman. *Sige,* victory; *man,* a man. A victorous man. Siegmann, from the same roots.

Sieler. *Sie,* the sea; *lǽr* doctrine. Sea-knowledge.

Siemers. *Sie,* the sea; *mersc,* a marsh, a fen. A sea-marsh.

Siemon. *Sie,* the sea; *mon,* a man. A seafaring man.

Sier. *Sieran,* to lie in wait for, to plot, to conspire.

Sifer. *Sie*, the sea; *fer*, a journey. A sea journey.

Sigmund. *Sige*, victory; *mund*, a hand. A victorious hand.

Silbert. *Sigel-beorht*, from *sigel*, or *sigl*, the sun, and *beorht*, bright. Sun-bright.

Sill. *Sigl*, a necklace.

Sillady. *Sill*, Sill; *hlǽfdie*, a mistress. Sill's mistress.

Siller. *Sigl*, a necklace, a brooch, an ornament; *ere*, an agent. A jeweller.

Silliman. *Sill*, Sill; *man*, a servant. Sill's servant.

Sills. *Sill*, Sill; *s* for *sun*, son. Son of Sill.

Silpath. *Sigl*, the sun; *pæth*, a path. The sun-path; sunny path.

Sillsby. *Sills*, Sill's; *by*, a habitation. Sill's home.

Silver. *Silfer*, silver.

Silverberg. *Silfer*, silver; *beorg*, a hill, a mountain. A mountain of silver.

Silvers. *Silver*, Silver; *s* for *sun*, son. Son of Silver.

Silverstine. *Silferes*, genitive of *silfer*, silver; *tine*, a tine, a tooth of a harrow. A silver tine.

Silverthorn. *Silfer*, silver; *thorn*, a thorn. A silver-thorn. Silverthorne, from the same roots.

Simard. *Sima*, a judge; *ard*, an ensign of office. A judge.

Sime. *Sima*, a bond, a reconciler, a judge. Syme, a kindred term.

Simes. *Sime*, Sime; *s* for *sun*, son. Son of Sime. Simms, Sims, Symes, from the same roots.

Simington. *Sima*, a reconciler; *ing*, expressive of action; *tun*, house. Home of reconciliation. Simmington, Symington, alike in derivation.

Simkin. *Sim*, Sime; *cyn*, kin, relation. Sime's relation. Simpkin, of similar meaning.

Simkins. *Simkin*, Simkin; *s* for *sun*, son. Son of Simkin. Simpkins, from the same roots.

Simkis. *Sima*, a judge; *cys*, pure. An upright judge.

Simler. *Sima*, a judge; *lær*, doctrine. Judicial knowledge.

Simmer. *Sima*, a bond; *ere*, an agent. A notary.

Simmers. *Simmer*, Simmer; *s* for *sun*, son. Son of Simmer.

Simmon. *Sima*, a bond; *mon*, a man. A bond-man.

Simmond. *Sima*, a bond; *mund*, a protection. A bond-protection.

Simmonds. *Simmond*, Simmond; *s* for *sun*, son. Son of Simmond. Simonds, Symonds, kindred names.

Simmons. *Simmōn*, Simmon; *s* for *sun*, son. Son of Simmon. Simmins, Symons, doubtless, of like parentage.

Simpson. *Simp*, Sime; *sun*, son. Son of Sime. Simson, from the same roots.

Sindall. *Sin*, sin; *dál*, a valley. Valley of sin.

Sine. *Sin*, sight, vision, appearance.

Siner. *Sin*, a vision; *ere*, an agent. One who sees visions; a dreamer.

Sines. *Sine*, Sine; *s* for *sun*, son, Son of Sine.

Singer. *Singan*, to sing, to play upon an instrument, to say, to pronounce; *ere*, an agent. A singer; a musician; a soothsayer.

Singerly. *Singer*, Singer; *lic*, like. Resembling Singer.

Singler. *Singan*, to sing, to play upon an instrument; *lær*, doctrine. Music-knowledge.

Singley. *Sing*, Sing; *ley*, from *lic*, like. Resembling Sing.

Sings. *Sing*, Sing; *s* for *sun*, son. Son of Sing.

Sink. *Sinc*, collection, heap, gain, treasure, riches, silver.

Sinn. *Sin*, or *synne*, sin.

Sinnamon. *Sina*, genitive of *sina*, sinews; *mon*, a man. A man of sinews; an athlete. Synnamon, Synamon, of similar derivation.

Sinning. *Sinn*, Sinn; *ing*, an offspring. Son of Sinn.

Sinns. *Sinn*, Sinn; *s* for *sun*, son. Son of Sinn.

Sithen. *Sidhan,* times, courses.

Sithens. *Sithen,* Sithen; *s* for *sun,* son. Son of Sithen.

Six. *Six,* six.

Sixsmith. *Six,* Six; *smidh,* an artificer, a smith, a workman. Six's workman.

Sixte. *Sixte,* sixth.

Skean. *Sceán,* shone. Skeehan, Skeen, from the same radix.

Skeffington. *Sceafa,* a shaving instrument; *ing,* expressive of action; *tún,* a house. A place where shaving is done.

Skelly. *Scell-ig,* from *scell,* a shell, and *ig,* an adjective termination. Shelly.

Skerl. *Scer,* a ploughshare; *el,* indicative of a person. A plowman.

Skerratt. *Scer-geát,* from *scer,* a ploughshare; *geát,* an opening, a gap. A gap made by a ploughshare; a furrow.

Skinner. *Scin,* the skin; *ere,* an agent. One who removes the skin; a skinner.

Skipton. *Scip,* a ship; *tún,* a town. A ship-town.

Slack. *Sleac,* slow, remiss, idle, sleepy.

Slade. *Slǽd,* a slade, plain, open tract of country.

Slagle *Slæge,* slaying, slaughter; *el,* indicative of a person. A slayer; a murderer.

Slater. *Slát,* slit; *ere,* an agent. One who slits, or cuts.

Slauch. *Slǽc,* slack, slow, remiss, idle, sleepy.

Slaugh. *Slæge,* slaying, slaughter, striking, beating, dashing together, a knock.

Slaw. *Sláw,* slow, idle, lazy.

Slawson. *Slaw,* Slaw; *sun,* son. Son of Slaw.

Slaymaker. *Slæ,* a weaver's reed, a slay; *mac-ere,* a maker. A slay-maker.

Slayman. *Slæ,* a slay; *man,* a man. A man who uses the slay; a weaver.

Slayton. *Slæ,* a slay; *tún,* a house, a habitation. A house where weaving is done.

Sleeper. *Slǽp-ere.* A sleeper.

Slick. Slicc, a mallet, a hammer.
Slider. Slidor, a slider.
Slifer. Slifer, slippery.
Sloan. Slán, pronounced *slōn*, sloes. Also, from *slán*, to strike, to fight, to slay, to throw. Sloane, from the same roots.
Sloanaker. Slán, sloes; *æcer*, a field. A field of sloes. Slonaker, a kindred name.
Sloat. Slát, pronounced *slōte*, torn, bitten, broken through. Slote, of the same derivation.
Slocomb. Slá, pronounced *slō*, a sloe; *comb*, a valley. A sloe-valley.
Slocum. Slá, a sloe; *cumb*, or *coom*, a valley. A sloe-valley.
Sloman. Slá, a sloe; *man*, a man. A collector of sloes.
Slough. Slog, a slough, a hollow place.
Slow. Sláw, slow, idle, lazy.
Slowe. Sláwe, slow, idle. Slowey, from the same radix.
Slowman. Sláw, slow, lazy; *man*, a man. A slow man; a lazy man.
Slugg. Slóg, slew, killed.
Smack. Smæc, smack, taste, savor.
Small. Smæl, small, slender, thin, narrow.
Smalley. Smale, a slender person.
Smallman. Smæl, small; *man*, a man. A small man.
Smallwood. Smæl, thin; *wud*, a forest. A thin forest.
Smeal. Smea, little, fine, subtle; *l* for *el*, indicative of a person. A subtle person.
Smeaton. Smeat, beaten; *tún*, a city. A beaten city. Smeeten, of kindred significance.
Smedley. Smédh-lic, smoothly.
Smick. Smic, smoke, vapor.
Smiley. Smilte, serene, placid, fair, smooth, calm.
Smith. Smidh, any one who strikes with a hammer, an artificer, a carpenter, a smith, a workman. Smyth, from the same radix.

Smithman. *Smidh-the,* a smithy, a work-shop; *man,* a man. The man of the workshop.

Smithing. *Smith,* Smith; *ing,* an offspring. Descendant of Smith.

Smithson. *Smith,* Smith; *sun,* son. Son of Smith.

Smock. *Smoc,* a smock, a farm-laborer's blouse.

Smocker. *Smoc,* a smock; *ere,* an agent. One who wears a smock.

Smythe. *Smidh-the,* a smithy, a workshop.

Snader. *Snæd,* a shaft, a pole, the handle of a scythe; *ere,* an agent. One who uses a snead, or sneed. Sneeder, a cognate term.

Snare. *Sneáre,* a snare, a loop, a noose.

Sneade. *Snæd,* a pole, a shaft, the handle of a scythe. Sneed, of like derivation.

Sneath. *Snæd,* a pole, a shaft, the handle of a scythe.

Sneden. *Snæd-en,* to cut, to cut off, to amputate. Snethen, from the same radix.

Snediker. *Snæd,* cut, shorn; *æcer,* a field. A mown field.

Sneer. *Snear,* active, quick, nimble.

Snelbaker. *Snel-bæc-ere,* from *snel,* active, cheerful; *bæc-ere,* a baker. An active, cheerful baker. Snellbaker, from the same roots.

Snell. *Snel,* or *snell,* quick, active, cheerful, bold, brave.

Snelling. *Snell,* Snell; *ing,* offspring. Descendant of Snell.

Sneyd. *Snid,* I cut, I amputate, I slay.

Snider. *Snid-ere,* a cutter, hewer, pruner. Snyder, from the same derivation.

Snodgrass. *Snod,* a fillet, a cap, a hood; *græs,* grass. A straw fillet; a straw cap.

Snow. *Snáw,* snow.

Snowdon. *Snáw-dan,* to snow.

Snowdon. *Snáw-dún,* from *snáw,* snow; *dún,* a mountain, a hill. A snow mountain.

Soden. *Soden,* perfect participle of *scódham,* to boil, to agitate, to cook. Boiled; agitated; cooked.

Soder. *Seod,* a little sack, a bag, scrip; *ere,* an agent. A sack-maker. Soeder, of like significance.

Soding. *Seod,* a bag, a sack; *ing,* expressive of action. Sack-making.

Sodman. *Seod,* a bag, a sack; *man,* a man. A sack-maker; a bag-dealer.

Soeffing. *Seofung,* sighing, sobbing, lamentation.

Somer. *Sumer,* summer. Sommer, Summer, from the same radix.

Somers. *Somer,* Somer; *s* for *sun,* son. Son of Somer. Sommers, Summers, equivalents.

Somerset. *Somer-setl,* from *sumer,* summer, and *setl,* a seat. A summer seat. Sommerset, a kindred term.

Sorg. *Sorg,* sorrow, care, anxiety.

Sorig. *Sorhg,* sorrow.

Souder. *Sódh,* truth; *ere,* an agent. One who speaks the truth.

Souders. *Souder,* Souder; *s* for *sun,* son. Son of Souder.

South. *Súdh,* south.

Southcott. *Súdh,* south; *côte,* a cottage. A south-cottage.

Southern. *Súdh-erna,* southern.

Southwark. *Súdh-geweorc,* from *súdh,* south, and *geweorc,* a fortress, a work. A south-work; a south-fortress.

Southwell. *Súdh,* south; *wel,* a well. A south-well.

Southwick. *Súdh,* south; *wic,* a camp. A south-camp.

Southwood. *Súdh,* south; *wud,* wood. A south-wood.

Southworth. *Súdh,* south; *weordh,* worth, price, value. South-worth; southern value.

Sower. *Sawere,* a sower.

Sowerby. *Sower,* Sower; *bý,* a dwelling, a habitation. Sower's dwelling.

Sowers. *Sower,* Sower; *s* for *sun,* son. Son of Sower.

Sox. *Socks,* from *socces,* genitive of *socc,* a sock, a woolen wrapper for the feet. Belonging to a sock.

Spackman. *Spæc,* speech ; *man,* a man. A speaker; an orator.

Spader. *Spád,* a spade ; *ere,* an agent. One who uses a spade ; a digger.

Spadone. *Spǽdan,* to speed, to prosper, to succeed.

Spaeter. *Spǽtan,* to spit ; *ere,* an agent. A spitter. Spaetter, from the same roots.

Spahn. *Span,* a span.

Spang. *Spange,* a little lock, a clasp.

Spangler. *Spange,* a lock, a clasp ; *lǽr,* doctrine. Lock-knowledge.

Spannagel. *Span,* a span ; *nægel,* a nail. A span-nail.

Spare. *Spær,* spare, frugal, moderate, small. Spare, from the same derivation.

Sparhawk. *Spear-hafoc,* from *spear,* a spear, lance, dart, and *hafoc,* a hawk. A sparrow-hawk.

Sparmaker. *Speare,* a spear ; *mac-ere,* a maker. A spear-maker.

Sparman. *Speare,* a spear ; *man,* a man. A Spearman. Spearman, from the same.

Sparrow. *Spearwa,* a sparrow.

Spearshott. *Speare,* a spear ; *scot,* a shot. A spear-shot.

Speakman. *Spéac,* speak ; *man,* a man. A speaker.

Spealler. *Spell,* history, story, speech, opinion, language ; *ere,* an agent, An historian ; a lawyer ; a linguist.

Spear. *Speare,* a spear. Speer, Speir, from the same root.

Spearing. *Spear,* Spear ; *ing,* an offspring. A descendant of Spear. Spering, a kindred word.

Spears. *Spear,* Spear ; *s* for *sun,* son. Son of Spear.

Speck. *Specca,* a blot, a blemish, a spot.

Specketer. *Specca,* a blot ; *etere,* an eater, a consumer. A blot-consumer ; a blotter.

Spedden. *Spéd-an,* to speed, to prosper, to succeed.

Speece. *Spæc,* speech.

Spect. *Spel,* a history, a narrative, a story.

Speers. *Speer*, Speer ; *s* for *sun*, son. Son of Speer.

Spellman. *Spell*, history, narration ; *man*, a man. A narrator.

Spicer. *Spic*, bacon; *ere*, an agent. A hog-butcher. Spicker, an analogous term.

Spillard. *Spill-an*, to spill, to destroy, to kill ; *ard*, an ensign of office. A destroyer; an executioner.

Spiller. *Spill-an*, to spill, to destroy ; *ere*, an agent. A destroyer.

Spillin. *Spill-ing*, a wasting, a consuming, spoiling, destruction.

Spillinger. *Spill-ing*, consuming, spoiling ; *ere*, an agent. A consumer ; a spoiler.

Spillman. *Spill-an*, to spill, to kill ; *man*, a man. An executioner ; a hangman ; a murderer.

Spindler. *Spindel*, a spindel, a needle ; *ere*, an agent. One who uses a spindle.

Spooner. *Spoon*, chips, tinder, touchwood ; *cre*, an agent. A fire-man.

Spor. *Spor*, a heel, a spur.

Sporer. *Spor*, a spur ; *ere*, an agent. One who uses a spur ; a rider.

Sporl. *Spor*, a spur ; *el*, indicative of a person. A rider.

Sprang. *Sprang*, sprang, leaped.

Spranger. *Sprang*, sprang ; *ere*, an agent. A springer ; a leaper.

Springer. *Spring*, a spring, a leap ; *ere*, an agent. A leaper.

Springfield. *Spring*, a spring, a fountain ; *feld*, a field, a plain. A springy field.

Springman. *Spring*, a spring, a leap ; *man*, a man. A leaper.

Springs. *Spring*, Spring ; *s* for *sun*, son. Son of Spring.

Springstead. *Spring*, a spring, a fountain ; *stede*, a place, a station. A spring-place.

Springthorpe. *Spring*, a spring, a fountain; *thorpe*, a village. A spring-village.

Spurr. *Spura*, a spur.

Stack. *Stáca*, a stake, a pile.

Stackel. *Stáca*, a stake, a pile; *el*, indicative of personality. One tied, or burnt at a stake.

Stacker. *Stáca*, a stake; *ere*, an agent. One who constructs a fence or a palisade. Staker, a kindred name.

Stackhouse. *Stáca*, a stake; *hús*, a house, a building. A building with a palisade; a fortress.

Stacpoole. *Stáca*, a stake; *púl*, a pool, a lake. A staked lake.

Staff. *Stæf*, a staff, stick, support, a letter, writing. Staffe, from the same root.

Staffner. *Stæf*, a staff; *nere*, refuge, preservation. Staff-preservation.

Stafford. *Stæf-ford*, from *stæf*, a stick, a pole; *ford*, a ford. A staff used in wading through a stream.

Stager. *Stæger*, a stair, step, degree.

Stagers. *Stager*, Stager; *s* for *sun*, son. Son of Stager.

Stagg. *Stæg*, a rope in the fore-part of a ship.

Stagger. *Stæg*, a rope in the fore-part of a ship; *ere*, an agent. One who has charge of the rope in the fore-part of a ship.

Staggers. *Stagger*, Stagger; *s* for *sun*, son. Son of Stagger.

Stainrook. *Stán*, a rock; *róc*, a rook. A rock-rook; a rook that dwells upon rocks.

Stains. *Stán-es*, genitive of *Stán*, a stone. From Staines, Middlesex, on the banks of the Thames, England, from a boundary stone placed here to denote the extent of the jurisdiction claimed by the city of London on the river Thames.

Stainsby. *Stains*, Stains; *bý*, a dwelling. Stains'. habitation.

Stakes. *Stake*, Stack; *s* for *sun*, son. Son of Stack.

Staley. *Stæl*, a stall, a room; *ig*, expression of an adjective. Roomy.

Stall. *Stæl*, a stall, place, seat, room.

Stallman. *Stæl*, a stall; *man*, a man. One who keeps a stall.

Stamford. *Stæng*, a stake, a pole; *ford*, a ford. A pole-ford.

Stanbridge. *Stán-brcig*, from *stán*, a stone, and *bricg*, a bridge, A stone-bridge; a paved way.

Stancliff. *Stán-cleof*, from *stán*, a stone, and *cleof*, a cliff. A stone-cliff; a rock.

Standbridge. *Stand*, a stand, a station; *bricg*, a bridge. A toll-bridge.

Standen. *Stand*, a stand; *en*, significant of a participle. Stood.

Standfield. *Stand*, a station; *feld*, a field. A station-field.

Standing. *Standan*, to stand, to continue; *ing*, expressing action. Standing; continuing.

Standish. *Stand*, a stand; *isc*, a termination of an adjective used substantively. A stand.

Standley. *Stand*, a stand; *ley* for *lic*, like. Resembling a stand.

Standring. *Stand*, a station; *hring*, a ring. A station-ring. Standering, a kindred term.

Stanfield. *Stán*, a stone; *feld*, a plain. A stone-plain.

Stanford. *Stán-ford*, from *stán*, a stone, and *ford*, a ford. A stone-ford.

Stang. *Stæng*, a bar of wood, a pole, a lever, a club. In Derbyshire, England, the word was used to denote a large pole employed in removing new-made hay.

Stanger. *Stæng*, a pole, a lever; *ere*, an agent. One who uses a lever.

Stanley. *Stán*, a stone; *lic*, like. Resembling stone.

Stansberry. *Stánes*, genitive of *stán*, a stone; *berige*, a berry. The berry of a stone; a stone-fruit. Stansbery, from the same roots.

Stansbury. *Stánes*, genitive of *stán*, a stone; *byrig*, a city. A city of stone; a stone-city.

Stansfield. *Stánes*, of stones; *feld*, a field. A field of stone; a stone-field.

Stanton. *Stán*, a stone; *tún*, a town. A stone-town. Stant, possibly, a contraction of the name. Staunton, from the same roots.

Stanwood. *Stán*, a stone; *wud*, a wood. A stone-wood.

Stanz. *Stants*, from *Stant*, Stant, and *s* for *sun*, son. Son of Stant.

Stapleford. *Stapel*, a step, a prop, a trestle; *ford*, a ford. A trestle-ford.

Stapler. *Stapel*, support; *ere*, an agent. A supporter.

Staples. *Stapeles*, genitive of *stapel*, a trestle. Belonging to a trestle.

Stapleton. *Stapel*, a step, an elevated place; *tún*, a mansion. A mansion reached by steps.

Stark. *Stearc*, stark, strong, severe, hard, austere, sharp.

Starkweather. *Stearc*, severe; *wedher*, weather. Severe weather.

Starling. *Stærn*, a starling; *ling*, a termination indicative of image, example.

Starn. *Stærn*, a starling. Starne, of like significance.

Starr. *Steorra*, a star.

Starrs. *Starr*, Starr; *s* for *sun*, son. Son of Starr.

Staub. *Staub*, a worthless vessel, one unable to stand

Staubes. *Staubes*, genitive of *staub*, a useless vessel. Belonging to a worthless vessel.

Stead. *Stæde*, a place, station, stead.

Steadham. *Stede*, steady, stable, firm; *hám*, a house. A firm house.

Steadman. *Stede*, steady, stable; *man*, a man. A steady man. Stedman, a kindred term.

Stearn. *Stearn*, the stern. Stearne, Sterne, of like derivation.

Stearns. *Stearn*, Stearn ; *s* for *sun*, son. Son of Stearn.

Stebbing. *Steb*, a boll, a trunk ; *ing*, originating from. Offspring of a trunk ; a shoot ; a branch.

Stebbins. *Stebbing*, Stebbing ; *s* for *sun*, son. Son of Stebbing.

Steed. *Stéda*, a steed, a stallion.

Steel. *Stýl*, steel. Steele, from the same radix.

Steeling. *Steel*, Steel ; *ing*, an offspring. Son of Steel.

Steelman. *Stýl*, steel ; *man*, a man. A steel-man ; a dealer in steel.

Steelwagon. *Stýl*, steel ; *wægen*, a wagon, a car. A steel-wagon ; a car for the conveyance of steel.

Steen. *Sténe*, a stone.

Steenburg. *Sténe*, a stone ; *beorg*, a mountain, a hill. A stone-hill.

Steenson. *Steen*, Steen ; *sun*, son. Son of Steen.

Steere. *Stýre*, a rule, direction, regulation, government. Steer, from the same root.

Steeringer. *Stcór-an*, to steer ; *ing*, implying action ; *ere*, an agent. One who has charge of the steering ; a pilot.

Steers. *Steer*, Steer ; *s* for *sun*, son. Son of Steer.

Steever. *Stæf*, a staff, a stick ; *ere*, an agent. One who uses a staff ; an old man.

Steffen. *Stefen*, a voice, message, sound, tone, concert, agreement. Steffan, of like meaning.

Steffe. *Stef*, a staff.

Steffens. *Steffen*, Steffen ; *s* for *sun*, son. Son of Steffen.

Steffler. *Stef*, a staff ; *lær*, doctrine. Staff-knowledge.

Steger. *Stegher*, a step, a stair.

Stell. *Stell*, a place, seat, room. Stelle, doubtless, from the same root.

Stellwagen. *Stell*, a seat ; *wægen*, a wagon, a car. A carriage. Stelwagon, of kindred signification.

Stem. *Stemn,* a voice, a command, a set time. Steman, of like derivation.

Stemme. *Stemne,* a voice, a command.

Stemmler. *Stemn,* a voice; *lēr,* doctrine. Voice-knowledge. Stemler, from the same roots.

Stempel. *Stemn,* a voice, a command; *el,* indicative of a person. A leader; a commander.

Steng. *Stenge,* a bar, a pole, a lever.

Stengel. *Stenge,* a lever; *el,* implying a person. A person that uses a lever. Stengle, a slightly varied form.

Stenger. *Stenge,* a bar, a pole; *ere,* an agent. One who uses a steng.

Stephen. *Stefen,* a voice, message, sound, tone. Stephan, from the same.

Stephens. *Stephen,* Stephen; *s* for *sun,* son. Son of Stephen. Stevens, a kindred term.

Stephenson. *Stephen,* Stephen; *sun,* son. Son of Stephen. Stevenson, from the same roots.

Sterk. *Sterc,* stark, rough, rigid.

Sterling. *Steóran,* to direct; *ling,* a termination denoting the condition of a person. In a condition to direct. Stirling, an equivalent word.

Stern. *Stern,* severe, hard, austere.

Sterner. *Stern,* severe; *ere,* an agent. A severe person.

Sternfield. *Stern,* rough, hard; *feld,* a field. A rough field.

Sterns. *Stern,* Stern; *s* for *sun,* son. Son of Stern.

Sterr. *Ster,* history.

Steward. *Stiward,* from Icelandic *stia,* work, and Anglo-Saxon *weard,* a guard. One who has the guard of work. Anciently, *stede-weard,* from *stede,* place, station, stead, and *weard,* a guard, guardianship, watch: that is, one who has the guardianship of a place. Stewart, of like kinship.

Sticker. *Stice,* a puncture, a stab; *cre,* an agent. A butcher.

Stickle. *Sticca*, a stick; *le* for *el*, indicative of a person, or expressive of the action of a person. The word originated from the practice of prize-fighters, who placed seconds with staffs, or *sticks*, to interpose occasionally: hence, to interpose.

Stickler. *Stickle*, to stickle, to interpose; *ere*, an agent. One that interposes; a sidesman to fencers; a pertinacious contender. Formerly, one who stood by to prevent the shedding of blood in a contest between two persons: so called, from the *sticks*, or staves, in his hands, with which he interposed between the combatants.

Stickley. *Stickler*, a stickler; *lic*, like. Resembling a stickler; stickler-like.

Stickling. *Stickle*, to stickle; *ing*, denoting an action. The action of a stickler.

Stickney. *Stician*, to stick, to adhere; Irish *neac̄*, an agent. One that sticks to another; an adherent.

Stidfole. *Stide*, firm, fast; *fole*, a foal, a colt. A fast foal.

Stidham. *Stide*, firm; *hám*, house An established house.

Stiff. *Stif*, stiff, hard.

Stiger. *Stigan*, to ascend, to rise, to climb; *ere*, an agent. A climber.

Stigale. *Stigel*, a stile.

Stileman. *Stigel*, a stile; *man*, a man. A man who has charge of a stile.

Stiles. *Stigale*, Stigale; *s* for *sun*, son. Son of Stigale.

Still. *Stille*, still, quiet, fixed, firm.

Stilley. *Still-ice*, stilly, quietly.

Stilling. *Still-ian*, to make still, to tranquilize; *ing*, implying action. Tranquilizing.

Stillings. *Stilling*, Stilling; *s* for *sun*, son. Son of Stilling.

Stillman. *Stille*, quiet; *man*, a man. A quiet man.

Stillwagon. *Stille*, fixed; *wægen*, a wagon. A stationary wagon.

Stillwell. *Stille*, quiet; *wel*, a well. A quiet well; an unused well. Stelwell, a cognate term.

Stilson. *Stille,* quiet, fixed; *sun,* son. A quiet son; a dead son.

Sting. *Stineg,* sting, prick, a biting, or stinging.

Stinger. *Stingan* to sting, to prick, to stab; *ere,* an agent. He who, or that which, stings, or pricks.

Stock. *Stoc,* a stock, stem, trunk, block, stick. *Stock,* past participle of *stician,* to stick: hence *stock,* in its multifarious meanings, implies fixedness.

Stocker. *Stoc,* stock; *ere,* an agent. One who has stock.

Stockham. *Stoc,* stock, stem; *hám,* a farm. A stock-farm; a nursery of trees.

Stockler. *Stoc,* stock, stem; *lær,* learning, knowledge. Stock-lore; tree-knowledge.

Stockley. *Stoc,* stock; *lic,* like. Stock-like; trunk-like; thick; stubbed; stocky.

Stockman. *Stoc,* stock, stem; *man,* a man. A stockman; a keeper of stock; a nurseryman.

Stocks. *Stock,* Stock; *s* for *sun,* son. Son of Stock.

Stockton. *Stoc,* stock; *tún,* a farm. A stock-farm.

Stockwell. *Stock,* a stock, stem, trunk, stick; *well,* a well. A well found in a wooded place.

Stoddard. *Stod,* a post, a stand, a pillar; *ard,* an ensign of office. A post-sign. Stoddart, doubtless, from the same roots.

Stoffer. *Stof,* a club; *ere,* an agent. One who uses a club; a warrior.

Stokely. *Stock,* past participle of *stic-ian,* to stick, to push, to poke, and, hence, to stir; a person who sticks, pushes, or pokes is a *sticker,* or a stoker; *lic,* like. Stoker-like. Stokley, a cognate form.

Stoker. *Sticker,* one who, or that which, *sticks,* pushes, or stirs, as it were, a fire. In Ireland, such a person was a *stoca,* a servant-boy.

Stokes. *Stoke,* Stoke; *s* for *sun,* son. Son of Stoke.

Stone. *Stán,* a stone.

Stoneham. *Stán,* stone; *hám,* house. A stone-house.

Stonehill. *Stán,* a stone; *hill,* or *hyl,* a hill. A stone-hill.
Stoneman. *Stán,* a stone; *man,* a man. A quarryman.
Stoner. *Stán,* a stone; *ere,* an agent. A stone-breaker.
Stones. *Stone,* Stone; *s* for *sun,* son. Son of Stone.
Stony. *Stǽn-ig,* or *stǽn-iht,* stony.
Stoop. *Stoppa,* a pot, a vessel, a cup.
Stoops. *Stoop,* Stoop; *s* for *sun,* son. Son of Stoop. Stoopes, a kindred form.
Storck. *Storc,* a stork. Storch, Stork, from the same radix.
Storm. *Storm,* or *steorm,* a storm, a tempest.
Storms. *Storm,* Storm; *s* for *sun,* son. Son of Storm.
Stott. *Stotte,* a hack, jade, a worthless horse.
Stotten. *Stotte,* a jade; *en,* an adjective termination. Jadish; vicious.
Stotts. *Stott,* Stott; *s* for *sun,* son. Son of Stott. Stotz, of similar derivation.
Stow. *Stow,* a place, dwelling-place, habitation.
Stowman. *Stow,* a place; *man,* a man. The man of the place; the proprietor.
Strack. *Strac,* straight, rigid, violent.
Stracker. *Strac,* rigid, violent; *ere,* an agent. A stern man; a violent man.
Strader. *Strade,* imperfect of *stredan,* to spread; *ere,* an agent. One who spreads, or straddles. Or, from *strǣde,* a stride; *ere,* one who. One who strides.
Stradinger. *Strade,* spread; *ing,* implying action; *ere,* an agent. A straddling person.
Stradling. *Strade,* spread; *ling,* denoting state or condition of a person. Act of one who straddles.
Strand. *Strand,* a strand, beach, shore.
Strang. *Strang,* strong, powerful, valiant, severe, rigid. Strong, from the same root.
Stratton. *Strǣte,* what is spread, a couch, a bed; *tún,* a house. A bed-house; an inn.
Straw. *Streow,* or *strēaw,* straw, hay, a bed.

Strawbridge. *Streaw*, a bed; *bryeg*, a bridge. A bridge that is flat like a bed.

Street. *Strǽt*, street, way, course, public road, mark.

Streeter. *Strǽt*, a way, a road; *ere*, an agent. A foot-traveler.

Streeton. *Strǽt*, a street; *tún*, a town. A city or town of streets.

Streets. *Street*, Street; *s* for *sun*, son. Son of Street.

Strenger. *Streng*, a string, sinew; *ere*, an agent. A sinewy man.

Stricker. *Strica*, a stroke; *cre*, an agent. One who makes a strike; a striker.

Strickland. *Astricen*, a participle from *astrican*, to smite; *land*, a land, a region. A smitten region. Or, from *stric*, plague, sedition, and *land*, land. A plague-land; a land of sedition.

String. *String*, a string, sinew, chord, cord, rope, line, race.

Stringer. *String*, a chord, the string of a musical instrument; *ere*, an agent. A musician.

Stringfellow. *String*, a string; *felaw*, a companion. A string-companion; a band-fellow.

Stringfield. *String*, a line; *feld*, a field. A fenced field.

Styer. *Styre*, ruling, direction, regulation, government, discipline, punishment.

Styers. *Styer*, Styer; *s* for *sun*, son. Son of Styer.

Styler. *Styl*, steel; *ere*, an agent. Steel-maker.

Styles. *Styles*, genitive of *styl*, steel. Belonging to steel.

Styring. *Styer*, Styer; *ing*, offspring. Son of Styer.

Sugden. *Súg*, a sow; *den*, a valley. Sow-valley.

Sugg. *Súg*, a sow.

Sulger. *Sulg*, a plough, a ploughshare; *ere*, an agent. One who ploughs; a ploughman.

Sullwin. *Sul*, a plough; *wine*, a friend, a disciple. A disciple of the plough; a farmer.

Summ. *Sum*, some, one, some one, any.

Summerfield. *Sumer,* or *somer,* summer; *feld,* a field. A summer-field; a field of grass and flowers. Sommerfield, of like derivation.

Sumner. *Sumer,* summer, by the insertion of an *n* between *m* and *e,* becomes the name under consideration, and affords a good illustration of one of the many attempts made to disguise the origin of names.

Sundberg. *Sund,* floating; *beorg,* a mountain. A floating mountain; an iceberg.

Sunderland. *Sunder,* sunder, separate, different; *land,* land. A separate land; a land that has been sundered, from *sundrian,* to sunder, or separated.

Sutton. *Súdh,* south; *tún,* town. South-town.

Suwald. *Súdh,* south; *wald,* wood. South-wood.

Swallow. *Swalewe,* a swallow.

Swan. *Swan,* a swan. Swann, from the same radix.

Swank. *Swânc,* imperfect of *swincan,* to toil, to labor. Labored; toil-worn.

Swanson. *Swan,* Swan; *sun,* son. Son of Swan.

Swanton. *Swan,* a swan; *tún,* town, a dwelling. A swan-dwelling.

Swarbrig. *Swǽr,* heavy; *brig,* a bridge. A heavy bridge.

Swartley. *Swart,* black; *lic,* like. Resembling black.

Sweat. *Swet,* sweat, blood, gore.

Sweater. *Swet,* sweat; *ere,* an agent. One who sweats; a laborer.

Sweatman. *Swet,* sweat; *man,* a man. A man that sweats; a toiler.

Sweet. *Swét,* sweet, pleasant.

Sweeten. *Swéten,* from *swét-an,* to sweeten. Made sweet; sweetened.

Sweeting. *Sweet,* Sweet; *ing,* an offspring. Descendant of Sweet.

Sweetland. *Swét,* pleasant; *land,* a land. A pleasant land.

Sweetman. *Swét,* pleasant; *man,* a man. An agreeable man.

Sweetwood. *Swét,* pleasant; *wud,* a wood. A pleasant wood.

Swegan. *Swég-an,* to sound, make a noise, to howl as the wind.

Sweigard. *Sweig,* a noise; *ard,* an ensign of office. One whose office is to make a noise, as evidenced by an ensign; a town-crier. Sweigert, Swigert, of like derivation.

Sweiger. *Sweig,* a noise; *ere,* an agent. A noisy fellow. Or, from *sweig-an,* to make a noise, and *ere,* an agent.

Swenck. *Swenc,* temptation, condemnation.

Swenson. *Swein,* a swain, a herdsman, a servant; *sun,* son. Son of a swain; son of a herdsman.

Swift. *Swift,* swift, nimble.

Swigler. *Swiga,* silence; *lǣr,* learning, knowledge, doctrine. Silence-doctrine.

Swiler. *Swil-ian,* to swill, to wash; *ere,* an agent. One who swills; a swiller; a drunkard.

Swilkey. *Swilce,* moreover, seeing, indeed, further.

Swindell. *Swin,* a song, a lay; *dǣl,* a dale, a valley. A song-valley.

Swindells. *Swindell,* Swindell; *s* for *sun,* son. Son of Swindell.

Swinden. *Swin,* a song; *den,* a valley. A song-valley.

Swineford. *Swin,* swine, a pig; *ford,* a ford. Swineford.

Swinehart. *Swin,* swine; *heort,* a termination denoting hearty, hearted, brave. Swine-hearted; brave as swine.

Swing. *Swing,* a whip, a blow, a stripe.

Swink. *Swinc,* labor, inconvenience, fatigue, trouble, affliction, torment, temptation, banishment.

Swinker. *Swinc,* labor, torment; *ere,* an agent. A laborer; a tormentor.

Swinton. *Swin,* a song; *tún,* a house. A song-house. Swint, perhaps, a contraction.

Swire. Swir, a column, a pillar.
Swope. Swope, a whip, a scourge.
Syckelmoore. Sicel, a sickle; *mór*, a moor, a heath. A sickled heath.
Syle. Sýl, a sill, a ground-post, a post, a pillar, a column.
Sypher. Sýfer, pure, decent, sober, abstinent, chaste.

T.

Tadly. Táde, a toad; *lic*, like. Toad-like.
Taessel. Tǽsel, teasel, the fuller's herb.
Tafel. Tæfel, a dice or gaming table, a game at table or dice.
Tag. Tæg, a bag, a chest, a coffer, a cupboard. Tage, Tagg, Tague, kindred names.
Taggart. Tæg, a bag, a chest; *geard*, a measure. Chest-measure.
Tagle. Tægel, a tail.
Tams. Irish *tam*, slow, sluggish; Anglo-Saxon *s* for *sun*, son. Son of Tamm; a slow son.
Tapking. Tæpp, a tap; *cyncg*, a king. A tap-king; a drinking king.
Tappan. Tæppan, to tap, to draw out, to drink.
Tappen. Tæppen, indicative of a participle from *tæppan*, to tap, to draw out, to drink. Tapped; drawn out; drank.
Tapper. Tæpp-ere, a tapper, butler, vinter.
Tapping. Tæpp, a tap; *ing*, expressive of action. Tapping; drawing out.
Tarbert. Tare, tar; *beorht*, glistening. Tar-glistening.
Targett. Targe, a shield, a buckler; *ett*, little, small. A little shield.
Tar. Tare, tar, balsam, pitch.
Tarring. Tarr, Tarr; *ing*, expressive of origin. Descendant of Tarr.
Tarton. Tare, tar, pitch; *tún*, a farm. A tar-farm.
Taswell. Tas, a tass; *well*, a well. A mow of corn.

Tate. *Tät,* soft, tender.

Tatham. *Tät,* soft, tender; *hám,* a home. A tender home. Tatem, perhaps, an abbreviated form of the word.

Tatlow. *Tät,* soft, tender, and *low,* a low, a bellow, from *hlowan,* to low, to bellow. A tender low; a soft bellow.

Tatman. *Tät,* soft, tender; *man,* a man. A tender man.

Taw. *Taw,* tow.

Taws. *Taw,* Taw; *s* for *sun,* son. Son of Taw.

Teal. *Teale,* an excuse.

Teamer. *Teáma,* a voucher, a witness, a leader.

Tees. *Tǽse,* right, kind, benevolent, gentle. Teese, of like import.

Teesdale. *Tǽse,* gentle; *dǽl,* a dale, a valley. A gentle dale.

Telford. *Tele,* imperfect of *tellan,* to esteem. An esteemed ford.

Telle. *Tele,* reputed, esteemed. Tell, of like significance.

Teller. *Tellan,* to tell, to relate; *ere,* an agent. A teller; a relater.

Temple. *Tempel,* Latin *templum,* a temple.

Templeman. *Tempel,* a temple; *man,* a man. A templeman; a priest.

Templeton. *Tempel,* a temple; *tún,* a house, a town. A temple-house; a church; a town of temples. When the Angles and Saxons settled in Britain, they had idols, altars, temples, and priests. These temples were surrounded with enclosures, and were profaned if lances were thrown into them. It is probable, therefore, that they obtained their word for temple directly from the Latins, and not from the Norman-French after the Conquest by William.

Thacher. *Thecere,* from *thæc,* a thach, a thatch, a roof, and *ere,* an agent. A thatcher; a roofer. Thatcher, from the same derivation.

Thatford. *Theód,* people's; *ford,* a ford. People's ford.

Thaw. *Theáw,* custom, manner, habit, behavior.

Thegen. *Thegen,* a servant, attendant, disciple, scholar, soldier, officer, knight, nobleman.

Thein. *Theign,* a servant, attendant, disciple, officer, nobleman.

Thissell. *Thistel,* a thistle. Thistle, a kindred term.

Thole. *Thól,* the thole, a piece of wood to support the oars.

Tholey. *Thól,* the thole; *lic,* like. Thole-like.

Thorman. *Thor,* Thor; *man,* a servant. A servant of Thor. Thor was one of the principal idols of the Saxons, Germans, etc. He was their Jupiter.

Thorn. *Thorn,* a thorn. Thorne, an equivalent name.

Thornberg. *Thorn,* a thorn; *beorg,* a hill. A thorn-hill; a thorny hill. Thornburg, from the same roots.

Thornberry. *Thorn,* a thorn; *berige,* a berry. A thorny berry; a prickly berry.

Thornhill. *Thorn,* a thorn; *hyll,* a hill. A thorny hill.

Thornley. *Thorn,* a thorn; *lic,* like. Thorn-like.

Thornton. *Thorn,* a thorn; *tún,* a farm. A thorny farm.

Thorp. *Thorpe,* a thorp, village. Thorpe, a kindred name.

Thrall. *Thræl,* a slave, a bondman.

Thrasher. *Thærsc-ere,* from *thærsc-an,* to thrash, and *ere,* an agent. A thrasher.

Threlfall. *Threal,* a servant; *fæl,* pure, clean, good, true. A good servant.

Thress. *Thræs,* or *thres,* a hem, a frill.

Thur. *Thur,* Thor.

Thurber. *Thur,* Thor; *beorh,* a mountain. Thor's mountain.

Thuring. *Thur,* Thor; *ing,* offspring. Descendant of Thor.

Thurman. *Thur,* Thor; *man,* a servant. Thor's servant.

Thurston. *Thures,* genitive of *Thur,* Thor; *tún,* house. Thor's house.

Thurwanger. *Thur,* Thor; *wangere,* a pillow. Thor's pillow.

Tiegman. *Tíge*, a tie, a band; *man*, a man. One who uses a band; a surgeon.

Tiel. *Tigle*, a tile.

Tier. *Tier*, a tier, rank, series, heap.

Tiers. *Tier*, Tier; *s* for *sun*, son. Son of Tier.

Tilburn. *Til*, station; *burne*, a bourn, stream, brook. A station near a stream.

Tilden. *Til*, a station; *den*, a valley. A valley-station.

Till. *Till*, a station.

Tillman. *Till*, a station; *man*, a man. A station-master. Tilman, a cognate name.

Tillyer. *Till-an*, to till, to cultivate; *ere*, an agent. A tiller; a cultivator.

Tilton. *Til*, station; *tún*, town. A station-town.

Tindall. *Tin*, tin; *dál*, a valley. A tin-valley. Tindel, from the same root.

Tine. *Tine*, a tine, tooth of a harrow.

Tines. *Tine*, Tine; *s* for *sun*, son. Son of Tine.

Tinney. *Tin-ig*, resembling tin.

Tinsley. *Tines*, genitive of *tin*, tin; *lic*, form, like. Tin-like; form of tin. Tinley, of similar derivation.

Tinsman. *Tines*, genitive of *tin*, tin; *man*, man. A dealer in tin; a seller of tin.

Toft. *Toft*, a croft, a homestead.

Tool. *Tól*, a tool, an instrument. Toole, from the same root.

Toon. *Tún*, pronounced *toon*, a field, dwelling, house, mansion, yard, farm, village, class, course, town. Toone, of like derivation.

Tooney. *Tún-ig*, from *tún*, a town, and *ig*, an adjective termination implying resemblance. Townish.

Toorish. *Torr*, a tower; *isc*, an adjective termination signifying resembling. Tower-like.

Toothaker. *Tódh-ece*, the toothache; *ere*, an agent. One who has the toothache.

Topham. *Top*, a ball, a tuft at the top of anything; *hám*, a home. A hilly home.

Topley. *Top*, a ball; *lic*, like. Resembling a ball.

Tophs. *Top*, a ball; *liss*, favor. Ball-favor.

Topping. *Top*, a ball; *ing*, implying action. Balling.

Torbeort. *Tor*, a tower, a high hill, rock, peak, tor; *beorht*, glistening, shining. A glistening peak.

Torr. *Tor*, a tower, rock, peak, tor.

Torrey. *Tor-ig*, from *tor*, a tower, a hill, a rock; *ig*, an adjective termination. Towering; hilly; rocky.

Tower. *Tor*, a tower, a high hill.

Towers. *Tower*, Tower; *s* for *sun*, son. Son of Tower.

Town. *Tún*, a field, a dwelling, house, mansion, farm, village, town, city. Towne, from the same radix.

Towner. *Tún*, a town; *ere*, an agent. A dweller in a town; a townsman.

Townley. *Tún*, a town; *lic*, like. Resembling a town.

Towns. *Town*, Town; *s* for *sun*, son. Son of Town.

Townsend. *Túnes*, genitive of *tún*, a town; *end*, termination of masculine nouns denoting a man. A townsman.

Townson. *Town*, Town; *sun*, son. Son of Town.

Trager. *Trag*, evil, bad; *ere*, an agent. An evil person; a sinner.

Treadway. *Træd*, trod; *wæg*, a way. A trodden way. Or, from *tred*, a step, and *wæg*, a way. A step-way; a stairs. Tredway, of like derivation.

Treadwell. *Tred*, a step; *well*, a well. A step-well.

Tree. *Treow*, or *treo*, a tree, a club.

Tregea. *Tréga*, vexation, tribulation, contumely, loss, misery, torment. Trego, perhaps, from the same root.

Tresch. *Treisc*, tragical. Tresck, from the same root.

Trescher. *Treisc*, tragical; *ere*, an agent. A tragedian. Tresher, an equivalent name.

Treude. *Treúdh*, troth, truth, league, pledge, covenant.

Trewin. *Tré*, vexation, tribulation; *win*, a man. A man of tribulation.

Trexler. *Treise*, tragical; *lár*, knowledge, learning. Tragedy.

Treischbock. *Treise*, tragical; *bóc*, a book. A book of tragedy.

Trimmingham. *Trymming*, confirming, fortifying, establishing; *hám*, a house. A house of confirmation.

Troth. *Treówdh*, troth, truth.

Trout. *Truht*, a trout. Troutt, an equivalent name.

Troutman. *Truht*, a trout; *man*, a man. A trout-fisher.

Trow. *Treów*, trust, faith, pledge, covenant.

Trowbridge. *Treówe*, faithful; *brieg*, a bridge. A faithful bridge.

Trowell. *Treów*, trust, faith; *el*, indicative of a person. A trusty person; a faithful person.

True. *Trýwe*, true, faithful.

Trueman. *Trýwe*, true; *man*, a man, a servant. A true man; a faithful servant. Truman, of similar import.

Tudor. *Tudor*, issue, offspring, seed, progeny, posterity, family. Tuder, a kindred name.

Tuman. *Tú*, two; *man*, a man. Twin-man; twin-brother.

Tumbleston. *Tumb-ian*, to tumble; *stán*, a rock. A rock that tumbles; a tumbling rock.

Tunis. *Túnes*, genitive of *tún*, a town. Belonging to a town.

Tunison. *Túnes*, genitive of *tún*, a town; *sun*, son. Son of a town; a townsman.

Tunney. *Tún*, a town; *ig*, an adjective termination. Townish. Tunny, of similar derivation.

Tuohy. *Tuoege*, two.

Turkington. *Turk*, from Irish *torc*, a boar; *ing*, implying a descendant; *tún*, house. Home of a descendant of Turk. Torkington, of similar significance.

Turland. *Tur*, a tower, a high hill, a peak; *land*, a land. A hilly land.

Turley. *Tur*, a tower; *lic*, like. Resembling a tower; tower-like; towering.

Turnbolt. *Turnian,* to turn; *bolt,* a bolt. A turned bolt.

Turnbull. *Turnian,* to turn; *bull,* a stud, a brooch. A turned brooch.

Turner. *Turnian,* to turn; *ere,* an agent. A turner.

Turnpenny. *Turnian,* to turn; *penig,* a penny. A turned penny.

Turpin. *Tur,* a rock; *pinn,* a pen. A rock pen; a steel pen.

Turtle. *Turtel,* or *turtle,* a turtle, a turtle-dove.

Tussey. *Tusc,* the canine, or eye-tooth, a tusk; *ig,* denoting an adjective. Tusky.

Tustin. *Tusc,* a tusk; *tine,* a tine. Tine of a tusk.

Tuston. *Tusc,* a tusk; *tún,* a house, a dwelling. A tusk-house.

Twaddell. *Twæde,* double, two-fold; *dǽl,* a dale, a valley. A twin-valley.

Tway. *Twá,* twice, double.

Tweed. *Twæde,* double, two-fold.

Tweedale. *Tweo,* double; *dǽl,* a dale, a valley. A twin-valley.

Tweedie. *Twæde,* double, two-fold.

Tweedle. *Twæde,* double; *le,* for *el,* indicative of a person. A twin.

Twitman. *Ætwitan,* to tease, to reproach, to blame, to upbraid; *man,* a man. A person who upbraids another.

Twibill. *Twy-bill,* a twibill, a pole-axe.

Twiford. *Twy-ford,* a double ford. Applied to the name of places near a river where two branches had to be forded.

Twigg. *Twig,* two, double.

Twigs. *Twig,* Twig; *s* for *sun,* son. Son of Twig.

Twiney. *Twin,* thread, twine, fine linen; *ig,* expressive of an adjective. Resembling twine.

Twining. *Twin-an,* to twine, to twist; *ing,* implying action. Twining; twisting.

Twitchell. Twiccian, to twitch; *el*, a termination denoting a person. A person that twitches; a nervous, restless person.

Tyber. Tiber, a sacrifice, gift, offering, victim.

Tye. Ty, instructs, teaches, imbues, inures.

Tyer. Ty, instructs, teaches; *ere*, an agent. An instructor; a teacher.

Tylacher. Ty, instructs; *lach*, a garment; *ere*, an agent. A sewing-teacher; a tailor. Tylacker, a kindred name.

Tymon. Ty, instructs; *mon*, a man. A man that instructs; a pedagogue.

Tynan. Tynan, to hedge in, to enclose, to shut.

Tyne. Tyne, ten.

Tyner. Tyne, ten; *ere*, an agent. A person of ten years of experience.

Tyre. Tyr, a leader, prince, glory, splendor.

Tyrell. Tyr, a prince; *el*, an ending denoting a person. A princely person.

Tyson. Tye, Tye; *sun*, son. Son of Tye.

U.

Ulm. Ulm, an elm.

Ulman. Ulm, an elm; *man*, a man. An elm-man; a propagator of the elm.

Ulmer. Ulm, an elm; *ere*, an agent. A cultivator of the elm.

Ulric. Ulph-ric, from *ulph*, help, aid, assistance, and *ric*, rich, powerful. Rich, or powerful in help. Ulrick, a cognate term.

Umstead. Hulme, for *holm*, the deep sea, abyss, ocean, water, and *stede*, a place. Ocean-place. Umsted, an analogous name.

Underdown. Under, under; *dun*, a mountain, a hill. An under hill.

Underhill. Under, under; *hyll*, a hill. An under hill.

Underwood. *Under,* under; *wud,* wood. Under-wood; undergrowth.

Unger. *Ungr,* hunger.

Ungerer. *Ungr,* hunger; *ere,* an agent. A hungry person.

Upham. *Upp,* high, lofty; *hám,* a house. A lofty home.

Upmann. *Upp,* high; *mann,* a man. A man high in position; a man of rank; a superior.

Upp. *Upp,* high, lofty.

Upright. *Up-riht,* upright, erect.

Upson. *Up,* Upp; *sun,* son. Son of Upp.

Upton. *Upp,* high, lofty; *tún,* a town. A lofty town.

Ustick. *Ust,* a tempest; *ig,* an adjective termination. Tempestuous; stormy.

Uth. *Udh,* pronounced *uth,* termination of the feminine noun *geogudh,* youth.

Uting. *Ut,* Utt; *ing,* an offspring. Descendant of Utt.

Utt. *Ut,* out, without, abroad.

Uttley. *Utt,* Utt; *lic,* like. Resembling Utt.

W.

Wade. *Wád,* a ford.

Wadsworth. *Wádes,* genitive of *wád,* a ford; *weordh,* value, price. Valuable ford.

Waer. *Wær,* an enclosure, a fishpond, a wear, a wave.

Waesch. *Wæsc,* a washing.

Wagel. *Wægel,* a gill, a little vessel.

Wagener. *Wægen-ere,* a wagoner, driver of a car. Waggener, Wagner, Wagoner, kindred terms.

Wager. *Wæg,* a wey, weigh, weight; *ere,* an agent. A weigher.

Wagstaff. *Wæg,* a balance; *stæf* a staff, stick, pole. A balance-pole.

Wainwright. *Wæn-wyrhta,* a wheelwright.

Wake. *Wæcce,* wake, watch, vigil. A watching.

Wakefield. *Wæcan,* to awake, arise, to be born; past participle *wacen,* awakened; *feld,* a field. An awakened field.

Wakeley. *Wǣc-lic,* from *wǣc,* weak, and *lic,* like. Weak-like; weakly. Wakelee, of similar derivation.

Wakeling. *Wǣc,* weak; *ling,* implying the condition of a person. A weakling; a feeble creature.

Walborn. *Wæl,* or *wal,* slaughter, carnage, death; *born,* born. Dead-born; stillborn.

Walee. *Wale,* a veil.

Walch. *Walch,* a foreigner, a stranger, a servant, a slave.

Walcher. *Walch,* a foreigner, a stranger; *ere,* an agent. A foreigner.

Wald. *Wald,* a forest, wood, grove, weald, wild, wold. Walde, of like import.

Waldeck. *Wald,* a wood; *ig,* implying an adjective. Woody.

Walden. *Wald,* wood; *en,* an adjective termination. Woody.

Walder. *Wald,* a forest; *ere,* an agent. A forester.

Walderford. *Walda,* a ruler; *ford,* a ford. The ruler's ford.

Walderly. *Walda-lic,* from *walda,* a ruler, and *lic,* like. Resembling a ruler.

Waldie. *Wald,* a wood; *ig,* denoting an adjective. Woody.

Waldis. *Wald,* a wood; *isc,* like. Wood-like.

Waldman. *Wald,* a wood; *man,* a man. A woodman. Waldmann, a kindred name.

Waldner. *Wald,* a wood, a forest; *nere,* a refuge. Wood-refuge.

Waldron. *Wald,* a wood; *rond,* a border. A wood-border.

Walds. *Wald,* Wald; *s* for *sun,* son. Son of Wald.

Waley. *Wæl,* a well, *ig,* implying an adjective. Well-like.

Walfish. *Wæl,* a well; *fisc,* a fish. A well-fish.

Walford. Wáll, a rampart; *ford,* a ford. A rampart-ford; a moat.

Walk. Wcolc, imperfect of *wealcan,* to roll, turn, tumble, revolve, turn up and down. Rolled; tumbled; revolved; turned up and down.

Walker. Weolc, rolled, revolved, turned up and down; *ere,* an agent. One who turned up and down; a walker.

Walkley. Walk, Walk; *lic,* like. Resembling Walk.

Wall. Weall, or *wáll,* a wall, a rampart.

Wallace. Wáll, a rampart, a bulwark; *læce,* a surgeon. The surgeon of a rampart. Wallack, Wallick, of like derivation.

Wallen. Wáll, a wall; *en,* a termination denoting an adjective. Wall-like.

Waller. Wáll, a wall; *ere,* an agent. A waller; a mason.

Wallers. Waller, Waller; *s* for *sun,* son. Son of Waller.

Walley. Wáll, a wall; *ig,* denoting an adjective. Wall-like.

Wallgren. Wáll, a wall; *gréne,* green. Wall-green.

Wallin. Wáll, a wall; *in,* an inn, a dwelling. A walled dwelling.

Walling. Wáll, a wall; *ing,* an offspring. Descendant of Wall.

Wallington. Walling, Walling; *tún,* house. Home of Walling.

Wallis. Weallisc, foreign, Welsh.

Walliser. Weallisc, Welsh; *ere,* an agent. A Welshman.

Walls. Wall, Wall; *s* for *sun,* son. Son of Wall.

Wallum. Wáll, a wall; *um* for *hám,* a house, a dwelling. A walled house.

Walmsley. Wælmes, genitive of *wælm,* heat, anger; *lic,* form, likeness. Form of anger; resembling heat.

Wain. Wǽn, a wain, wagon, carriage.

Walnut. Wáll, a wall; *hnut,* a nut. A walled nut.

Walraun. Wáll, a wall; *hræfen,* a raven. A wall-raven.

Walsh. *Weallise,* Welsh. Welch, Welsh, Welsch, from the same radix.

Walstead. *Wäll,* a wall; *stede,* a place. A walled, or fortified place.

Walstrum. *Wäll,* a wall, a rampart; *streom,* a stream. A walled stream; an aqueduct.

Walt. *Wald,* a wood, a forest.

Walter. *Wald,* a forest; *ere,* an agent. A forester. Walther, doubtless, a kindred name.

Walters. *Walter,* Walter; *s* for *sun,* son. Son of Walter.

Waltman. *Wald,* a wood; *man,* a man. A wood-man; a hunter.

Waltoe. *Wäl,* a wall; *tæ,* a toe. A wall-toe; the toe used in scaling a rampart.

Waltun. *Wäl,* a wall; *tún,* a dwelling. A walled dwelling.

Waltram. *Wald,* a wood; *ram,* a ram. A wooden ram; a battering-ram.

Walwork. *Wäll-geweorc,* from *wäll,* a wall, and *geweorc,* work. Wall-work.

Wamalong. *Woma,* a sound; *long,* long. A continued sound.

Wambold. *Wam,* crime; *bóld,* audacious. An audacious crime.

Wampole. *Wam,* a stain; *pol,* a pole. A stained pole; a bludgeon.

Wanamaker. *Wana,* deficient, lacking, imperfect; *macian,* to make; *ere,* an agent. An unskilled mechanic.

Wandall. *Wan,* deficient, wanting, void; *dál,* a valley. An empty valley. Wandell, of like significance.

Wanner. *Wann,* pale, livid, dusky, dark; *ere,* an agent. A wan person.

Warbrick. *Wár,* caution; *bric,* a bridge. A caution-bridge.

Warburton. *Wǣr-borh,* a pledge for the payment of the were or fine for slaying a man; *tún,* a town. A town's pledge for the payment of the were or fine for slaying a man.

Ward. *Weard*, a warden, ward-keeper, guardian, watchman.

Warder. *Weard*, watch, vigilance; *ere*, denoting an agent. A watchman.

Wardin. *Weardin*, a watch-tower.

Wardle. *Weard*, a guard, guardianship, watch; *le* for *el*, implying a person. A watchman.

Wardrop. *Weard*, a warden; *rop*, broth, pottage. A warden's pottage.

Ware. *Ware*, a harbor, a haven. Or, from *wǣr*, an enclosure.

Wareham. *Wǣr-hám*, from *wǣr*, an enclosure, and *hám*, a house, a dwelling. A fortified dwelling. Waream, an abbreviated form of the same.

Warfield. *Wær*, war; *feld*, a field, a plain. A battlefield.

Warford. *Wǣr*, an enclosed place; *ford*, a ford. An enclosed ford.

Waring. *Ware*, Ware; *ing*, an offspring. Son of Ware. Or, from *wǣring*, a wall.

Wark. *Wærc*, work, labor, fatigue, suffering, pain, grief, anguish.

Warley *Wær*, war; *lic*, like. Warlike.

Warman. *Wær*, war; *man*, a man. A warrior.

Warmuth. *Wær*, war; *múdh*, mouth. War-mouth; declaration of war.

Warne. *Wearn*, a keeping off, obstacle, resistance, refusal, denial.

Warner. *Warnian*, to warn,; *ere*, an agent. One who gives warning.

Warnig. *Wearn*, obstacle, resistance; *ig*, denoting an adjective. Opposing; resistful. Warnick, Warnecke, Warnock, kindred terms.

Warr. *Wearr*, a knot, a wart.

Warrick. *Wearr-ig*, or *wearr-iht*, knotty, rough.

Warris. *Wearr*, a knot, a wart; *isc*, implying like. Knot-like; hard; rough.

Warth. *Warodh*, a shore, a weed on the shore.

Warthman. *Warodh*, a shore; *man*, a man. A shore-man; a land-man.

Wartman. *Weart*, a wart; *man*, a man. A warty man

Warwick. *Wǽring-wic*, from *wǽring*, a bulwark, and *wic*, a dwelling. A fortified dwelling.

Wasch. *Wæsc*, a washing.

Wasrott. *Wæs*, water; *rot*, a mastiff. A water-mastiff.

Washam. *Wæsc*, a washing; *hám*, a house. A wash-house; a laundry.

Washburne. *Wæsc*, a washing; *burne*, a stream, brook, river, well. A washing stream. Washburn, from the same root.

Washington. *Wæsc-ing*, a washing; *tún*, a house. A washing house.

Waste. *Wæsten*, or *wéste*, a desert.

Water. *Wæter*, water.

Waterall. *Wæter*, water; *all*, all. All-water; a deluge.

Waterbury. *Wæter*, water; *byrig*, a city. A watery city; a watering-place.

Waterfield. *Wæter*, water; *feld*, a plain. A watery field; a meadow.

Waterford. *Wæter*, water; *ford*, a ford. A watery ford; a ford that is not dry.

Waterhouse. *Wæter*, water; *hús*, a house. A spring-house.

Waterman. *Wæter*, water; *man*, a man. A water-man; a boatman.

Waters. *Water*, Water; *s* for *sun*, son. Son of Water. Watters, a cognate term.

Waterson. *Water*, Water; *sun*, son. Son of Water. Watterson, of like derivation.

Watford. *Wæt*, wet, moist; *ford*, a ford. A wet ford; a water-ford.

Watkin. *Wæt*, water, liquor, drink: *cyn*, akin. Akin to water.

Watkins. Watkin, Watkin; *s* for *sun*, son. Son of Watkin.

Watkinson. Watkin, Watkin; *sun*, son. Son of Watkin.

Watt. Wæt, wet, moisture, drink, liquor, water.

Wattis. Wæt, water; *isc*, like. Water-like.

Watton. Watt, Watt; *tún*, house. House of Watt.

Watts. Watt, Watt; *s* for *sun*, son. Son of Watt.

Wattson. Watt, Watt; *sun*, son. Son of Watt. Watson, a slightly abbreviated form of the name.

Wax. Weax, or *wæx*, wax.

Waxler. Weax, wax; *lær*, doctrine. Wax-knowledge.

Way. Wæg, or *weg*, a way, passage, road.

Wayland. Wæg, a road; *land*, land, ground. Road-land; a highway.

Waylen. Wæg, a road; *lén*, a loan. Loan, or leased road.

Wayman. Wæg, road; *man*, a man. A road-man; a wayfarer; a traveler.

Wayne. Wæn, a wain, wagon, carriage.

Waysz. Ways, from *Way*, Way, and *s* for *sun*, son. Son of Way.

Weaber. Wæbb, a web; *cre*, an agent. One who, or that which, makes a web; a weaver.

Weadley. Wæd, a garment, apparel, weeds; *lic*, form. Form of weeds; garment-like.

Weagle. Wægel, a gill, a little vessel.

Weak. Wæc, weak.

Weakley. Wæc-lic, from *wæc*, weak, and *lic*, like. Weakly; foolishly; vilely.

Weaks. Weak, Weak; *s* for *sun*, son. Son of Weak.

Weand. Wænd, or *wend*, a turn, a change.

Wear. Wear, a knot, a wart. Weare, of similar derivation.

Wears. Wear, Wear; *s* for *sun*, son. Son of Wear.

Weart. Weart, a wart.

Weaser. Wæs, water; *cre*, an agent. A waterer.

Weatherby. Wæder, or *weder*, weather, storm, tempest; *bý*, a habitation, a dwelling. A signal dwelling; a weather-house.

Weatherhead. Wæder, storm; *heáfd*, a head. Storm-head.

Weatherley. Wæder, weather, storm; *lic*, like. Weather-like; storm-like. Wetherly, of like meaning.

Weaver. Wæfre, or *wyfre*, a weaver.

Webb. Webb, a web, cloth, tapestry.

Webber. Webb-ere, from *webb*, a web, and *ere* an agent. A weaver.

Weber. Web, a web, cloth, tapestry; *ere*, an agent. A weaver. Weeber, of similar import.

Webster. Web, a web, cloth; *ster* from *steóre*, direction, a noun-ending denoting direction, guidance. Web-direction.

Wecker. Wæccer, watchful, lively.

Weckerly. Wæccer-lic, from *wæccer*, watchful, and *lic*, like. Watchful-like; watchfully. Weckerley, a kindred term.

Weddell. Wed, a pledge, a promise; *dál*, a dale. A promised dale. Wedell, from the same roots.

Weder. Weder, weather, the air, firmament, storm, tempest. Or, from *weder*, a wether.

Wedge. Wecg, a wedge.

Wedig. Weód, a weed; *ig*, an adjective termination. Weedy.

Wedinger. Weódung, a weeding; *ere*, an agent. One who, or that which, weeds; a weeder.

Wedlock. Wed-lác, from *wed*, a pledge, and *lác*, a gift. A pledge-gift.

Wedman. Wed, a pledge; *man*, a man. A pledge-man; a married man. Wedmann, of like meaning.

Weed. Weód, herb, grass, pasture, a weed.

Weeden. Weód-ian, to weed; *weód-en*, perfect participle. Weeded; rid of weeds.

Weeder. Weód-ere. A weeder.

Weedstram. *Weód,* a weed; *stream,* a stream, a river. A weedy stream.

Weekes. *Weoces,* genitive of *weoc,* a week. Weeks, a kindred term.

Weckley. *Weoc,* a week; *lic,* like. Week-like; weekly. Weekly, of similar derivation.

Weer. *Wér,* a fine for slaying a man, the price or value of a man's life. Every man was valued at a certain sum, which was called his *wér,* and whoever took his life was required to pay this *wér* to the family or relatives of the deceased. Perhaps the name is derived from *wér,* an enclosure.

Weest. *Weast, wæst,* or *west,* west.

Weger. *Weg,* a wey, a weight; *ere,* an agent. A weigher.

Wegman. *Weg,* a wey, a weight; *man,* a man. A weigher.

Weightman. *Wiht,* weight; *man,* a man. A weigher.

Welbank. *Well,* a well, a fountain; *banc,* a bench, bank, hillock. A well-bank. Wellbank, a kindred name.

Welchman. *Weallisc,* Welsh; *man,* a man. A Welshman.

Welcher. *Wealcere,* a fuller, a walker. Welker, of similar derivation.

Welcom. *Wel-cuma,* a pleasure-comer, one received with gladness, a beloved guest.

Welle. *Well,* a well, a fountain.

Weller. *Wellere,* a hollow, a bosom.

Wellers. *Weller,* Weller; *s* for *sun,* son. Son of Weller.

Welles. *Welle,* Welle; *s* for *sun,* son. Son of Welle. Wells, Welz, from the same roots.

Welling. *Well,* Welle; *ing,* an offspring. Descendant of Welle.

Wellington. *Welling,* Welling; *tún,* house. Home of Welling.

Wellwood. *Well,* rich, flourishing; *wud,* wood. A flourishing wood.

Welman. *Wel,* rich, wealthy; *man,* a man. A wealthy man.

Welmesley. *Welmes,* genitive of *welm,* heat, fire; *lic,* form. Form of heat; fire-like.

Welstead. *Wel,* a well; *stæde,* a place, a station. A well-place.

Welton. *Wel,* rich, flourishing; *tún,* a city. A flourishing city.

Wemmer. *Wemere,* a harlot.

Wenban. *Wen,* a wen, a tower; *bán,* a bone. A wen-bone.

Wence. *Wencle,* a maid, a daughter. Wence, Wenk, of similar derivation.

Wendel. *Wend,* a turn, change; *el,* implying a person. One who turns, or changes; a fickle person. Wendell, Wendle, from the same roots.

Wendling. *Wend,* a turn, a change; *ling,* a termination denoting the state of a person. Turning; changing.

Wenner. *Wenn,* a wen; *ere,* an agent. A wen-doctor.

Wenger. *Wengere,* a pillow, a bolster.

Wenhold. *Wen,* pleasure; *hold,* friendship. A pleasure-friendship.

Wenrich. *Wen,* joy, pleasure; *rice,* power, dominion. Pleasure-dominion.

Wensel. *Wen,* pleasure; *sel,* palace, hall. Pleasure-hall.

Wensler. *Wenes,* genitive of *wen,* pleasure; *lár,* doctrine. Pleasure-knowledge.

Wensley. *Wenes,* genitive of *wen,* pleasure; *lic,* form. Form of pleasure; joy-like.

Wentling. *Wente,* the Gwents, or Welsh; *ling,* a termination denoting the state or condition of a person. Welsh-state.

Wentworth. *Wente,* the Gwents, or Welsh; *weordh,* dignity. Welsh dignity.

Werfel. *Wer,* a man; *fel,* skin. Man's skin.

Wermouth. *Wer,* a man; *múdh,* the mouth. Mouth of man.

Werner. *Wernan,* to warn; *ere,* an agent. One who warns; a warner.

Wernley. *Wern,* a squirrel; *lic,* like. Squirrel-like.

Werson. *Wer*, a man; *sun*, son. Son of man.

Werst. *Werst*, worst.

Wert. *Wert*, wort, an herb, plant.

Wertman. *Wert*, an herb; *man*, a man. An herb-man.

Wertz. *Werts*, from *Wert*, Wert, and *s* for *sun*, son. Son of Wert.

Wesley. *Wes*, the west; *lic*, like. Resembling the west; westernly.

Weslyn. *Wesline*, a rough coat.

Wesson. *Wes*, the west; *sun*, son. A western son.

West. *West*, the west. Weste, of like meaning.

Westscott. *West*, the west; *scot*, payment. The western payment.

Westall. *West*, the west; *all*, all, whole. Wholly west.

Westbrook. *West*, the west; *bróc*, a brook. A western brook.

Westcott. *West*, the west; *côte*, a cottage. A western cottage. Westcote, of like derivation.

Wester. *West*, the west; *ere*, an agent. A western man. Or, from *wéste*, a desert, and *ere*, an agent. A man of the desert.

Westerman. *Western*, a desert place; *man*, a man. A desert-man.

Westholt. *West*, the west; *holt*, a forest. A western forest.

Westing. *West*, west; *ing*, an offspring. Descendant of West.

Westly. *West*, west; *lic*, like. West-like; westernly.

Westney. *Westan-ig*, from *westan*, west, and *ig*, an island. Western island.

Weston. *West*, the west; *tún*, a town. A western town.

Westwood. *Westan-wudu*, from *westan*, western, and *wudu*, wood. Western wood.

Weter. *Weter*, water.

Wetherald. *Wedher*, a wether, a ram; *ald*, old. An old wether; an old ram.

Wetherbee. *Wedher*, weather; *beo*, a bee. A weather-bee. Weatherbee, a kindred name.

Wetherell. *Wedher*, weather; *ell*, all. All weather; weather for all. Wetherill, doubtless, from the same roots.

Wetherhold. *Wedher*, weather; *hold*, pleasant. Agreeable weather.

Wetmer. *Wet*, wet; *mere*, a sea. A wet sea.

Wetmore. *Wet-mór*, from *wet*, wet, and *mór*, a moor. A wet moor.

Wetstone. *Wet*, wet; *stæn*, a stone. A wet stone.

Wetton. *Wet*, wet; *tún*, a town. A wet town.

Wheat. *Hwǽte*, wheat.

Wheatcroft. *Hwǽte*, wheat; *croft*, a small field. A wheat field.

Wheatland. *Hwǽte*, wheat; *land*, land. Wheat land.

Wheatley. *Hwǽte*, wheat; *lic*, like. Resembling wheat.

Wheaton. *Hwǽte*, wheat; *tún*, farm. A wheat farm.

Wheeler. *Hweohl*, or *hweol*, a wheel, circle, the world; *ere*, an agent. A wheeler. Or, from *hweolere*, a diviner.

Wheelock. *Hweohl*, a wheel; *loc*, a lock. A wheel-lock.

Whelan. *Hwélan*, to become foul, to putrefy.

Whelen. *Hwélen*, a participle derived from *hwélan*, to become foul. Made foul.

Whetham. *Hwet*, wet; *hám*, house. Wet house; water-house. Whithem, Whittem, other forms of spelling.

Whetstone. *Hwet-stán*, from *hwet*, sharpening, and *stán*, stone. Whetstone.

Whipp. *Hweop*, a whip.

Whipper. *Hweop*, a whip; *ere*, an agent. One who whips; a whipper.

Whippey. *Hweop*, a whip; *ig*, an adjective termination. Whip-like.

Whipple. *Hweop*, a whip; *el*, a termination expressive of an inanimate object. A whip-like bar.

Whistler. *Hwistlere*, a whistler, a piper. Whisler, an abbreviated form of the name.

Whitaker. *Hwit*, white; *æcer*, a field. A white field. Whitecar, Whittaker, of like import.

Whitall. *Hwitel*, a white mantle; a priest's cope. Whital, Whittle, cognate terms.

Whitby. *Hwit*, white; *by̆*, a habitation. A white habitation.

Whitcomb. *Hwit*, white; *comb*, a valley. A white valley.

White. *Hwite*, white. Whyte, from the same root.

Whitchurch. *Hwite-cirice*, from *hwit*, white, and *cirice*, a church. A white church.

Whitecraft. *Hwite*, white; *cræft*, trade, occupation. A white trade.

Whitefield. *Hwite*, white; *feld*, a field. A white field. Whitfield, of similar meaning.

Whiteford. *Hwite*, white; *ford*, a ford. A white ford.

Whitehead. *Hwite*, white; *heáfod*, a head. A white head.

Whitehill. *Hwite*, white; *hyll*, a hill. A white hill.

Whitehouse. *Hwite*, white; *hús*, a house. A white house.

Whiteley. *Hwite*, white; *lic*, like. Resembling white. Whitely, Whitley, of like derivation.

Whiteline. *Hwite*, white; *lin*, flax. White flax. Or, from *hwite*, white, and Latin *linea*, a line: hence, a white line.

Whiteling. *Hwite*, white; *ling*, a termination denoting state of a person. Whiteness. Whitling, a kindred term.

Whitelock. *Hwite*, white; *locc*, a lock, hair. White hair. Whitlock, from the same roots.

Whiteman. *Hwite*, white; *man*, a man. A white man. Whitman, kindred name.

Whitenack. *Hwite*, white; *naca*, a skiff. A white skiff.

Whitesell. *Hwite*, white; *sel*, a hall. A white hall. Whitzell, of similar import.

Whiteside. *Hwite*, white; *side*. a side. A white side.

Whitesides. *Whiteside*, Whiteside; *s* for *sun*, son. Son of Whiteside.

Whiting. *White*, White; *ing*, an offspring. Descendant of White.

Whitmore. *Hwit,* white; *mór,* a moor. A white moor.

Whitnall. *Hwiten,*—participle from *hwitian,* to whiten,—made white or whitened; *all,* all. All whitened.

Whitney. *Hwiten,* whitened; *ig,* an adjective termination. Whitish; somewhat white.

Whitnight. *Hwit,* white; *niht,* night. A white night; a moonlit night.

Whiton. *Hwit,* white; *tún,* a farm. A white farm.

Whitson. *Hwit,* white; *sun,* son. A white son; a pale son.

Whitten. *Hwiten,* from *hwit-ian,* to whiten. Whitened.

Whittenberg. *Hwiten,* whitened; *beorg,* a hill. A whitened hill.

Whittendale. *Hwiten,* whitened; *dál,* a valley. A whitened valley.

Whittig. *Hwit,* white; *ig,* an adjective termination. Whitish. Whittick, Whitty, of like derivation.

Whittingham. *Whitting,* Whiting; *hám,* house. Home of Whiting.

Whittington. *Whitting,* Whiting; *tún,* house. House of Whiting.

Whitworth. *Hwit,* white; *weordh,* honor, dignity. White, or unsullied honor.

Whorf. *Hwearf,* a wharf, a shore.

Why. *Hwy,* why, wherefore, indeed.

Whyard. *Hwy,* why; *ard,* indicating an ensign. One who asks for reasons; a questioner.

Wiard. *Wi,* an idol; *ard,* indicative of an ensign. An idolater.

Wibberley. *Wibba,* a worm; *lic,* like. Worm-like.

Wible. *Wibil,* a weasel, a beetle.

Wicemann. *Wic,* a castle; *mann,* a man. Man of the castle. Wichmann, of similar derivation.

Wichelmann. *Wicelian,* to stagger, to reel; *mann,* a man. A staggering man.

Wick. *Wic,* a dwelling-place, mansion, village, street, convent, camp, castle, fortress.

Wickel. *Wicele,* present indicative first person of *wicelian,* to stagger, to reel.

Wickersham. *Wic,* a camp; *ere,* an agent; *wiceres,* genitive of *wicere,* a soldier; *hám,* a house. A soldier's home.

Wicks. *Wick,* Wick; *s* for *sun,* son. Son of Wick. Wickes, from the same roots.

Wickfield. *Wic,* a camp; *feld,* a field, a plain. A campfield; a tented plain.

Wickham. *Wic,* a camp; *hám,* home. A camp-home.

Wickman. *Wic,* a camp; *man,* a man. A camp-man; a soldier.

Widdall. *Wid,* grass; *dál,* a valley. A grass-valley.

Widdifield. *Widisc,* grassy; *feld,* a field, a plain. A grassy plain.

Widdis. *Wid,* grass; *isc,* an adjective termination denoting like. Grassy.

Widdows. *Widewe,* a widow; *s* for *sun,* son. Son of a widow. Widdoes, a cognate term.

Wideman. *Wid,* wide, broad, famous; *man,* a man. A broad man; a famous man. Widemann, Widman, Widmann, of like import.

Widemer. *Wid-mǣre,* from *wid,* far, and *mǣre,* famed. Far-famed. Widmer, from the same roots.

Widener. *Wid,* grass; *nere,* a refuge. A grass-refuge. Widner, a cognate term.

Widger. *Wicg,* a horse, a steed; *ere,* an agent. A horseman; a warrior.

Widley. *Wid,* wide; *lic,* like. Widely.

Wiese. *Wiese,* wise, prudent.

Wigand. *Wigend,* a warrior, a soldier.

Wiggan. *Wiggan,* to carry on war, to fight, to contend.

Wiggins. *Wiggin,* Wiggan; *s* for *sun,* son. Son of Wiggan.

Wigham. *Wig,* war; *hám,* a house. A war-house; castle; tower; fortress.

Wight. *Wiht,* a creature, wight, animal.

Wightman. *Wiht-man,* from *Wiht,* the Isle of Wight, and *man,* a man. A man of the Isle of Wight.

Wigley. *Wig-lic,* from *wig,* war, and *lic,* like. War-like.

Wigman. *Wig-mann,* from *wig,* war, and *mann,* a man. A war-like man; a warrior; a soldier.

Wigmore. *Wig,* battle; *mór,* a moor. A battle-moor.

Wigo. *Wiga,* a soldier, a warrior.

Wigton. *Wig,* a battle; *tún,* town. A battle-town.

Wike. *Wic,* a dwelling-place, mansion.

Wilbank. *Wil,* a prefix denoting pleasant; *banc,* a bank. A pleasant bank.

Wilbraham. *Wilbra,* Wilbur; *hám,* house. House of Wilbur.

Wilbur. *Wil,* pleasant; *búr,* a bower. A pleasant bower. Wilber, from the same roots.

Wilby. *Wil,* pleasant; *bȳ,* dwelling. A pleasant dwelling.

Wilcock. *Wil,* good, well; *cocc,* a cock. A well-bred cock.

Wilcocks, *Wilcock,* Wilcock; *s* for *sun,* son. Son of Wilcock. Wilcox, a kindred term.

Wild. *Wild,* following its own will and impulse, wild, powerful. Wilde, of similar meaning.

Wildermore. *Wild,* wild; *mór,* a moor. A wild moor; an uncultivated moor.

Wilder. *Wild,* wild; *ere,* an agent. One who, or that which, is wild.

Wildes, *Wild,* Wild; *s* for *sun,* son. Son of Wilde. Wilds, of like derivation.

Wildey. *Wild-ig,* from *wild,* wild; *ig,* an adjective termination. Wild-like; wildly. Willdey, from the same roots.

Wilding. *Wild,* wild; *ing,* expressing action. Growing wild.

Wildman. *Wild,* wild; *man,* a man. A wild man. An uncivilized man.

Wile. *Wile,* a wile, craftiness.

Wileman. *Wile,* a wile, craftiness. A wily man; a crafty man.

Wilen. *Wilen,* or *wilhen,* a maid, a foreign woman, a female slave.

Wiler. *Wile,* a wile; *ere,* an agent. A trickster.

Wiles. *Wile,* Wile; *s* for *sun,* son. Son of Wile.

Wiley. *Wile,* wile; *ig,* an adjective termination. Wily; tricky; crafty. Wilie, from the same roots.

Wilfong. *Wil,* well; *fong,* received. Well-received.

Wilfonger. *Wil,* well; *fong,* received; *ere,* an agent. One who is well received.

Wilford. *Wil,* pleasant; *ford,* a ford. A pleasant ford.

Wilgus. *Wiliges,* genitive of *wilig,* a willow. Belonging to a willow.

Wilhare. *Wil,* pleasant; *harra,* a lord. A pleasant lord. Wilher, from the same roots.

Wilhelm. *Wil,* well, pleasant; *helm,* a crown. An easy crown; a happy monarch. Or, from *will,* a will, and *helm,* a helmet. A will-helmet; an undaunted helmet.

Wilkening. *Wil,* pleasant; *cyn,* people; *ing,* offspring. Descendant of pleasant people.

Wilkens. *Wilken,* pleasant people; *s* for *sun,* son. Son of pleasant people. Wilkes, Wilks, possibly, contractions of the same name.

Wilkinson. *Wilken,* pleasant people; *sun,* son. Son of pleasant people.

Will. *Will,* will, mind, disposition, affection, consent.

Willahan. *Will-an,* of one's will, willingly. Willian, from the same root.

Willand. *Willende,* willing, wishing. Willang, doubtless, from the same radix.

Willans. *Willan,* Willahan; *s* for *sun,* son. Son of Willahan.

Willard. *Wil-laueord,* from *wil,* good, pleasant, and *laueord,* a lord. A kind lord; a beneficent master. Willauer, Williard, from the same.

Willdon. *Wil-dòn,* from *wil,* well, and *dòn,* to do. To do well; well-done.

Willeman. *Wille,* a well; *man,* a man. A well-man; a well-borer. Williman, Willman, of like import.

Willemin. *Willan,* to will; *mine,* the mind. A willing mind. Willimen, a kindred term.

Willems. *Willem,* Wilhelm; *s* for *sun,* son. Son of Wilhelm.

Willer. *Willan,* to will, to wish; *ere,* an agent. One who wills, or wishes; a willer; a wisher. Willar, another form of the name.

Willers. *Willer,* Willer; *s* for *sun,* son. Son of Willer.

Willes. *Wille,* Will; *s* for *sun,* son. Son of Will.

Willess. *Will,* a will; *leas,* free from. Free from will.

Willet. *Wil,* a well, a fountain; *lyt,* little. A small fountain. Or, from *will,* mind, and *lyt,* little. A little mind. Willett, of like derivation.

Willets. *Willet,* Willet; *s* for *sun,* son. Son of Willet. Willetts, Willitts, from the same roots.

Willey. *Will-ice,* contraction of *willendlice,* from *willende,* willing, and *lice,* like. Willing-like; willingly. Willi, Willie, perhaps, corruptions of the name.

William. Old History German for Wilhelm. See Wilhelm.

Williams. *William,* William; *s* for *sun,* son. Son of William.

Williamson. *William,* William; *sun,* son. Son of William.

Willig. *Will,* will; *ig,* an adjective termination. Willing; desirous; prone. Willey, Willi, and Willie, may be derived from the same roots. See Willey.

Willimeit. *Willa,* will; *miht,* might, power. Will-power.

Willing. *Will,* will; *ing,* an offspring. Descendant of Will.

Willinger. *Willing,* willing; *ere,* an agent. A servant of Willing.

Willingmyre. Willing, from *willende,* willing; *myre,* a mare. A willing mare; a ready mare. Willingmeyer, from the same roots.

Willings. Willing, Willing; *s* for *sun,* son. Son of Willing.

Willis. Willice, willingly.

Willman. Will, a will; *man,* a man. A will-man; a man of will; a resolute man. Willeman, Williman, may be traced to the same roots. See Willeman.

Willmanns. Willmann, Willman; *s* for *sun,* son. Son of Willman.

Willmarth. Will, mind; *mǣrdh,* wonders. Mind-wonders. Wilmarth, a kindred name.

Willmunder. Will, mind; *mundian,* to protect; *ere,* an agent. A mind-protector; an instructor; a teacher; a physician.

Willoughby. Wilige, what is made of willow, a basket; *by,* a habitation. A house where baskets are made; a basket-factory.

Willow. Wilig, or *wileg,* a willow.

Wills. Will, Will; *s* for *sun,* son. Son of Will.

Willsey. Willes, Will's; *ig,* an island. Will's island. Wilsey, from the same roots.

Willson. Will, Will; *sun,* son. Son of Will. Wilson, from the same roots.

Wilmer. Wil, well; *mǣre,* famed. Well-famed; distinguished; illustrious.

Wilmerton. Wilmer, Wilmer; *tún,* house. Home of Wilmer.

Wilmoore. Wil, pleasant; *mór,* a moor. A pleasant moor. Wilmore, from the same roots.

Wilmot. Wil, pleasant; *mót,* an assembly. An agreeable assembly. Wilmott, a kindred term.

Wilsher. Wilsc, Welsh; *ere,* an agent. A Welshman.

Wilsky. Wilsc-ig, from *Wilsc,* Welsh, and *ig,* an adjective termination. Welsh.

Willsleger. *Willes*, genitive of *will*, mind, affection; *leger*, disease, couch. Disease of the mind; couch of affection.

Wilsman. *Willes*, genitive of *will*, mind; *man*, a man. A man of mind.

Wilstach. *Wil*, a well; *stác*, a pole. A well-pole.

Wilt. *Wilt*, from *willan*, to will, to wish. Wilt; willest; wishest.

Wiltbank. *Wilt*, willest; *banc*, a bank. A bank thou willest, or wishest; a wished-for bank.

Wilten. *Wiltún*, contraction of *Willy-tún*, from *Willy*, the name of a river, and *tún*, town. Town on the river Willy. Willy is, perhaps, from *wilie*, a basket, or *wilig*, a willow.

Wiltshire. *Wiltún-scire*, from *Wil*, Willy, and *tún*, town; *scire*, a shire, a district. Wiltonshire; Wilton-district.

Winch. *Wince*, a winch, a reel to wind thread upon. Winsch, from the same root.

Winchell. *Wincel*, a corner. Winsel, doubtless of like import.

Winchester. *Win-ceaster*, from *win*, wine; *ceaster*, a castle. A wine-castle.

Wind. *Windan*, to wind, to bend, to twist, to twine.

Winder. *Winde*, what winds round, a winder, a reel. Or, from *windan*, to wind, and *ere*, an agent. One who winds; a winder.

Windisch. *Windan*, to wind; *isc*, an adjective termination denoting external quality of a thing. Winding; flexuous.

Windle. *Windel*, dative *windle*, anything twined, a basket.

Windpipe. *Wind*, wind; *pip*, a pipe, a flute. A wind-pipe.

Windrim. *Wyn-drim*, or *wyn-dreám*, from *wyn*, joy, and *drim*, or *dreám*, joy, rejoicing. Great joy, exultation.

Windsor. *Wind*, wind; *sór* sorrow, grief. Wind-sorrow. Windser, from the same roots.

Wine. *Win*, wine.

Wineland. *Win*, wine; *land*, a region. Wine-region.

Winelander. *Win,* wine; *land,* a region; *ere,* an agent. A resident of a wine region.

Winfield. *Win,* wine; *feld,* a field. A wine-field; a vineyard.

Winfree. *Win,* wine; *freó,* free. Wine free; abstaining from wine.

Wing. *Winge,* a wing.

Wingart. *Win-geard,* from *win,* wine, and *geard,* a garden. A wine-garden; a vineyard. Wingert, a kindred name.

Wingate. *Win,* wine; *geát,* a gate, a door, an opening. A wine-gate; an opening to a wine-cellar.

Winig. *Win,* wine; *ig,* an adjective termination. Wine-like; vinous.

Wink. *Wincian,* to bend one's self, to nod, to wink.

Winkel. *Wincle,* a wilk, cockle, shell-fish.

Winkelmann. *Wincle,* a wilk, a cockle; *mann,* a man. A wilk-man; a cockler.

Winkler. *Wincle,* a wilk, a cockle; *ere,* an agent. A wilk-man; a cockler.

Winkley. *Wincle,* a cockle; *lic,* like. Resembling a cockle.

Winline. *Winn,* acquisition, possession, winning; Latin *linea,* a line. Acquisition-line; border-line; winning-line.

Winn. *Winn,* contention, strife, war, trouble, acquisition, possession, winning. Winne, from the same radix.

Winnel. *Winn,* a contest; *el,* implying a person. A contestant; a rival; a fighter.

Winnemoore. *Winn-an,* to win, to conquer, to subdue; *mór,* a moor. A conquered moor.

Winner. *Winna,* a rival, an enemy, a fighter. Or, from *winn,* contest, war, and *ere,* an agent. A contestant; a warrior.

Winners. *Winner,* Winner; *s* for *sun,* son. Son of Winner.

Winnett. *Win,* pleasure; *nett,* a net. A pleasure net.

Winnig. Winn, contention, war, labor; *ig,* an adjective ending. Contentious; war-like; laborious. Winnie, a slightly modified form of the name.

Winning. Winn, Winn; *ing,* offspring. Descendant of Winn.

Winpenny. Winn, labor, winning; *pening,* a penny. Labor-penny; win-penny; winning penny.

Winrick. Win, winning; *rice,* power, kingdom. Winning power.

Winring. Win, winning; *hring,* a ring. Winning ring. Or, from *win,* pleasure, and *hring,* a ring. A pleasure-ring; a wedding-ring.

Winship. Wine-scipe, from *wine,* a friend, and *scipe,* a termination denoting form, condition, state, office, dignity. A society of friends; a fraternity.

Winslow. Win, contest; *släw,* slow, idle, lazy. A slow contest. Or, from *win,* pleasure, and *släw,* idle. An idle pleasure.

Winsmore. Wines, genitive of *win,* contention; *mór,* a moor. A contending moor.

Winstanley. Wine, a friend; Stanley, Stanley. Stanley's friend. See Stanley.

Winston Wines-tún, from *wines,* genitive of *win,* wine, and *tún,* a house. A house of wine; a wine-house; a tavern.

Wint. Wint, from *wintan,* to wind. Winds.

Winter. Winter, winter, a year. The Anglo-Saxon, and other northern nations, reckoned by winters instead of years.

Winterbottom. Winter, winter; *botm,* bottom. Winter's close.

Winterbourn. Winter, winter; *burne,* a brook. A winter brook.

Winterer. Winter, winter; *ere,* an agent. One who, or that which, winters in a certain place.

Winterfield. Winter, winter; *feld,* a field, a plain. A wintry field.

Winterhall. Winter, winter; *heal*, a palace. Winter-palace.

Winterhalter. Winter, winter; *healtian*, to halt; *cre*, an agent. One who, or that which, halts for the winter; a winter sojourner.

Winterholer. Winter, winter; *hole*, a hole; *cre*, an agent. One who, or that which, seeks winter-quarters in holes.

Winternight. Winter, winter; *niht*, night. A winter night.

Winters. Winter, Winter; *s* for *sun*. Son of Winter.

Wintersteen. Winter, winter; *stæn*, or *stén*, stone. A winter stone.

Winther. Windh, from *winnan*, to labor; *cre*, an agent. A laborer.

Winton. Win-tún, from *win*, wine, and *tún*, a house. A wine-house; a tavern.

Wire. Wir, wire.

Wireback. Wir, wire; *bæc*, a back. A wire-back. Wire-bach, from the same roots.

Wireman. Wir, wire; *man*, a man. A worker in wire.

Wirgman. Wirg, wicked, cursed; *man*, a man. A wicked man.

Wirsing. Wirs, worse; *ing*, expressing action. Making worse.

Wirth. Wirdh, from *weordhan*, to be made. Is made.

Wischan. Wiscan, to wish, to adopt.

Wischman. Wiscan, to wish; *man*, a man. A man that wishes; a wisher. Wischmann, Wishman, from the same roots.

Wisdom. Wis-dóm, from *wisa*, a sage, and *dóm*, opinion. Opinion of a sage; wisdom.

Wise. Wis, wise, prudent; a wise man, a hero, a prince.

Wisely. Wis-lice, from *wis*, wise, prudent, and *lice*, like. Wise-like; wisely; prudently.

Wiseman. Wis, wise, prudent; *man*, a man. A wise man; a prudent man. Wisman, from the same roots.

Wiser. *Wisa*, a sage, a philosopher, a wise man, a leader, guide, director. Or, from *wis*, wise, and *ere*, an agent. One who, or that which, is wise or prudent.

Wisham. *Wis*, wise, prudent; *hám*, home. A wise home.

Wishart. *Wis*, wise, prudent; *heort*, a termination denoting hearty, hearted, brave. Wise-hearted.

Wisher. *Wisc-ere*, from *wiscan*, to wish; *ere*, an agent. A wisher.

Wisenger. *Wisung*, making wise, instruction, command, a governing, regulator; *ere*, an agent. Wisdom-maker; instructor; commander; governor; regulator.

Wisler. *Wis*, wise, prudent; *lár*, doctrine. Wise doctrine. Wissler, a kindred term.

Wismer. *Wis*, wise; *mǽre*, famed. Wise-famed; famous for wisdom.

Wisner. *Wis*, wise; *nere*, a refuge. A wise refuge.

Wisse. *Wisse*, for *wiste*, past of *witan*, to know, to be conscious. Knew; was conscious.

Wissman. *Wisse*, knew, was conscious; *man*, a man. A man that knew; a wise man.

Wist. *Wiste*, past of *witan*, to know. Knew; was conscious.

Wister. *Wiste*, knew; *ere*, an agent. One that knew. Wistar, from the same root.

Wiswell. *Wis*, wise; *well*, much. Exceedingly wise.

Witchel. *Wicce*, a witch, an enchantress; *el*, a termination denoting a person. A witch; an enchantress.

Witcher. *Wicce*, a witch, an enchantress. Witscher, of kindred derivation.

Witcraft. *Wit*, mind, wit, understanding; *cræft*, continuance. Mind-continuance; invention.

Witham. *Wit*, mind, wit; *hám*, house. Home of wit; the brain.

Witheat. *Wit*, mind; *hát*, heat, fervor. Mind-fervor.

Witman. *Wit*, wit; *man*, a man. A witman; a man of wit. Wittman, of kindred significance.

Witmer. *Wit,* wit; *mǽre,* famed. Wit-famed. Wittmer, a cognate term.

Witsil. *Wit,* wit; *scl,* best. Best wit.

Witt. *Witt,* wit, mind, understanding. Witte, from the same radix.

Wittig. *Witt-ig,* from *witt,* wit, and *ig,* an adjective termination. Witty; wise.

Wittingham. *Witting,* Wittig; *hám,* house. Home of Wittig.

Wittkamp. *Witt,* wit; *camp,* a contest. A wit-contest.

Wittkorn. *Witt,* wit; *corn,* a grain. A wit-grain; a grain of wit.

Wittland. *Witt,* wit; *land,* a land. A land of wit.

Wittrook. *Witt,* wit; *róc,* a rook. A witty rook.

Witts. *Witt,* Witt; *s* for *sun,* son. Son of Witt.

Wittwer. *Witt,* wit; *wer,* a man. A witty man. Witwer, from the same roots.

Woddrop. *Wod,* a wood; *drop,* a drop, a spot. A wood-spot.

Wogan. *Wógan,* to woo, to marry.

Wolbert. *Wól,* mischief; *beorht,* glistening. Glistening with mischief.

Wolbold. *Wól,* mischief; *báld,* audacious. Audacious mischief.

Wolcott. *Wól,* disease; *cóte,* a couch, a bed. A diseased couch.

Wolf. *Wulf,* a wolf. Wolfe, Wolff, Woolf, Wulf, Wulff, from the same root.

Wolfel. *Wulf,* wolf; *el,* a termination denoting a person. A wolfish person; a ravenous person.

Wonder. *Wunder,* a wonder, a miracle.

Wonderly. *Wunder-lic,* from *wunder,* wonder, and *lic,* like. Wonder-like; wonderful; wondrous.

Woudle. *Wund-cl,* a wound.

Wouhart. *Won,* lacking; *heort,* heart. Lacking heart; faint-hearted.

Wood. Wude, wood.

Woodall. Wude, wood; *call*, all. Well-wooded.

Woodbridge. Wude, wood; *bricg*, a bridge. A wooden bridge.

Woodburn. Wude, wood; *burne*, a stream. A wooded stream.

Woodbury. Wude, wood; *bury*, from *byrig*, a city, a town. A wooded town.

Woodcock. Wude, wood; *coc*, or *cocc*, a cock, a male fowl, or bird. A woodcock; a bird that affects wooded places.

Woodelton. Wudelic-tun, from *wudelic*, woody, wild; *tun*, a farm. A woody, or wild farm.

Wooder. Wudere, a wooden shoe.

Woodfall. Wude, a wood; *fealle*, a trap. A wood-trap.

Woodhead. Wude, a wood; *heafd*, head. A wood-head; a wooden head.

Woodhouse. Wude, wood; *hus*, a house. A wood-house.

Woodhull. *Wude*, wood; *hul*, a hill. A wooded hill.

Woodington. Wudiende, present participle of *wudian*, to cut wood; *tun*, a farm. A wood-cutting farm.

Woodland. Wudu-land, from *wudu*, or *wude*, wood, and *land*, land, region. A woodland; a wooded region.

Woodlands. *Woodland*, Woodland; *s* for *sun*, son. Son of Woodland.

Woodley. Wudu-lic, from *wudu*, wood, and *lic*, like. Wood-like; woody; wild.

Woodman. Wudu-mann, from *wudu*, wood, and *mann*, a man. A woodman; a wood-ward.

Woodmansee. *Wudu-mann-seo*, from *wudu-mann*, a woodman, and *seo*, the sight of the eye. A woodman's vision.

Woodnutt. Wude, wood; *hnut*, a nut. A wood-nut.

Woodring. *Wude*, wood; *hring*, a girdle. A wood-belt; a belt of woods.

Woodrow. *Wude*, wood; *ræwa*, a row. A wood-row; a line of woods.

Woodruff. *Wude*, wood; *róf*, a roof. Woodroof, Woodroff, Woodroffe, from the same roots.

Woods. *Wood*, Wood; *s* for *sun*, son. Son of Wood.

Woodside. *Wude*, wood; *side*, side. Side of a wood.

Woodsides. *Woodside*, Woodside; *s* for *sun*, son. Son of Woodside.

Woodson. *Wood*, Wood; *sun*, son. Son of Wood. Or, from *wude*, wood, and *sun*, son. Son of the woods.

Woodstocker. *Woodstock*, from *wude*, wood, and *stóc*, a place; *cre*, an agent. A resident of Woodstock—a woody place.

Woodward. *Wudu-weard*, from *wudu*, wood, and *weard* a ward, a guardian. A wood-ward; a woodman.

Woodworth. *Wude*, wood; *weordh*, value. Wood-value.

Woody. *Wudu-lic*, from *wudu*, wood, and *lic*, like. Woodlike; woody; wild. Or, from *wud*, wood, and *ig*, an adjective termination. Woody; wild.

Wooldridge. *Wold*, a wood; *hrycg*, a ridge. A wooden ridge.

Woolery. *Wülle*, wool; *rice*, a region. A wool-growing region. Woolrey, from the same roots.

Woolford. *Wüll*, wool; *ford*, a ford. A wool-ford; a place where the wool-bearers crossed the stream.

Wooliscroft. *Wülles*, genitive of *wüll*, wool, sheep; *croft*, a croft, a field. A wool-field; a sheep-pasture.

Woollard. *Wüll*, wool; *hlaford*, a lord. A wool-lord; a wool-master.

Woollerton. *Wüll*, wool; *erc*, an agent; *tün*, house. Home of a wool-grower.

Woolley. *Wüll-ic* from *wüll*, wool, and *ic* for *lic*, like. Woollike; woolly; hairy.

Woolman. *Wüll*, wool; *man*, a man. A woolman; a dealer in wool.

Woolsey. *Wülles*, genitive of *wüll*, wool, sheep; *ig*, an island. Isle of wool, or sheep.

Woolson. Wüll, wool; *sun,* son. Son of wool; offspring of a sheep.

Woolston, Wülles, genitive of *will,* wool; *tün,* town. A wool-town.

Woolworth. Wüll, wool; *weordh,* value. Wool-value.

Wopson. Wóp, a whoop, weeping, cry, bewailing, lamentation; *sun,* son. A weeping son.

Worden. Worden, or *weordhan,* to become, to be, to happen, to come to pass.

Work. Weorc, work, labor, fatigue, suffering, pain.

Workman. Weorc, work, labor; *man,* a man. A workman; a laborer.

Worknot. Weorc, work; *not,* for *nota,* office. A work-office.

Wormley. Worm, a worm; *lic,* like. Worm-like; spiral.

Wormsley. Wormes, genitive of *worm,* a worm; *lic,* form. Form of a worm; worm-like; spiral. Or, from *worms,* corruption, and *lic,* like. Corruption-like.

Worn. Worn, a number, multitude, body, company, band, troop, crowd, herd, power, force. Worne, from the same radix.

Worrall. Worold, the world. Worrell, Worl, from the same derivation.

Worsley. Wyers, worse; *lic,* like. Worse-like.

Worst. Wærst, or *wyrst,* worst.

Worth. Weordh, worth, value, price, honor, dignity.

Worthington. Weordh-ung, honoring, worshipping; *tün,* a house. A worshipping-house.

Worthline. Weordh, wealthy, honorable; *line,* a line. An honorable line.

Wosser. Wosa, a leader.

Wotherspoon. Wodh-spónere, from *wodh,* eloquence, song, and *spónere,* an enticer. Song-enticer.

Wrangham. Wrang, wrong; *hám,* house. Wrong home.

Wrede. Wræde, a latch, buckle, clasp, restraint, control, fastness, haft, handle.

Wren. Wrenna, a wren, a small bird.

Wrench. *Wringe*, an instrument to wring or strain, a press.

Wrensley. *Wrænnes*, extravagance, luxury, lust, lechery; *lic*, like. Extravagantly; luxuriously.

Wright. *Wryhta*, a wright.

Wrightley. *Wryhta*, a wright; *lic*, like. Resembling a wright.

Wrightson. *Wright*, Wright; *sun*, son. Son of Wright.

Wrigley. *Wrige*, covered, hidden; *lic*, like. Covered-like; hidden-like.

Writt. *Writ*, a writ, scripture, writing, letter.

Wroth. *Wrádh*, wrath, anger.

Wulton. *Wull*, wool; *tún*, town. A wool town.

Wunder. *Wundr*, or *wundor*, wonder.

Wunderly. *Wundr*, wonder; *lic*, like. Wonder-like. Wunderle, from the same roots.

Wunning. *Wun-ung*, from *wun-ian*, to won, to dwell, to inhabit. A woning; a dwelling; a habitation.

Wurst. *Wurst*, worst. Wust, a kindred term.

Wurster. *Wurst*, worst; *ere*, an agent. One who, or that which, is the worst. Wuster, perhaps, from the same radix.

Wurtele. *Wurt*, a wort, an herb; *el*, implying a person. An herb collector; an herbalist.

Wurts. *Wurtes*, genitive of *wurt*, a wort, an herb. Belonging to an herb. Wurtz, another spelling of the name.

Wyche. *Wyc*, a habitation, city, castle, fortress.

Wyckoff. *Wyc*, a dwelling-place, habitation, city, castle, fortress; *cofa*, a room, a chamber. A castle-chamber.

Wylie. *Wyllic*, from *wyl*, a well, a fountain, and *lic*, like. Like a well; as a fountain.

Wyman. *Wi*, an idol; *man*, a man. An idolater. Wymann, of like derivation.

Wynkoop. *Wyn*, joy, pleasure, light; *copp*, or *cuppa*, a cup. A pleasure-cup.

Wynn. *Wyn*, joy, pleasure, delight.

Wynne. *Wyne*, one that gives pleasure, a friend.

Wyss. *Wiss*, a wise man, a hero, a prince.

Y

Yard. *Ierd*, a yard.

Yardley. *Ierd*, a yard; *lic*, like. Yard-like.

Yarnall. *Gearn*, yarn, spun wool; *eall*, all, whole. All yarn; entirely woollen.

Yateman. *Iát*, or *geát*, a gate; *man*, a man. A gate-keeper. Yeatman, Yetman, from the same roots.

Yates. *Iátes*, or *geátes*, genitive of *iát*, a gate. Belonging to a gate. Yeats, of like derivation.

Yeager. *Ia*, yea, yes; *gare*, ready. A ready yes; a ready reply.

Yeagle. *Iagul*, pronounced *yeagul*, a gargle.

Yeakle. *Iac*, a cuckoo; *el*, indicative of personality. A person like a cuckoo; a simpleton.

Yeakley. *Iac*, a cuckoo; *lic*, like. Cuckoo-like; wild; careless; lascivious. Yeckley, of similar meaning.

Yeamans. *Ie*, a river; *man*, a man; *s* for *sun*, son. Son of a river-man.

Yeansson. *Geean*, yearning; *s* for *sun*, son. Son of yearning.

Yearick. *Gear*, a year; *icg*, or *ig*, an adjective termination. Yearly. Yearicke, Yerrick, from the same roots.

Yearly. *Gear-lic*, from *gear*, a year, and *lic*, like. Year-like; yearly.

Yearred. *Geard*, or *yrd*, a hedge, enclosure, garden, yard, earth, world.

Yearsley. *Geares*, genitive of *gear*, a year; *lic*, form. Form of a year; yearly.

Yeasler. *Ysele*, a fire-spark, spark, ember, hot ashes; *ere*, an agent. A fire-maker; a fireman; a stoker.

Yeather. *Y'dh*, what rises up, a wave, a flood; *ere*, an agent. That which rises up; a wave; a flood.

Yeaton. *Geat*, a gate; *tún*, a house. A gate-house.

Yeatts. *Geátes*, genitive of *geát*, a gate. Belonging to a gate. See Yates.

Yegen. *Yg-buend*, from *yg*, or *ig*, an island, and *buend*, an inhabitant. An inhabitant of an island; an islander.

Yeingest. *Iungest*, or *geongest*, comparative of *iung*, or *geong*, young. Youngest.

Yeiter. *Y'tte*, past of *ytan*, to out, to drive out, to expel, to banish; *ere*, an agent. One expelled; an exile.

Yellard. *Yl*, or *il*, a hedgehog, a porcupine; *land*, land. Land of the hedgehog, or porcupine.

Yenner. *Ynner*, inner.

Yenz. *Yntsa*, an ounce.

Yeo. *Ieo*, or *geo*, formerly, of old.

Yeomans. *Yeoman*, from *ieo*, or *geo*, of old; *man*, a man, and *s* for *sun*, son. Son of a man of old; son of a yeoman; son of a tiller of the soil.

Yeomanson. *Yeoman*, a yeoman; *sun*, son. Son of a yeoman.

Yepson. *Yppe*, plain, open, manifest; *sun*, son. A plain, open, staightforward son.

Yerg. *Earg*, or *eorg*, inert, weak, timid, wretched.

Yerger. *Earg*, timid, *ere*, an agent. One who, or that which, is timid.

Yerges. *Yerg*, Yerg; *s* for *sun*, son. Son of Yerg. Yerkes, perhaps, corruption of the same.

Yergey. *Earg*, inert, timid; *ig*, an adjective termination. Timid; inert.

Yerpe. *Eorp*, a wolf.

Yettinger. *Yting*, a way, a journey; *ere*, an agent. A wayfarer; a journeyer. Perhaps, from *get-ung*, getting, and *ere*, an agent. A getter.

Yetter. *Get*, imperfect of *getan*, to get; *ere*, an agent. A getter.

Yewdall. *Iw*, the yew tree; *dál*, a valley. The valley of the yew.

Yheaulon. *Hyew*, hue; *lon*, for *lond*, land. Land of hue.

Yhost. *Gást*, breath, spirit, ghost. Yoast, Yost, like it, a corruption of the original.

Yingling. *Ging*, young, tender; *ling*, a termination denoting state or condition of a person. Youth; tenderness.

Yoce. *Ioc*, or *geoc*, a yoke.

Yochum. *Ioc*, a yoke; *hum*, for *hám*, a house. A yoke-house. Yocam, Yocum, Yokam, from the same roots.

Yockel. *Ioc*, a yoke; *el*, a termination denoting a person. One who has charge of a yoke of oxen; a farmer; a bumpkin.

Yoder. *Gǽd*, a goad; *ere*, an agent. One who uses a goad.

Yonker. *Iunga*, or *geonga*, a youth. A young fellow; a youngster. Or, from *iuneer*, a younker, a young nobleman, one that is young, a young fellow. Younker, of like kinship.

Young. *Iung*, or *geong*, young, tender. Younk, from the same root.

Youngblood. *Iung*, young; *blódh*, or *blód*, blood. Young blood.

Younger. *Geongra*, comparative of *geong*, young, tender. Younger; more tender.

Younginger. *Young*, Young; *ing*, an offspring; *ere*, an agent. A descendant of Young.

Youngling. *Geong-ling*, a youngling, a boy.

Youngman. *Geong*, young; *man*, a man. A young man; a youth.

Younk. Corruption of Young. See Young.

Yuker. *Iuc*, a yoke; *ere*, an agent. One who, or that which, is yoked; a companion; a yoke-mate.

From the Anglo-Norman.

HISTORY—NORMAN CONQUEST.

The Normans, or Northmen, were primarily of the Norse, or Scandinavian, branch of the Teutonic race. They were active, enterprising men—merchants, navigators, soldiers. Restless under the restraints of a power that was slowly and surely consolidating the Scandinavian kingdoms, they broke away from its influence, and boldly ventured forth, conquered the Shetland Islands, the Orkneys, and the Hebrides, founded the kingdom of Caithness in Scotland, settled Iceland, discovered Greenland, and colonized Vinland, which is supposed to be on the coast of New England.

In 911, Rolf, or Rollo, the Ganger, with his daring band of vikings, obtained a footing in the fertile valley of the Seine. The province, which was afterwards called Normandy, was received by him as a fief from Charles the Simple. Friendly relations were soon established, and Rollo became the king's vassal with the title of duke, and subsequently married his daughter. The Normans were brought under French law and customs, became Christians, adopted the French language, married into French families, and caught the French spirit.

Edward the Confessor dying without issue in 1066, Harold, his brother-in-law, succeeded to the throne. But William, seventh Duke of Normandy, whose aunt, Emma, had been married to Ethelred II of England, claimed it by hereditary right and by the promise of both Edward and Harold.

Determined to establish his claim, he set sail with thirty thousand followers for the coast of England. On October

14, 1066, he met and defeated Harold, near Hastings, and was soon afterwards crowned king at Westminster. This was the only conquest—and British soil has throbbed to the clatter and tramplings of four—that reached down to the people of the island and thoroughly leavened them. The admixture of a new blood and a new spirit with theirs proved the greatest good that ever befell them. It can be considered as nothing short of a regeneration, for it made the English nation of to-day, the English language, and the English literature.

The modern Englishman owes to his Teutonic ancestry his love of justice and fair play, his religious nature, his physical robustness and intellectual vigor, his love of liberty, and to his French lineage—and we must not lose sight of the fact that, though originally Teutonic, the Normans had been metamorphosed by their life in France—his manner, his tact, his administrative genius, his poetic skill, and his artistic nature. In him are most happily blended the two races, forming a composite better than either component, greater even than both elements while in separation. The changes which Anglo-Saxon thus underwent are vital, fundamental, and, we may say, revolutionary.

Expressive of the change thus effected, a new name is needed. Before 1066, writers refrained from calling the dominant people of the island, or their language, by any other term than Anglo-Saxon. But after the union of the people and of the languages, no name expresses the new condition of things so well as English. As thus applied, English denotes always the race resulting from the marriage of the two peoples, or the speech resulting from the union of the two tongues.

ANGLO-NORMAN LANGUAGE.

The Anglo-Saxons and the Normans lived side by side. It must not be supposed, however, that either the two peoples or the two languages were welded instantaneously. They grew together, and the growth was slow. There were special reasons why such should be the case. The conqueror was of alien blood. National animosity existed between him and the conquered. In the north, more especially than in the south, William's conquest was ruthless. Harvests were destroyed, cattle killed or carried off, implements of husbandry sacrificed, towns and villages burned, and the inhabitants slain or driven across the border. The entire soil was confiscated, and the land, upon condition of military service, parcelled out among a score or more of great vassals, among hundreds of inferior crown vassals, and among the higher clergy. The meanest Norman was raised to opulence and influence in the new dominion. By the establishment of this modified feudal system, the masses were reduced to a species of serfdom. They became mere tillers of the soil. Shoals of Norman ecclesiastics came across the Channel, and the people were forced to accept religious instruction and consolation from the strangers. Everywhere, in the palace and among the nobility, in the law courts and the schools, as authority dictated, another language than their own prevailed. A keen sense of the scorn with which their lack of culture and their "barbarous tongue" were regarded, added to a painful consciousness of their social and political degradation, only served the more to heighten their aversion to the strangers, and to make the problem of coalescence slow and difficult.

But the influences at work were not wholly those of repulsion. Living together as they did, they had to meet each other in the field and in the town. They were forced to buy from each other and to sell to each other. Time could not but lessen the arrogance of the one, and modify the moroseness of the other. Definite rights were gradually acquired by the subject race. His services became limited, and could be commuted for money considerations. The ownership of his hut and of the plat of ground surrounding it, and the privilege of using the waste land of the manor for the pasturage of his cattle, which were mere indulgences at first, grew into rights that could be pleaded at law. The serf became a power. He was struggling to grow to a copyholder, and the copyholder, to a freeholder. Such things had their effects. The military strength of the nobles waned, the courts of the feudal baronage were shorn of their influence, and the feudal system was fast sinking into decay. In education, as well as in material things, the Anglo-Saxons were improving. Intermarriages were common, and strong social and national feelings were springing up, before which their mutual antagonism was giving away.

The vast possessions, partly hereditary and partly acquired by marriage, held by the English kings in France, served but to aid this feeling. To hold these against the French kings required not only a united people, but a people unified by the strong sentiment of nationality. And to make progress against the encroachments of their own kings the nobility were forced to make common cause with the people. To what extent the interests of barons and commons were identified may be seen from the provisions of the Great Charter extorted from King John in 1215.

For a long time after the Conquest there existed in England the singular spectacle of two languages declining to coalesce and yet spoken by two peoples living together. Neither language would give way to the other. How little these two languages had blended in the vocabulary of authors, may be seen when it is said that Layamon's *Brut*, a poem of thirty-two thousand lines, written in 1205, does not contain a hundred and fifty French words; and that in the *Ormulum*, a poem of twenty thousand lines, which appeared in the year of Magna Charta, hardly fifty French words are found. But the difficulties in the way of coalescence were slowly diminishing. Such as were political have already been spoken of, but those more properly linguistic will now be considered.

This period was, to the subject race, one of general depression. Very little literature, and that of an indifferent quality, was produced. Their language was no longer spoken, and their standards in it forgotten. Anglo-Saxon had been banished from the schools, was no longer used at the palace and castles of the nobles, or in the courts. Few were writing it. It seems to have been left in the care, if care it can be called, of those ignorant of its literature and grammar, and familiar only with the vocabulary employed in colloquial speech. The effect of all this upon the language can be easily inferred. A large fraction of the vocabulary, the more dignified and scholarly portion, fell into neglect and then into oblivion. The grammatical inflections, denoting case, person, number, tense, of the words kept in circulation, almost entirely perished. These inflections would only be retained by those who knew their importance, but they sloughed off as the words fell from the tongues of those who were ignorant of them. When, then, this Anglo-Saxon speech had forced itself upon the Normans, as it had fairly done by the latter half of the fourteenth century, it was far easier to master than would have been the case immediately after 1066. Nearly one-half of the words in the vocabulary before the Conquest, it is estimated, dropped out of it in the three hundred years immediately following, and it is certain that the grammar had been vastly simplified. With one-half of its words lost, and the remaining half nearly flectionless, the work of learning the language was made comparatively easy for the Norman.

This forcing of the tongue of a conquered people upon its conquerors was a signal achievement and of far-reaching consequences. Upon the authority of John of Trevisa, we are told that, after the great pestilence of 1349, the instruction of youth was revolutionized. John Cornwall changed the instruction in the grammar-school from French into English, and was followed by Richard Pencrich and others, so that in 1335 in all the grammar-schools of England the children were being taught English rather than French. In 1362 French was exchanged for English in the courts of law, Parliament having passed an act that year ordering that in all the courts "all pleas * * * shall be pleaded, shewed, defended, answered, debated, and judged in the English tongue." Great writers had now arisen—Wyclif, 1324-1384, in prose; Chaucer, 1340-1400, in poetry. They wrote in English, and their influence upon the plastic language of their day, and upon all subsequent writers, is simply incalculable.

The adoption of the Anglo-Saxon by the Norman was greatly facilitated by the fact that the French he was using was not the French of Paris, but the degenerate tongue of Normandy, which was at best but provincial. But during the centuries of its use in England it had been kept from free contact with the dialect of Normandy, and so had deteriorated even from the imperfect standard. Even the Norman himself had grown ashamed of it, and was not unwilling to part with it.

When it is said that by 1400, or even earlier, English was generally used, it is meant a speech not in existence by itself till long after the Norman Conquest, a speech neither Anglo-Saxon nor French, but Anglo-Saxon and French. It was a speech to which both of these languages contributed, to form which both of these were combined. The adoption of words was not all done by the Norman. While he borrowed many from the Saxon, the Saxon borrowed some from the Norman. English may, therefore, be considered a compromise, a compound. It is one speech after the union, but not univocal, not all of a piece, every speaker of which being bilingual.

The tongue brought over by the Conqueror has been called Norman-French. It is in reality Latin. Just before the Christian era Julius Cæsar subdued the people then in possession of Gaul, what is now France, and imposed upon them his language, which was that of Rome. This language, used for a thousand years by a people to whom it was not the vernacular, was acquired by the Normans, of still another alien stock, and by them introduced into England. Spoken a whole millennium by people whose mother-tongue it displaced, and from them learned by strangers, it is not at all unreasonable to suppose that the words had lost much of their original form and meaning. Proofs, in the words themselves, are not wanting to sustain the assertion. Outwardly they were almost invariably shortened. By a dropping of vowels or consonants, or of both, two or three syllables had been squeezed into one, as some examples will conclusively show. French *sûr*, our *sure*, came originally from the Latin *securus* ; French *règle*, our *rule*, from Latin *regula* ; French *île*, English *isle*, from *insula*. And not unfrequently the final and unaccented syllable or syllables seem not to have been caught by the subject Gaul, or, if caught by his ear, were not retained on his tongue. The Latin *domina*, for instance, appears in French as the truncated *dame ; medius* as *midi ;* and *malum*, as *mal*. Though changed, yet it must be patent to all that the French words are **Latin**, as their essential identity with the words used by Horace and Virgil unmistakably show.

NAMES—THEIR DERIVATION.

A.

Avis. *Avis*, advice, opinion. Avise, from the same radix.
Auter. *Auter*, an altar.
Ayler. *Ayel*, a grandfather; *ere*, an agent. An active grandfather.
Ayles. *Ayeles*, genitive of *ayel*, a grandfather. Belonging to a grandfather.

B.

Batchelor. *Bachelor*, an unmarried man, a knight, one who has taken his first degree in a college.
Bayard. *Bayard*, a bay horse, a blood-horse; so called in Chaucer, and in old romances. Byard, abbreviation of the term.
Beauford. *Beau*, beautiful; *ford*, a ford. A beautiful ford.
Belfield. *Bel*, beautiful; *feld*, a field. A beautiful field.
Belford. *Bel*, beautiful, good; *ford*, a ford. A good ford.
Bellamy. *Bel amy*, from *bel*, good, and *amy*, a friend. A good friend.
Bellenere. *Belle*, beautiful; *nere*, a refuge. A beautiful refuge.
Bokel. *Bokel*, a buckle.
Borell. *Borel*, coarse cloth of a brown color, made of plain, coarse stuff. Borel folk, borel men, were laymen.
Bortel. *Bordel*, a brothel.
Bos. *Bos*, a protuberance.

Bosek. *Bos,* a protuberance; *ig,* an adjective termination. Bossy. Bose, Bosee, from the same roots.

Boser. *Bos,* a protuberance; *ere,* an agent. One who, or that which, has a protuberance.

Boshart. *Bos,* a protuberance; *heort,* a hart. A humped hart.

Bossard. *Bosard,* a buzzard, a species of hawk unfit for sporting. Bossart, Bossert, identical in derivation and meaning.

Boswell. Latin *bos,* an ox; *well,* a well, a fountain. An ox-well; a well where oxen are watered.

Bosworth. *Bos,* an ox; *weordh,* value, price. Ox-value.

Botler. *Botel,* or *botelle,* a bottle; *ere,* an agent. A bottler. Butler, from the same radix.

Bottle. *Botel,* or *botelle,* a bottle.

Brear. *Brere,* a briar, a bramble.

Brearey. *Brere,* a bramble; *ig,* an adjective termination. Briery; brambly; full of briars; rough.

Brearley. *Brere,* a bramble; *lic,* like. Bramble-like; briery.

Brinton. *Brin,* a sprig, a slip; *tun,* a house, an enclosure. A hot-bed; a green-house; a nursery.

Buffett. *Buffette,* a blow.

Burdon. *Burdoun,* a humming noise, the base in music.

C.

Cappell. *Capel,* a horse.

Caron. *Caroigne,* carrion, dead, or putrefied flesh.

Carrick. *Carrik,* a large ship.

Case. *Cas,* chance, condition, circumstance.

Casler. *Cas,* chance; *lár,* doctrine. Doctrine of chance.

Casely. *Cas,* chance; *lic,* like. Chance-like; accidental. Casley, from the same root.

Casey. *Cas,* chance, condition; *ig,* an adjective termination. Accidental; conditional.

Cattell. *Catel,* goods, chattel.

Cellerier. *Celerer*, the officer in a monastery who had the care of the provisions.

Chambers. *Chamberes*, genitive of *chamber*, a chamber, a room, an apartment. Belonging to a chamber.

Chambley. *Chamb*, for *chamber*, a chamber; *ley*, for *lic*, like. Chamber-like.

Chesser. *Ches*, chess; *ere*, an agent. A chess-player.

Chessman. *Ches*, chess; *man*, man. A chessman; a piece used in chess.

Chesson. *Ches*, chess; *sun*, son. A son fond of chess.

Chestney. *Chesteyn*, a chestnut. Chestin, perhaps, from the same root.

Clary. *Clarré*, wine mixed with honey and spices, and afterwards strained till it is clear. Clarey, of like relationship.

Clerke. *Clerk*, one who has received school-learning.

Clink. *Clinke*, a ring, to tinkle.

Clinker. *Clinke*, to tinkle; *ere*, an agent. That which tinkles.

Coate. *Cote*, a coat.

Compayre. *Comperé*, a gossip, a near friend.

Coates. *Coate*, Coate; *s* for *sun*, son. Son of Coate.

Cope. *Cope*, a cloak.

Couch. *Couche*, to lay, place; past participle *couched*, laid. *Couched* with pearls means laid or trimmed with pearls. *Couch*, also, a bed.

Colpe. *Coulpe*, a fault.

Crowne. *Crown*, crown of the head, top of the head. Crown, from the same radix.

Curtis. *Curteys*, or *curteis*, courteous, polite.

D.

Dresser. *Dresse*, to address, to apply; *ere*, an agent. One who addresses, or applies himself to any task.

Drury. *Druerie*, courtship, gallantry, love, a mistress.

F.

Fay. *Fay*, faith, confidence, trust. Faye, from the same radix.

Fayer. *Fay*, faith; *ere*, an agent. One who has faith; a believer.

Fayle. *Fay*, faith; *le*, for *el*, denoting a person. A person of faith; a believer.

Fein. *Feyne*, to feign, to pretend.

Fey. *Fey*, faith, trust, confidence.

Feyer. *Fey*, faith; *ere*, an agent. One that has faith; a believer.

Feyhl. *Fey*, faith; *hl*, for *el*, denoting a person. A believer.

Floyd. *Floyte*, a flute.

Forster. *Forster*, a forester, an officer of the forest. Foster, a kindred term.

Fowl. *Fowel*, a fowl, a bird.

Fowler. *Fowel*, a fowl; *ere*, an agent. One who pursues or traps wild fowl.

Fowles. *Fowle*, Fowl; *s* for *sun*, son. Son of Fowl.

Foyle. *Folye*, folly, foolish conduct, indiscretion.

Franklin. *Frankeleyn*, the father of a family. This is the application in Chaucer's time. Spencer uses the term in the sense of a freeholder, but in Queen Elizabeth's day it denoted a yeoman, or a man above a vassal, but not a gentleman.

Frearson. *Frere*, a friar; *sun*, son. Son of a friar.

G.

Gabb. *Gabbe*, to jest, to talk idly, to lie.

Gaylord. *Gaylard*, gay, licentious. Perhaps from *galliard*, a sprightly kind of dance.

Gentil. *Gentil*, gentlemanlike, gentlemanly. Gentel, Gentle, of like kinship.

Gentry. *Genterye,* gentility. Chaucer spelt the word with the additional e's. Even at the present day it is not unusual to find some writing the name—Gentery.

Gerry. *Gery,* changeable, inconstant, uncertain.

Geyler. *Gylour,* a deceiver.

Glose. *Glose,* a comment, an interpretation.

Grace. *Grace,* favor, kindness, good-will, benignity.

Gracey. *Grace,* favor, kindness; *ig,* an adjective termination. Gracious; kind.

Grange. *Graunge,* a farm-house.

Granger. *Graunge,* a farm-house; *ere,* an agent. One who has a farm-house; a farmer.

Greeley. *Gree,* pleasure, satisfaction, prize, grade; *lic,* like. Pleasurable; satisfactory; estimable; gradual.

Greaser. *Grees,* grease, ointment; *ere,* an agent. An anointer.

Greasly. *Grees,* grease; *lic,* like. Grease-like; unctuous.

Grone. *Grone,* to groan, to grunt.

Groner. *Grone,* to groan, to grunt; *ere,* an agent. A groaner; a grunter.

Groning. *Grone,* to groan, to grunt; *ing,* expressive of action. Groaning; grunting.

H.

Hamburg. *Hamburgeon,* diminutive of *hauberg,* a coat of mail.

Hamburger. *Hamburgeon,* a coat of mail; *ere,* an agent. One who wears a coat of mail; a warrior.

Haire. *Haire,* hair-cloth.

Hackney. *Hakeney,* a hackney, an ambling horse, or pad.

Harney. *Harneys,* armor, furniture.

Hauberger. *Hauberg,* a coat of mail; *ere,* an agent. An armor-bearer; a knight; a warrior.

Houpt. *Houped,* hooped, hollowed, shoaled.

K.

Keep. *Keep*, care, attention.

L.

Lacey. *Laas*, or *lace*, a lace, a net, a snare ; *ig*, an adjective termination. Resembling a lace, or net.
Large. *Large*, spacious, free, prodigal.
Larger. *Larger*, comparative of *large*, spacious, prodigal. More spacious ; more prodigal.
Largey. *Large*, large, prodigal ; *ig*, an adjective termination. Large ; prodigal.
Largly. *Large*, large, free ; *lic*, like. Large-like ; largely ; freely.
Layard. *Liard*, a name of a horse, belonging originally to a horse of a gray color. A gray horse.
Lodge. *Loge*, a lodge, a habitation.
Logerman. *Loge*, a lodge ; *ere*, an agent ; *man*, a man. A person who lodges, or is lodged ; a lodger.
Logue. *Loge*, a lodge, a habitation.
Loos. *Loos*, praise, approval.
Luce. *Luce*, the fish called a pike.

M.

Mallison. *Malisoun*, a malediction, a curse.
Maner. *Manere*, carriage, behavior, kind, sort.
Maris. *Marreys*, a marsh.
Mauger. *Maugré*, in spite of.
Marvill. *Mervaille*, marvel, wonder. Marvel, from the same radix.

N.

Nice. *Nice*, foolish, simple, silly. Nyce, a kindred term.
Noon. *Noon*, the ninth hour of the natural day, nine o'clock in the morning, the hour of dinner.
Norris. *Norice*, a nurse.
Nowell. *Nowel*, Christmas.

O.

Oliphant. *Olifaunt*, an elephant.
Oliver. *Oliver*, olive-trees.
Opie. *Opye*, opium.

P.

Paase. *Paas*, a foot-pace.
Paramore. *Paramour*, love, gallantry.
Pardee. *Pardé*, a common oath, literally, by God. Purdie, of like kinship.
Parvis. *Parvis*, a portico before a church. Purvis, perhaps, from the same root.
Pass. *Passe*, to surpass, to excel, to pass sentence.
Peer. *Peere*, a peer, an equal.
Pergin. *Peregrine*, wandering.
Perry. *Perrye*, jewels, precious stones.
Person. *Persone*, a man, a parson, a rector of a church.
Pierie. *Pierrie*, jewels, precious stones.
Pile. *Pile*, *pyle*, to rob, to plunder. Pyle, from the same radix.
Platt. *Platte*, or *plat*, flat, plain.
Pleydell. *Plye*, to bend; *dál*, a dell, a valley. An undulating valley.
Poke. *Poke*, a pocket, a bag.
Pollak. *Pollax*, a halberd. Pollock, Polock, from the same derivation.
Pomeltree. *Pomel*, any ball or round thing, as an apple; *treow*, a tree. An apple-tree.
Poynter. *Poynt*, the principal business, a point, a stop; *ere*, an agent. That which acts as a point, or a stop; a pointer.
Poynton. *Poynt*, a point, a stop; *tún*, a house. A point-house; a business place.
Prentis. *Prentys*, an apprentice. Prentiss, a kindred term.
Presley. *Prees*, a press, a crowd; *lic*, like. Crowd-like; dense; compact.

Freston. *Prest*, from *prese*, to press, to crowd; *tún*, a house. A crowded house.

Prevear. *Preve*, to try, to demonstrate by trial; *ere*, an agent. An experimenter; a demonstrator.

Price. *Prys*, price, value, praise.

Prime. *Prime*, the first quarter of the artificial day. Sometimes metaphorically used in Chaucer for the season of action or business. Perhaps, from *pryme*, daybreak.

Prow. *Prow*, profit, advantage.

Pye. *Pie*, a magpie, a prating gossip, a tell-tale.

Pyne. *Pyne*, pain, grief, sorrow.

Q.

Quint. *Queynt*, strange, cunning, artful, trim, neat.

Quinton. *Queynt*, neat, trim; *tún*, a house. A neat home.

R.

Raffles. *Rafles*, plays with dice.

Rampe. *Rampe*, to climb. Rempe, doubtless, from the same root.

Rampson. *Ramp*, Rampe; *sun*, son. Son of Rampe.

Ransom. *Raunsoun*, a ransom.

Rems. *Remes*, realms, regions.

Revel. *Revel*, entertainment, sport, festivity.

Ribaut. *Ribaude*, a low, profligate man.

Roche. *Roche*, a rock.

Rochester. *Roche*, a rock; *ceaster*, a castle. A rock-castle.

Rocholl. *Roche*, a rock; *ol*, a termination denoting a personal noun. A rock-dweller; a man of decision.

S.

Scollay. *Scolay*, to attend school, to study.

Sergeant. *Sergeaunt*, a squire attendant upon a prince or nobleman.

Spence. *Spence*, a store-room for wine or victuals. A buttery; a larder; a store-room.

Spencer. *Spence*, a store-room; *ere*, an agent. One who has charge of the spence.

Suel. *Sue*, to follow; *el*, implying a person. A follower.

T.

Tally. *Taille*, a tally, an account scored upon a piece of wood.

Talent. *Talent*, desire, affection.

Targett. *Targe*, a small shield; *et*, implying a diminutive. A small shield.

Timbers. *Timbres*, basins. *Timbesterre* was a term applied to a woman who played tricks with timbres, or basins of some sort or other, by throwing them up into the air and catching them upon a single finger; a kind of balance-mistress.

Tourison. *Tour*, a tower, and *sun*, a son. Son of a tower.

Tresse. *Tresse*, an artificial lock, or gathering of hair.

Tressley. *Tresse*, an artificial lock of hair; *lic*, like. Tress-like; gathered into a tress.

Tressler. *Tress*, a tress; *lár*, knowledge. Tress-knowledge.

V.

Verrey. *Verray*, true, faithful.

Voucher. *Vouche*, contraction of *vouchen sauf*, to vouchsafe; *ere*, an agent. One who vouches a thing safe. In Chaucer, such expressions as *voucheth sauf*, vouchsafe ye, and *the king vouches it save*, the king vouchsafes it, were of common occurrence.

W.

Waite. *Waite*, to watch. Wait, Waitt, Wayte, kindred terms.

Warden. *Wardeyn*, a guard, a keeper of a gate.

From the Scotch.

HISTORY—THE SCOT.

Who were the Scots? This is a question extremely difficult to answer. No satisfactory account of the origin of the appellation has been given. It has puzzled the most distinguished antiquaries, whose conjectures serve rather to perplex than clear up the difficulty. Nor is this surprising, when Varro and Dyonysius could not agree about the etymon of Italia, nor Plutarch and Selinus about that of Rome. All that is known with certainty is, that it was at first a term of reproach, and consequently framed by enemies, rather than assumed by the nation distinguished by that name. The Highlanders, who were the genuine descendants of the ancient Scots, are absolutely strangers to the name, and have been so from the beginning of time. All those who speak the Gaelic language call themselves *Albanich* or *Gael*, and their country *Alba* or *Gaeldochd*.

The Picts, who possessed originally the northern and eastern, and, in a later period, the more southern division of North Britain, were at first more powerful than the Caledonians of the west. It is therefore probable that the Picts, from principles of malevolence and pride, were ready to traduce and ridicule their weaker neighbors of Argyle. These two people spoke the same language—the Gaelic. In that language *Scot*, or *Scode*, signifies a corner or small division of a country. Accordingly, a corner of North Britain is the very name which Giraldus Cambrensis gives the little kingdom of Argyle, that the six sons of Muredus, King of Ulster, are said to have established in Scotland. *Scot*, in Gaelic, is much the same as *little* or *contemptible* in English; and *Scotlan* literally signifies a *small flock*, but metaphorically stands for a small body of men. *Scuit*, a wanderer, is also from the Gaelic, and a few writers suppose that this may have been the origin of the name of *Scot*, a conjecture which seems to be countenanced by a passage in Ammianus Marcellinus, where the men are characterized "*per diversa vagantes.*" All that can be affirmed is, that, for some one of the reasons stated above, the Picts or the Britons may have given, out of derision, the appellation of *Scots* to the ancestors of the Scottish nation.

At what time the inhabitants of the west of Scotland came to be distinguished by this name is uncertain. Porphyrius, the philosopher, is the first who mentions them, and this was about the year of the Christian era 267. Towards the middle of the fourth century Ammianus Marcellinus speaks of them along with other British nations.

Much discussion among antiquaries of note has taken place in regard to the origin of the Scots. Dr. Macpherson contends that they are of Caledonian, and Mr. Whitaker that they are of Irish extraction. Each supports his position with such arguments and authorities that an impartial inquirer is almost at a loss to know which to accept. What appears most probable is, that both are partly in the right and partly in the wrong. From what can be gleaned from past records the Scots seem to have been originally descended from Britons of the south, or from Caledonians, who, being pressed forward by new colonies from Gaul till they came to the western shore of Britain, passed over into Ireland probably one hundred years before the Christian era. Subsequently, about the year of Christ 320, they, or a large colony of them, returned under Fergus to Britain, and settled on the western coasts of Caledonia, from which place they had formerly migrated. As early as 340 they are found associated with the Picts in their expeditions into the Roman province, and for ninety or a hundred years afterwards Roman and British writers make frequent mention of their depredatory excursions.

The territory of the ancient Scots comprehended, before the annexation of Pictavia, all that side of Caledonia that stretched along the coast from the Frith of Clyde to the Orkneys. Towards the east their dominions were divided from those of the Picts by the high mountains running from Dumbarton to the Frith of Tain. In course of time the Scots, under the reign of Kenneth, son of Alpin, became so powerful as to subdue their neighbors the Picts, and to give their own denomination to all Caledonia, Pictavia and Valentia, which territories are still comprehended under the general name of Scotland.

Like those of all other nations, the historians of Scotland assume too great an antiquity for their countrymen, but are, however, much less extravagant in this particular than many others. According to them, the reign of Fergus, the first Scot monarch, is placed at 330 B. C. He was the son of Ferchard, an Irish prince, and is said to have been called into Scotland by the Caledonians to assist them against the Southern Britons, with whom they were then at war. Their language and manners he found to be the same as those of his countrymen. This happy condition of things rendered his position a very easy one. Placing himself at the head of his new allies, he engaged the Britons under their king, Coilus. Events proved him a brave and efficient leader. Coilus was defeated and killed, and victory soon settled upon the banners of the Scots. Shortly afterwards Fergus was declared, with the solemnity of an oath, king of the Scots. But he did not long enjoy his new dignity, for, being called to Ireland to quiet some commotions there, he was drowned on his return voyage at a place on the coast of Ireland, which was called for him, *Knock-Fergus*, or *Carrick-Fergus;* that is, Fergus's Rock.

Feritharis, brother of Fergus, succeeded to the throne to the prejudice of his nephews—Ferlegus and Mainus. His reign was not a peaceful one, for Ferlegus fomented strifes and dissensions, which failed of success, and only resulted, after the death of his uncle, in his being set aside from the succession. The throne was conferred upon his brother Mainus, Ferlegus having died in obscurity. The reign of Mainus and those of Dornadill and Nothat afford nothing remarkable. Reutha, Thereus, Jasina and Finnan then followed in regular succession, but no transactions of note marked their administrations, save that of the last, where we find the first beginnings of the Scottish Parliament. Durstus, Even and Gillus then succeeded, but their reigns were barren of interest. Even II, the nephew of Finnan, who came after Gillus, is said to have built the towns of Innerlochy and Inverness. He overcame Belus, king of the Orkneys, who had invaded Scotland. His son Ever, who next assumed the reins, became king at the time of the invasion of Britain by Julius Cæsar, and assisted the Britons against the common enemy. Even III, his successor, was a monster of cruelty and lust. His great wickedness occasioned a rebellion, and ended in his dethronement, imprisonment and death. Nothing memorable in the history of Scotland is met with from this time until that of Agricola, who having completed the conquest of the southern parts and in a great measure civilized the inhabitants, formed a like plan with regard to Scotland. Here he met a most formidable opposition, but Scotch valor was not proof against the discipline of Roman troops and the experience of their commander. The subsequent history of the Scot, his contact with the Dane, the Angles and the Saxons, and the Normans, must be left unmentioned. We have called attention to these people for the reason that they had in manner and language impressed the Scot of their days, and left an influence behind which is even felt in his progenitors of the present time. Our purpose at the beginning was to give but the history of the origin of the name and of those who had it imposed upon them, and this we have briefly, and it is to be hoped, successfully, accomplished.

SCOTCH—AS IT NOW EXISTS.

Modern Scotch, or the language as spoken even a hundred years ago, differs very materially from that in use by the Scots when Cæsar invaded Britain.

Like the Erse, the latter was an important branch of the Celtic, or Keltic, family of Indo-European languages, of which the Irish, now almost extinct, affords a good illustration.

Eighteen centuries, with their destructive and modifying influences, have been at work upon its structure till its genius has departed, never to return. The Anglo-Saxon and Anglo-Norman have supplanted many of its word-forms, and done away with its peculiarities of speech. What is now left of its former glory is but the shadow.

It is true we meet with Celtic words in current use, but time and neglect have so disfigured their physiognomies that even the practised mind of the philologist often fails to indicate their kinship.

Scotch words, or we might say with greater propriety and exactness Scottish words, for *Scotch* is seemingly nothing more than a corruption of *Scottish*, the English form of the Anglo-Saxon *Scyttisc*, vary their inflections as English words do. The changes, when there are changes, follow the usages of the Anglo-Saxon.

As should be expected, when is considered the influence of the Teutonic and Norman-French invasions, the sounds of certain letters, whether taken singly or in combination, must necessarily have varied. This, as we shall now see, has been the case.

Ch and *gh*, in Scotch, have always the guttural sound.

The sound of the English diphthong *oo* is commonly spelled *ou*.

French *u*, a sound which often occurs in the language, is marked *oo, ui*.

In genuine Scottish words the *a*, except when constituting a diphthong, or when followed by an *e* mute after a single consonant, sounds generally like the broad English *a* in *wall*.

The Scottish diphthong *æ* always, and *ea* very often, sound like the French *e* masculine, while the Scottish diphthong *ey* sounds like the Latin in *ei*.

NAMES—THEIR DERIVATION.

A.

Aiken. *Aik*, an oak; *en*, indicative of an adjective. Oaken.

Auld. *Auld*, old, ancient, of long duration.

B.

Baude. *Baud*, bold, courageous, brave.

Bauder. *Baud*, bold; *ere*, an agent. A bold person.

Bearne. *Bearn*, a child, a human creature.

Bent. *Bent*, long grass, wild fields where bents, etc, grow. Bente, a kindred term.

Bentley. *Bent*, long grass; *lic*, like. Resembling bent.

Bicker. *Bicker*, a kind of wooden dish, a short race.

Birkey. *Birkie*, a clever fellow.

Bonney. *Bonnie*, bonny, handsome, beautiful.

Blyth. *Blyth*, joy, sprightliness, liveliness. Blythe, another spelling of the word.

Bradley. *Brade*, or *braid*, broad; *lic*, like. Broad-like; broadly.

Brauley. *Braw*, brave; *lic*, like. Brave-like; bravely.

Brenner. *Brenn*, burn; *ere*, an agent. That which burns, or gives light.

Briggs. *Brigs*, bridges.

Brock. *Brock*, a badger.

Bunker. *Bunker*, a window-seat.

Burn. *Burn*, water, a rivulet.

Burney. *Burnie*, diminutive of *burn*, a rivulet. A small rivulet.

Buss. *Buss*, shelter, refuge, protection. Busse, a kindred name.

Bussell. Bussle, a bustle, great stir, tumultuous hurry.
Butt. Butt, outer room.
Byers. Byres, plural of *byre*, a cow-stable, a sheep-pen.

C.

Caddy. Caddie, a young person, a young fellow.
Caffey. Caff, chaff; *ig*, implying an adjective. Chaffy.
Cairns. Cairns, plural of *cairn*, a loose heap of stones.
Callan. Callan, a boy.
Canny. Cannie, gentle, mild, dexterous.
Carl. Carl, an old man, a churl.
Carlin. Carlin, feminine of *carl*. A stout old woman.
Cauldwell. Cauld, cold; *well*, a well. A cold well. Caldwell, Colwell, from the same roots.
Child. Chield, a fellow.
Clapp. Clap, clapper of a mill.
Clater. Clatter, an idle story.
Clash. Clash, an idle tale, the story of the day.
Collie. Collie, a general.
Core. Core, corps, party, clans.
Cotter. Cotter, an inhabitant of a cot-house, or cottage.
Cowton. Cowt, a colt; *tun*, a house. A colt's house.
Craft. Craft, in old husbandry, a field near a house, a croft.
Crap. Crap, a crop, to crop.
Crawford. Craw, a rook; *ford*, a ford. A rook-ford.
Creeley. Creel, a basket; *lie*, like. Resembling a basket. To have one's wits in a *creel*, is to be crazed, to be fascinated.
Crees. Crees, grease.
Crick. Cricke, an ant, any small insect.
Crouse. Crouse, cheerful, courageous.
Curley. Curlie, curled, hair falling naturally in ringlets.
Curling. Curling, a well-known game on ice. In Scotland, where it is practised, the player is called a *curler*.

D.

Dale. *Dale*, a plain, a valley. Deal, from the same root.
Dales. *Dale*, a plain; *s* for *sun*, son. Son of Dale.
Daley. *Dale*, a plain; *ig*, an adjective termination. Resembling a plain. Dealy, a kindred term.
Dawson. *Dawes*, days; *sun*, son. Son of days.
Dearie. *Dearie*, diminutive of *dear*, a dear. A little dear.
Dern, *Dern*, secret, hidden, sequestered.
Dolte. *Dolt*, stupefied, crazed.
Dool. *Dool*, sorrow. To sing *dool* is to lament, to mourn.
Dooley. *Dool*, sorrow; *ig*, an adjective termination. Sorrowful.
Doupe. *Doupe*, the backside, the side or part of anything that is out of sight, or that is not observed.
Douredoure. *Doure*, stout, durable, sullen, stubborn; *doure*, stout, durable, etc. Very stout; portly; obstinate.
Dow. *Dow*, am, or are able.
Dowie. *Dowie*, worn with grief, fatigue, etc., half asleep.
Dripps. *Dreips*, or *drips*, drops.
Duddy. *Duddie*, ragged.
Dyce. *Dyce*, dice, checker-work.

E.

Eldridge. *Elriche*, *Elritch*, wild, hideous, ghostly, lonesome, uninhabited, except by spectres.
Enburgh. *Enbrugh*, Edinburgh.

F.

Fae. *Fae*, a foe, an enemy.
Fallon. *Fallan*, falling.
Fallows. *Fallow*, a fellow; *s* for *sun*, son. Son of a fellow. Also, *fallows*, plural of *fallow*, a fellow.
Faust. *Faust*, a fault.

Fay. *Fay*, faith. Faye, of like kinship.

Fell. *Fell*, keen, biting, the flesh immediately underneath the skin, a moderately level field on the side or top of a hill.

Ferley. *Ferley*, or *ferlie*, to wonder, a wonder. Farley, from the same root.

Firth. *Firth*, or *frith*, a wood.

Flegel. *Fleg*, a kicker; *el*, denoting a personal name. A kicker; an opposer.

Fothergill. *Fother*, fodder; *gill*, from *giolla*, a servant. A fodder-servant.

Fow. *Fow*, or *fou*, full, fuddled, drunk.

Fyler. *Fyle*, to soil, to dirty; *ere*, an agent. One who soils, or is soiled.

G.

Gaber. *Gab*, the mouth; *ere*, an agent. One who uses the mouth; a prattler.

Gair. *Gair*, gear, dress, goods, effects, stuff.

Gash. *Gash*, wise, sagacious, talkative.

Gear. *Gear*, riches, goods of any kind.

Geary. *Gear*, riches; *ig*, an adjective termination. Rich; wealthy. Gearey, another spelling.

Glen. *Glen*, a dale, a deep valley.

Goff. *Gowff*, the game of Golf. A game played with a ball and a bat. It is a favorite game in Scotland and consists in driving the ball from one hole to another. The person who drives his ball into a hole with the fewest strokes is declared the winner.

Gowdy. *Gowd*, gould, gold; *ig*, an adjective termination. Gold-like; resembling gold.

Great. *Great*, great, intimate, familiar.

Greely. *Gree*, prize, victory; *lie*, like. Victorious. Greeley, of like derivation.

Greer. *Gree*, prize, victory; *ere*, an agent. One who gains the prize; the victor.

H.

Hagey. *Hag*, a scar; *ig*, implying an adjective. Resembling a scar.

Hale. *Hale*, whole, tight, healthy.

Haly. *Haly*, holy.

Haldeman. *Hald*, an abiding place; *man*, a man. A man that has an abiding place.

Hap. *Hap*, an outer garment, mantle, plaid. Happ, a kindred term.

Haphold. *Hap*, a plaid; *hold*, a captain. A captain invested with his plaid.

Harner. *Harn*, very coarse linen; *ere*, an agent. One who makes coarse linen.

Hasher. *Hash*, a fellow that neither knows how to dress nor act with propriety; *ere*, an agent. A fellow that does not dress becomingly.

Haugh. *Haugh*, a low, rich land, a valley.

Haughey. *Haugh*, a valley; *ig.* expressing an adjective. Valley-like.

Haughton. *Haugh*, a valley; *tun*, a town. A valley-town.

Haverley. *Haverel*, a half-witted person, half-witted.

Hawkey. *Hawkie*, a cow, properly one with a white face.

Hearse. *Hearse*, hoarse, rough, raucous.

Heather *Heather*, a heath, a place overgrown with heath, a low shrub belonging to the family of ericaceous plants.

Hecht. *Hecht*, promised, foretold, the thing promised, or offered.

Heckle. *Heckle*, a board in which is fixed a number of sharp pins used in dressing hemp, flax, etc. Heckel, a cognate term.

Helm. *Helm*, rudder of a vessel.

Helmer. *Helm*, rudder; *ere*, an agent. One who has the charge of the rudder; a helmsman.

Helmbold. *Helm*, rudder, helm; *bóld*, a house. The helmsman's house; pilot-house.

Helms. *Helm*, Helm; *sun*, son. Son of Helm.
Herd. *Herd*, to tend flocks, one who tends flocks.
Herder. *Herd*, to tend flocks; *ere*, an agent. One who tends flocks.
Herry. *Herry*, to plunder; most properly, to plunder birds' nests.
Hiney. *Hiney*, honey.
Hinger. *Hing*, to hang; *ere*, an agent. A hanger; a hangman.
Hitch. *Hitch*, a loop, a knot.
Hoff. *Howff*, a tippling house, a house of resort.
Hoole. *Hool*, outer skin or case, a nut-shell, a peascod, a pea-pod.
Hooley. *Hoolie*, slowly, leisurely.
Horney. *Hornie*, one of the many names of the devil.
Howe. *Howe*, hollow, a hollow, or dell.
Howkins. *Howkins*, diggings.
Howlett. *Howlet*, an owlet, a small owl.
Hoy. *Hoy*, to urge, to press forward. Hoye, of like derivation.
Hoyer. *Hoy*, to urge; *ere*, an agent. One who urges; an urger.
Hoyt. *Hoyte*, to amble crazily.
Hushen. *Hushion*, a cushion.

I.

Ilko. *Ilka*, each, every.
Ingle. *Ingle*, fire, fire-place.

K.

Kain. *Kain*, fowls, etc., paid as rent by a farmer.
Kames. *Kames*, combs.
Keel. *Keel*, a raddle.
Keeler. *Keel*, a raddle; *ere*, an agent. One who uses a raddle; a weaver.

Keeley. *Keel*, a raddle; *ig*, implying an adjective. Raddle-like; resembling a raddle.

Kett. *Ket*, matted hair, fleece of wool.

Kirk. *Kirk*, church. Kirke, of similar derivation.

Kirkbride. *Kirk*, church; *bryde*, a bride. The church's bride.

Kirkby. *Kirk*, church; *by*, a habitation. A habitation belonging to the church; a parsonage.

Kirker. *Kirk*, church; *ere*, an agent. A churchman.

Kirkham. *Kirk*, church; *hám*, house. Church-house.

Kirkland. *Kirk*, church; *land*, land. Church-land.

Kirkman. *Kirk*, church; *man*, a man. A churchman.

Kirkpatrick. *Kirk*, church; *Patrick*, Patrick. Church of St. Patrick.

Kirkwood. *Kirk*, church; *wud*, wood. Church-wood.

Kirn. *Kirn*, the harvest-supper, a churn.

Kitchen. *Kitchen*, anything that is eaten with bread, or that serves for gravy, soup, etc.

Kittle. *Kittle*, ticklish, lively, apt. As a verb, it signifies to tickle.

Knapp. *Knap*, to strike sharply. A smart blow.

Knapper. *Knap*, to strike sharply; *ere*, an agent. One who strikes a smart blow.

Kye. *Kye*, cows.

Kyle. *Kyle*, a district in Ayrshire. Doubtless from *kyel*—the equivalent of *kye*, cows, and *el*, a personal suffix—a cowherd.

L.

Laddey. *Laddie*, diminutive of *lad*, a small lad, or boy.

Laggen. *Lagen*, the angle between the side and the bottom of a wooden dish.

Lang. *Lang*, long.

Lear. *Lear*, learning, knowledge.

Linn. *Linn*, a water-fall, a precipice.

Lowe. *Lowe*, a flame.

Lounes. Lounes, plural of *loun*, a fellow, a ragamuffin, a woman of easy virtue.

Lowrie. Lowrie, abbreviation of Lawrence. Lowry, from the same name. Lawrence, from the Latin, belonging to the laurel; secondarily, victorious.

Lowse. Lowse, to loose.

Lum. Lum, the chimney.

Lunt. Lunt, a column of smoke, to smoke.

M.

Mair. Mair, more.

Malley. Mallie, Molly, nickname for Mary, a Hebrew word signifying bitter.

Mang. Mang, among.

Manse. Manse, the house where the minister lives, the parsonage.

Mavis. Mavis, the thrush.

Maw. Maw, to mow, a mow.

Mawby. Maw, to mow; *bý*, a house, a habitation. A mow-house; a chamber in a barn where hay is stored.

Mell. Mell, to meddle. Also, a mallet for pounding barley in a stone trough.

Meslin. Meslin, mixed corn.

Muckel. Muckle, great, big, much.

Murney. Murne, mourn; Irish *neac*, an individual. One that mourns; a mourner.

N.

Napey. Nappy, ale, to be tipsy. Naphey, perhaps, from the same root.

P.

Pack. Pack, intimate, familiar, twelve stone of wool.

Parle. Parle, speech, discourse, conversation.

Pechin. Pechan, the crop, the stomach.

Pickle. *Pickle*, a small quantity. Pickel, from the same radix.
Pine. *Pine*, pain, uneasiness.
Plews. *Plews*, or *pleughs*, ploughs.
Prigge. *Prig*, to cheapen, to dispute.
Pund. *Pund*, pound.
Pyle. *Pyle* (*a pyle o' chaff*), a single grain of chaff.

Q.

Quay. *Quay*, or *quey*, a young heifer, a cow from one to two years of age.

R.

Raible. *Raible*, to rattle nonsense.
Rash. *Rash*, a rush.
Reamer. *Ream*, cream, to cream; *ere*, an agent. One who skims the cream from anything.
Reck. *Reck*, to heed.
Redwood. *Red-wud*, stark mad.
Reid. *Reid*, a reed.
Reider. *Reid*, to advise; *ere*, an agent. One that advises; an adviser.
Reidy. *Reid*, a reed; *ig*, indicating an adjective termination. Reedy.
Rever. *Rever*, robber, pirate, rover.
Rief. *Rief*, or *reef*, plenty, abundance, randies, sturdy beggars.
Rigby. *Rig*, a ridge; *by*, a habitation. A ridge-house.
Riggs. *Rigs*, plural of *rig*, a ridge.
Rink. *Rink*, the course of the stones, a term in *curling* on ice.
Ripley. *Rip*, a handful of unthreshed corn; *lic*, like. Resembling a handful of unthreshed corn.
Ripp. *Rip*, a handful of unthreshed corn.
Routh. *Routh*, or *rowth*, plenty, abundance.

Rung. *Rung*, a cudgel. *Runge*, of like kinship.
Runger. *Rung*, a cudgel; *ere*, an agent. A cudgeller.

S.

Saul. *Saul*, soul. *Saull*, from the same root.
Sauter. *Saut*, salt; *ere*, an agent. One who salts; a salter.
Sax. *Sax*, six.
Scarborough. *Scar*, a cliff; *beorh*, a burrow. A cliff-burrow.
Shaw. *Shaw*, to show, a small wood in a hollow.
Sheen. *Sheen*, bright, shining.
Sheetz. *Sheits*, or *shetes*, sheets.
Shiel. *Shiel*, a shed.
Shill. *Shill*, shrill.
Shur. *Shure*, did shear, shore. *Shurr*, from the same root.
Siller. *Siller*, silver, money.
Simmer. *Simmer*, summer.
Simmers. *Simmer*, Simmer; *s* for *sun*, son. Son of Simmer.
Skerl. *Skirl*, to shriek, to cry shrilly.
Slade. *Slade*, did slide.
Slaw. *Slaw*, slow, tardy.
Smithers. *Smithers*, smothers.
Snell. *Snell*, bitter, biting.
Soutter. *Souter*, a shoemaker.
Speel. *Speel*, to climb.
Spier. *Spier*, to ask, to inquire.
Stang. *Stang*, an acute pain, a twinge, to sting.
Stangle. *Stang*, to sting; *el*, expressive of a personal name. That which stings.
Staut. *Staut*, to stand.
Stark. *Stark*, stout, stiff.
Steane. *Stean*, or *stane*, a stone.
Stell. *Stell*, a still.
Swank. *Swank*, stately, jolly. A tight, strapping young fellow or girl was called a *swankie*, or *swanker*.

T.

Taine. *Taine,* or *tane,* a token.
Tifft. *Tift,* a puff of wind.
Toomey. *Toom,* empty; *ig,* expressive of an adjective. Empty; unoccupied.

W.

Waley. *Walie,* ample, large, jolly.
Wambold. *Wam,* the womb, the belly; *bóld,* a house, a habitation. The womb-house; the abdomen.
Ward. *Ward,* watch, sentinel.
Wark. *Wark,* work.
Warley. *Warly,* worldly, eager in amassing wealth. Warlley, a cognate term.
Warris. *Warris,* wars.
Whidden. *Whidden,* running as a hare or cony.
Wicht. *Wicht,* powerful, strong, inventive, of superior genius.
Wiel. *Wiel,* a small whirlpool.
Wrangham. *Wrang,* wrong, to wrong; *hám,* a house. A wrong home; a wronged house.

Y.

Yerkes. *Yerkes,* or *yerks,* present indicative third person singular of *yerk,* to lash, to jerk. Lashes; jerks.
Yetter. *Yett,* a gate; *ere,* an agent. One who has charge of a gate; a gate-keeper. *Yett* was usually applied to a gate that commanded the entrance to a farm-yard or a field.

ADDENDA ET CORRIGENDA.

A.

Acker. *Acer*, an acre, a field. Aker, of like derivation.

Ackley. *A'c-lea*, from *ác*, an oak, and *leag*, a territory, a district. An oak-district. Oakley, from the same roots.

Acorn. *A'c-cærn*, from *ác*, an oak, and *cærn*, a corn. An oak-corn.

Adamson. Hebrew *Adam*, red earth; A. S. *sun*, son. Son of Adam; son of red earth. Adams, contracted form of the word.

Albertson. *Albert*, from *æl*, all, and *beorht*, bright; *sun*, son. Son of Albert; son of the all-bright, or illustrious. Alberts, of like kinship.

Albright. *Æl*, all; *beorht*, bright. All-bright; illustrious.

Alderson. *Alder*, an author, an originator; *sun*, son. Son of an author.

Anderson. Greek *aner*, French *andré*, a man; *sun*, son. Son of a man. Anders, Andrews, of like significance.

Antrim. Irish *antrim*, land of caverns. Very closely allied to *antrum*, the Latin for cave, den, grot, lurking-place.

Armstrong. *Earm*, arm; *strong*, strong. Arm-strong.

Ashburn. *Æsc*, an ash-tree, a ship; *burne*, a bourn, stream, creek, river. A stream bordered by ash-trees; a river navigable by ships.

B.

Barrow. *Beorh*, a heap, burrow or barrow, a heap of stones, a place of burial. Barrows, son of Barrow.

Bartram. *Beorht*, bright; *remn*, or *hrem*, a raven. A bright raven. Bertram, of like kinship.

Becker. *Béc*, a book; *ere*, an agent. A book-maker; a bookman. *Béc*, derivable from *bécc*, a beech-tree, as books were first made out of the beech. Becher, a name of analogous significance.

Beckman. *Béc*, a book; *man*, a man. A bookman; a book-maker. Bechman, a kindred term.

Beckley. *Béc*, book, or *béce*, beech; *lic*, like. Book-like; resembling the beech.

Berry. *Berige*, or *berie*, a berry, a grape.

Best. *Best*, best, most.

Bickel. *Bicce*, a bitch; *el*, implying personality. A woman in disgrace.

Bickley. *Bicce*, a bitch; *lic*, like. Resembling a bitch.

Bigg. *Byge*, or *bige*, a corner, a bay. Perhaps, from *byggan*, to big, to build: hence, great, large in bulk.

Bigley. *Byge*, a bay; *lic*, like. Resembling a bay.

Birch. *Birce*, or *byrce*, a birch-tree. Birkey, from the same radix.

Blackburn. *Blæc*, black; *beorn*, a prince, a king. A black prince. Or, from *blæc*, black, and *byrne*, a coat of mail. A black coat of mail.

Blade. *Blæd*, a blade, leaf, branch, twig. It also signifies a blowing, blast, breath, life, a favorable wind, success, prosperity, honor, reward, fame, glory.

Blading. *Blæd*, a blade, a leaf; *ing*, expressive of action. Leaf-producing.

Blakeley. *Blæc*, black; *lic*, like. Resembling black. Blakely, a kindred term.

Blakey. *Blæc*, black; *ig*, an adjective termination. Blackish.

Blakiston. *Blæc*, black; *isc*, an adjective termination denoting likeness; *tún*, town. A blackish town.

Blane. *Blægen*, a pustule. *Blain*, perhaps, from the same root.

Blaney. *Blægen*, a pustule; *ig*, an adjective termination. Full of pustules.

Blank. Blanc, white. Blanke, from the same root.

Blankley. Blanc, white; *lic*, like. White-like.

Blee. Bleo, color, hue, blee, complexion, beauty.

Blue. Bleo, blue, azure. Blew is, doubtless, from *bleow*, the past of *bláwan*, to blow, to breathe.

Boot. Bót, a boot, remedy, amend, atonement, offering, redress, compensation, cure. Boote, another spelling.

Booth. Ir. *both*, a house.

Borgman. Borg, a loan, a pledge; *man*, a man. A man who receives a loan, or one who gives a pledge; a bondsman.

Bostick. Bósig, a crib, a stall, a manger, a boose. Bostwick, from the same roots, both words, doubtless, being corruptions of the original.

Bower. Búr, a bower, cottage, dwelling, an inner room, bed-chamber, store-house.

Bowman. Boga, a bow, arch, corner, bending, band, horn, tail; *man*, a man. A bow-man; an archer.

Brick. Ir. *brice*, French *brique*, a brick. Earth or clay formed into regular blocks and burnt in a kiln or baked in the sun.

Bridge. Bricg, or *bryeg*, a bridge.

Bradbury. Brád, broad, vast; *beorh*, a barrow, or burrow. A vast barrow.

Braddock. Brád, broad; Gothic *dok*, a deep or gulfy place. A broad dock. Or, from *brád*, broad; *docce*, a dock, a kind of plant. A broad-leaved dock.

Bradford. Brád, broad; *ford*, a ford. A broad ford.

Bray. Ir. *breág*, fine. Or, from *breac*, ever.

Brightly. Beorht, bright; *lic*, like. Bright-like; with lustre; splendidly.

Bryan. Ir. *brig*, virtue, vigor, force; *an*, a personal termination. A virtuous person; a man of vigor.

Buckingham. Boccenham, from *bóccen*, an adjective derived from *bócce*, a beech, and *hám*, a house. A beechen house; a house surrounded by beech trees.

Burk. *Bearoc*, from *beaŕo*, a grove, a wood, a hill covered with wood. Burke, from the same root.

Burkley. *Bearoc*, a grove, a forest; *lic*, like. Forest-like.

Burr. *Búr*, a bower, dwelling, store-house. Also, from French *bourre*, the down on herbs and fruits. Most properly, from the Anglo-Saxon.

Burrell. *Búr*, a bower, a storehouse, a dwelling; *el*, a termination denoting both persons and inanimate objects. One who, or that which, dwells in a bower; a cottager; a storehouse.

Burrow. *Beorh*, a heap, a barrow, a heap of stones, a place of burial. Burrough, from the same radix.

C.

Cade. Ir. *céad*, a hundred, first. Perhaps, from *cat*, pronounced *cath*, or *cadh*, war, battle.

Cadic. Ir. *céad*, first; *eac*, for *neac*, an agent. The first man. Caddy, from the same roots. Probably, from *cat-aid*, a warrior.

Callow. *Calo*, or *caluw*, callow, bald, without hair.

Camley. Ir. *cam*, curved, crooked, bent; A. S. *lic*, like. Curved-like; crooked.

Camp. *Camp*, from Latin *campus*, a contest, battle, war, a camp.

Campbell. *Camp*, a camp; *bel*, a bell. A camp-bell. Possibly, from French *camp*, a camp, and *bel*, beautiful: hence, a beautiful camp.

Canby. *Can*, or *cann*, clearance; *by*, a habitation. A clearance-house.

Capp. *Cappa*, a cap, cope, priest's garment.

Carl. *Carl*, a male; chiefly used before words to denote the male, as *cwén* does the female. *Carl-catt*, meaning a male cat, and *carl-fugol*, a male or cock bird. Later, *carl* came to signify man, a married man, as well as the male of any kind.

Carley. *Carl,* a male, a man; *lic,* like. Male-like; resembling a man; churlish. Carle, from the same.

Carncross. Ir. *carn,* a heap of stones; *cros,* a cross. A cross composed of a heap of stones.

Carra. Ir. *cara,* a friend.

Carritt. Ir. *car,* dear; *aid,* a termination indicative of personality. A dear person; a friend.

Carter. *Cræt,* or *crat,* a carriage, a cart; *ere,* an agent. One who drives a cart or carriage; a carter; a teamster. In Anglo-Saxon, *cræt-wæn* was applied to a wain, a chariot. It is highly probable that *cræt* or *crat* is traceable through the Gaelic words *cairt* and *carr* to Latin *carrus,* a car, a chariot.

Caskey. Ir. *Caisg,* Easter; *eac,* an individual. One who celebrates Easter.

Caton. A. S. for the Latin *catus,* or *cautus,* cautious, weary, provident.

Cilles. *Cille,* a bottle; genitive *cilles,* of bottle. Belonging to a bottle.

Conrad. *Cón,* bold; *ræd,* counsel, reason, opinion. Bold counsel; courageous opinion.

Conway. *Cón,* bold; *wæg,* a way, a passage. A bold passage.

Cormac. Ir. *corb,* a chariot; *mac,* son. Son of a chariot; a charioteer. Cormick, Cormuck, barbarous spellings of the name.

Coulter. *Culter,* and not *colter,* a coulter. See page 67.

Crawford. *Cráw,* a crow, chough, jackdaw; *ford,* a ford. A crow-ford; a ford crossed by crows.

Crock. *Croc,* a crock, a pitcher.

Crook. *Cruc,* a crook, a crutch.

Crookes. *Crook,* Crook; *s* for *sun,* son. Son of Crook.

Crouch. Corruption of *cruc,* a crook, a crutch.

Crowley. *Cráw,* a crow; *lic,* like. Resembling a crow.

Culbert. *Col,* a helmet; *beorht,* bright. A bright helmet. Colbert, of like derivation.

Curby. *Cear,* anxious, careful; *by,* a habitation. An anxious home.

Curry. Ir. *curam,* care (applied in Irish to all over whom one has charge); *eac,* an agent, and not *lac.* A supervisor. See page 22.

D.

Dalby. *Dál,* a dale, a valley; *by,* a habitation. A valley-home.

Darby. Common name for *Diarmoid* in Limerick and Tipperary. See Dermod, page 23.

Darcey. *Dearc,* or *deorc,* dark, dusky; *ig,* an adjective termination. Dark; dusky.

Darkis. *Dearc,* dark; *isc,* an adjective ending. Darkish; dusky.

Darling. *Deór,* dear; *ling,* a termination denoting state or condition of a person. A person that is dear, or beloved.

Darlington. *Darling,* Darling; *tán,* house. Home of Darling.

Darley. *Deór,* dear; *lic,* like. Dear-like; dearly.

Davidson. *David,* Hebrew for "beloved;" *sun,* son. Son of David. Davids, a contracted form of the name.

Davies. *Davie,* Scotch for the Hebrew for "beloved;" *s* for *sun,* son. Son of Davie. Davieson, unabbreviated name, and Davis, a contraction thereof.

Daw. *Dæg,* a day; *dawe,* Old English for the same. Day, of like kinship.

Dawson. *Daw,* Daw; *sun,* son. Son of Daw.

Deacon. *Deacon,* or *diacon,* a deacon, a levite.

Deane. *Deane,* the Danes: so called from *dene,* a valley, a plain, for they are dwellers in a vale or plain. *Dean,* as commonly applied, is the same as *deacon,* a levite.

Denison. *Denis,* French of the Greek *Dionysos,* god of Nysos; *sun,* son. Son of Denis.

Denn. *Den,* a valley, a plain.

Derby. *Deór-by,* from *deór,* a deer, a beast, and *by,* a habitation. A deer-park.

Dilg. *Dilge,* present indicative of *dilgian,* to destroy.

Donald. Ir. *Donghal,* from *donn,* brown, and *gall,* stranger. Brown-haired stranger.

Donaldson. *Donald,* Donald; *sun,* son. Son of Donald.

Donnell. Ir. *Domhnall,* possibly *Donghal,* from *donn,* brown, and *gall,* stranger. Brown-haired stranger.

Donaghy. Ir. *Donoghoe,* from *Donnachu,* which is from *donn,* brown, and *ncac,* an individual, an agent. A brown-haired chief. Donnogh, Donahoe, Donahue, Donohoe, Donohue, from the same roots.

Douglass. Ir. *dhu,* from *dub,* black, dark; *glas,* green, gray. Dark green; dark gray.

Dugall. Ir. *dhu,* from *dub,* black; *gall,* a stranger. A black stranger. Dugald, from the same roots.

Downes. *Dúnes,* genitive of *dún,* a mountain, a hill. Belonging to a hill.

Douncy. *Dún-ig,* from *dún,* a mountain, a hill, and *ig,* an adjective ending. Mountainous; hilly. Downy, from the same derivation.

Durburrow. *Dur,* a door, a gate; *beorh,* a burrow, a place of burial. A door-burrow; a place of burial entered by door, or gate. Durborrow, Durborow, cognate terms.

E.

Earl. *Eorl,* not *earl,* noble, earl, man. See page 68.

Earley. *Eorl-lic,* from *eorl,* an earl, and *lic,* like. Earl-like; belonging to an earl.

Easby. *Eás,* genitive of *eá,* a river; *by,* a habitation. Habitation of a river; banks of a river.

Eastburn. *East,* eastern; *burne,* a river. An eastern river.

Eastman. *East,* eastern; *man,* a man. An eastern man.

Eck. *E'ce,* eternal, perpetual, everlasting.

Eckley. *E'ee-lic,* from *eee,* eternal, and *lic,* like. Eternal-like; everlasting.

Edgar. *Eádg,* happy, prosperous, blessed, rich, perfect; *gár,* a dart, javelin, spear, weapon. A prosperous spear. *Eádg,* contraction of the adjective *eád-ig,* which is derivable from the substantive *eád,* prosperity, happiness. It is highly probable that *eád* is an altered form of *eard,* earth, a man's prosperity and consequent happiness being measured by the extent of his earthly possessions. See page 68.

Edmund. *Eádmund,* from *eádg,* happy, and *mund,* hand, protection, defence. Happy defence.

Edson. *Eádg,* rich; *sun,* son. Rich son.

Edward. *Eádward,* from *eádg,* blessed; *weard,* guardian, watchman. A blessed guardian.

Egge. *Egge,* present indicative first person singular of *eggian,* to egg, to excite.

Eglee. *Egle,* troublesome, difficult, hateful. Or, from *egle,* a sprout, an ear of corn, a thistle.

Eggleson. *Egle,* troublesome; *sun,* son. A troublesome son.

F.

Farley. *Far-lic,* from *fær,* sudden, fortuitous, wonderful, and *lic,* like. Sudden; fortuitous; wonderful.

Ferguson. *Fergus,* Fergus; *sun,* son, Son of Fergus. See Fergus, page 25.

Fetter. *Feoter,* or *fetor,* a fetter.

Fetterling. *Feoter,* a fetter; *ling,* a termination denoting the state or condition of a person. Bondage.

Finan. Ir., *fionn,* fair, white; *an,* a personal ending. A fair person. Finian, kindred in derivation.

Fitler. *Fit,* or *fitt,* a song; *lár,* lore, learning, law. Song-lore.

Forder. *Ford,* a ford; *ere,* an agent. On who, or that which, fords a stream.

Fordham. *Ford,* ford; *hám,* house. Ford-house.

Fowler. Fugel-ere, from *fugel,* a bird, a fowl, and *ere,* an agent. One who pursues or traps wild fowl.

Freeborn. Freó-bearn, from *freó,* free, and *bearn,* born. One free born.

Fricka. Friga, Saxon Venus, the goddess of love. Or, which is more likely, from *fricca,* a crier or preacher. Frick, from the same radix. See Frick, page 70.

Frost. Frost, or *forst,* frost.

Fry. Frý, free, having liberty or authority. Frye, of similar derivation.

Fuller. Fullere, from *fullian,* to whiten, and *ere,* an agent. One that whitens anything; a bleacher.

Fullerton. Fuller, Fuller; *tún,* house. Home of Fuller.

Fullom. Fúle-hám, from *fúle,* foul, muddy, corrupt, and *hám,* a house. A muddy house; a corrupt home. Fullum, a cognate term.

G.

Gadd. Gád, or *gǽd,* a point of a weapon, a prick, a goad. Also, from *gád,* want, need, deficiency.

Gadsby. Gádes, genitive of *gád,* want, deficiency, need; *by,* a habitation. A needy home.

Gaff. Gaf, base, vile, lewd.

Gaffney. Gaf, base; Ir. *neac,* an individual. A base person.

Gale. Gale, a nightingale, is from *galan,* to sing, to enchant. Galey, of like derivation.

Galen. Galen, past participle of *galan,* to sing, to enchant.

Garlic. Gár-leac, from *gár,* a spear, and *leac,* a leek, an onion, an herb. Spear-leek; garlic.

Garman. Gár, a spear; *man,* a man. A spearman.

Garret. Gár, a spear; *rédhe,* cruel. A cruel spear.

Gillingham. Gillinga-hám, or *Gill-ingahám,* from *Gill,* Gill, and *ingahám,* residence of the sons. Home of the sons of Gill. See Gill, page 27.

Glade. Glade, a river, a brook. Or, *glade,* gladly.

Gladney. *Gláed*, purified, bright; Ir. *neac*, an individual. A purified person; a saint; an angel.

Glenney. *Glen*, a glen, a valley; Ir. *neac*, an individual. A dweller in a glen, or a valley.

Guildford. *Gild-ford*, from *gild*, a guild, society, or club where money was paid for support, and *ford*, a ford. A stock-ford.

H.

Haddock. *Hacod*, by the inversion of the letters in the last syllable became *hadoc*, and signifies a pike, mullet.

Hadley. *Heáfod-lic*, from *heáfod*, a head, and *lic*, like. Head-like; capital; chief. Headley, of like kinship.

Haines. *Heánes*, from *heáh*, high, and *nes*, a termination of feminine nouns denoting quality or state. Highness; height; top; end; pinnacle; fortress.

Haley. *Heálig*, from *heáh*, high, and *ig*, an adjective ending. High; lofty. Or, from *hál*, healthy, sound, whole, and *ig*, implying an adjective. Healthy; sound; wholly; holy.

Hallowell. *Heálig*, holy; *well*, a well. A holy well. Halliwell, from the same roots.

Hambright. *Hám*, home; *beorht*, bright. A bright home.

Hambrook. *Hám*, home; *bróc*, a rivulet. A home rivulet.

Hancock. *Hean*, worthless; *cocc*, or *coc*, a cock, a male bird. A worthless cock. See Hancock, page 72.

Handley. *Handle*, that which is used by the hand. A handle; a haft. Hanley, a kindred term.

Hane. *Heán*, high, lofty, sublime; chief, noble, excellent.

Hanna. *Heana*, poor, needy, humble, despised.

Hansbury. *Heán-burh*, from *heán*, high, lofty, and *burh*, a tower. A lofty tower.

Harbeck. *Hár*, hoar, hoary, gray; *béc*, a book. A hoary book.

Harbert. *Hár*, hoary, gray; *beorht*, glistening. Glistening with gray.

Harding. *Heard*, hard; *ing*, implying action. Hardening.

Hardick. Heard, hard; *ig*, an adjective termination. Hardy. Hardie, Hardy, from the same roots.

Hare. Hara, a hare. As hares are gray, the name was originally derived from *hár*, hoar, hoary, gray. *Hare*, an estuary, is a probable etymology.

Hargis. Heregas, armies, a host.

Harmer. Hearm, harm, damage, calamity; *ere*, an agent. One who, or that which, produces harm. Perhaps, from *harma*, a sling to support a wounded arm, an arm that has been harmed or damaged.

Hay. Hoeg, or *hég*, hay.

Hayes. Haye, Hay; *s* for *sun*, son. Son of Hay.

Hazel. Hæsel, or *hæsl*, a nut-tree, hazel. *Hæsel*, also, signifies a hat. The husk of the hazel-nut resembles a hat, but whether the plant took its name from the form of the covering of the nut, or the hat received its name from its resemblance to the covering, is a question. We incline to the latter belief.

Heany. Heane, poor, needy, humble, worthless, despised. Heeny, from the same root.

Heberton. Heber, a goat; *tún*, a house. A goat-house.

Heller. Helle, clear, eminent; *ere*, an agent. A man of eminence.

Heppe. Heope, a hip, fruit of the dog-rose.

Herman. Here-man, from *here*, an army, and *man*, a man. An army-man; a soldier.

Hill. Hill, or *hyll*, a hill.

Hilles. Hilles, or *hylles*, genitives of *hill* and *hyll*, a hill. Belonging to a hill.

Hocker. Hocer, or *hocor*, mocking, reproach.

Hood. Hód, a hood.

Hodge. Hog, prudent, careful, anxious.

Hodgson. Hog, prudent; *sun*, son. A prudent son.

Holcombe. Hel, a hole, cavern, den; *comb* a valley. A cavernous valley.

Holden. *Healden,* past participle of *healdan,* to hold, rescue, fasten, rule, govern. Held; ruled; governed.

Holland. *Hol,* a hole, a cavern; *land,* region. A cavernous land. Or, *hol,* hollow; *land,* land. A hollow land.

Hookey. *Hóc,* or *hooc,* a hook, a stick, or iron bent at the end; *iht,* an adjective termination. Hooked.

Hoopes. *Hópes,* genitive of *hóp,* a hoop, circle, company. Belonging to a hoop.

Hough. *Hoh,* or *hó,* a heel, hough, ham.

I.

Inger. *Ing,* Ing; *ere,* an agent. A descendant of Ing. According to Teuton mythology, Ing was the son of Tuisco, and is, without doubt, the name-father of the Anglo-Saxon and English.

Ingham. *Ing,* Ing; *hám,* house. Home of Ing.

Ingram. *Ing,* Ing; *remn,* or *hrem,* a raven. Ing's raven.

K.

Kane. Ir. *caton,* pronounced *cahon,* from *cat,* battle, and *an,* a termination denoting a personal noun. A warrior.

Kindall. *Cyn,* or *cin,* suitable; *dál,* valley. A suitable valley. Kendall, of like kinship.

Kettle. *Cetel,* a kettle.

Kidder. *Cidan,* to contend, quarrel, chide; *ere,* an agent. One who chides; a chider.

Kille. *Cile,* cold, coldness. Or, more likely, *cille,* a battle.

King. *Cyng,* king, ruler, prince.

Kingsbury. *Cynges,* genitive of *cyng,* king; *beorh,* a city. King's city.

Kingston. *Cynges,* genitive of *cyng,* a king; *tún,* town. King's town.

Kitchen. *Cicene,* a kitchen.

Knapp. *Cnæpp,* a top, cop, knop, button.

Knauf. *Cnáfa,* one begotten, an offspring, a son, boy, youth.

Knaup. *Cnápa,* son, boy, youth.

Knight. *Cniht,* a boy, youth, attendant, a military follower.

Knoll. *Cnoll,* a knoll, a hill, top, cop, summit.

Knott. *Cnott,* a knot, a fastening, knitting.

Knowles. *Cnolles,* genitive of *cnoll,* a knoll, a hill. Belongging to a knoll, or hill.

L.

Landes. *Landes,* genitive of *land,* land, ground, earth, field, country. Belonging to the country. Landis, of cognate derivation.

Lang. *Lang,* long, tall.

Langfeld. *Lang,* long; *feld,* a field. A long field.

Langham. *Lang,* long; *hám,* home. Long home.

Langley. *Lang-lice,* from *lang,* long, and *lice,* form. Form of long; a long time.

Lapp. *Lappa,* a lap, border, hem, piece, portion.

Lark. *Lauerc,* or *lawerc,* a lark.

Lau. *Láu,* a relict, a widow.

Lawman. *Lah,* law; *man,* a man. A man of the law; a lawyer.

Lawson. *Lah,* law; *sun,* son. Son of the law; a lawyer.

Lea. *Lea,* or *leag,* a law, a territory or district in which a particular law or custom was in force. See Lea, page 75.

Leak. *Leac,* a leek, an onion, garlic, an herb.

Light. *Liht,* light, bright, not heavy.

Lightham. *Liht,* bright; *hám,* home. A bright home.

Lillie. *Lilie,* a lily. Lilly, from the same radix.

Lillig. *Lilige,* a lily.

List. *List,* wisdom, science, power, faculty, art, deceit.

Lous. *Lús,* pronounced *loos,* a louse.

Lord. *Laucord,* or *hláford,* a lord, a master, a ruler.

Love. *Lóf,* praise. Or, from *luf,* love, favor, grace.

Lovely. *Lóf*, praise; *lic*, like. Praise-like; lovely. Or, from *luf-lic*, lovely.

Luff. *Luf*, love, favor, grace.

Lunger. *Lunger*, immediate, quick.

Lust. *Lust*, desire, will, power, pleasure, delight, exultation.

M.

McAlpin. Ir. *mac*, son; *ailpin*, from *ailp*, a lump, a height, and *in*, implying a diminutive. Son of a small lump, or height.

McArthur. Ir. *mac*, son; *Arthur*, Anglicised form of Ir. *ard*, high. Son of Arthur; son of the high.

McBride. Ir. *mac*, son; *brig*, virtue, vigor, force. Son of virtue; son of force. Anglo-Saxon *bride* is, doubtless, traceable to Ir. *brig.*

McCadden. Ir. *mac*, son; *catin*, pronounced *cathin*, or, possibly, corrupted into *cadhin*, a warrior. Son of a warrior.

McCandless. Ir. *mac*, son; Anglo-Saxon *candeles*, genitive of *candel*, a candle. Son of a candle. Candle is from the Latin *candeo*, I burn.

McCarrick. Ir. *mac*, son; *Carrick*, Carrick. Son of Carrick. See Carrick, page 21.

McCartney. Ir. *mac*, son; *cairt*, a cart; *neac*, an agent. Son of a carter.

McClay. Ir. *mac*, son; A. S. *clæg*, clay. Son of Clay; son of clay.

McClerk. Ir. *mac*, son; A. S. *clerc*, a clerk, a priest. Son of a priest.

McCombes. Ir. *mac*, son; A. S. *combes*, genitive of *comb*, a valley. Son of a valley. McComb, McCombs, McCoomb, McCoombs, of kindred derivation.

McCoon. Ir. *mac*, son; A. S. *coones*, genitive of *coon*, bold. Son of the bold.

McCord. Ir. *mac*, son; *coird*, genitive of *cord*, a string. Son of a string.

McCormac. Ir. *mac*, son; *cormac*, from *corb*, a chariot, and *mac*, a son; hence, a charioteer. Son of a charioteer.

McCourt. Ir. *mac*, son; *cuirte*, genitive of *cuirt*, a yard, an enclosed place. Son of an enclosed place. McCort, from the same roots.

McDade. Ir. *mac*, son; A. S. *dæde*, genitive of *dæd*, deed, action. Son of action.

McFeat. Ir. *mac*, son; *fearte*, genitive of *feart*, a feat, an achievement. Son of achievement.

McFeeters. Ir. *mac*, son; A. S. *fæteres*, genitive of *fæter*, a fetter. Son of a fetter.

McGade. Ir. *mac*, son; A. S. *gádes*, genitive of *gád*, a goad, a prick. Son of a goad.

McManus. Ir. *mac*, son; *manus*, most likely a corruption of A. S. *mannes*, genitive of *mann*, a man. Son of a man.

McMaster. Ir. *mac*, son; *maigistera*, genitive of *maigister*, a master. Son of a master.

Mader. *Mædere*, or *mæddere*, madder.

Madge. *Mæge*, a kinswoman, a daughter.

Madison. *Mæge*, genitive of *mæge*, a maid. Son of a maid.

Maiden. *Mæden*, a maiden, a virgin.

Mallow. *Malwe*, or *malu*, mallow. Mallow, name of a species of malvaceous plant.

Mear. *Mear*, a field. Also, from *mear*, or *mearh*, a horse. See Mear, page 76.

Mease. *Measse*, the mass. a feast, a festival.

Mennig. *Menigo*, a multitude, a host.

Mennis. *Mennisc*, human, manlike, mortal.

Merrill. *Mere*, the sea; Ir. *aill*, a wall, a cliff. A sea-wall; a sea-cliff.

Mood. *Mód*, mind, disposition, mood, passion, violence, force.

Moody. *Mód-ig*, from *mód*, mind, and *ig*, an adjective ending. Proud; courageous; bold; irritable; moody. Moodie, from the same roots.

Moon. *Món,* pronounced *moon,* wickedness. Or, from *móna,* the moon.

Mooney. *Mon-ig,* from *móna,* the moon, and *ig,* an island. Mona Island; Isle of the Moon.

Morley. *Mǽr-lic,* from *mǽr,* great, high, lofty, exalted, illustrious, famous; *lic,* like. Noble; lofty; glorious.

Morning. *Morgen,* the morning, morrow.

Morrow. *Morhgèn,* or *morgen,* the morning, morrow.

Morton. *Mór,* moor, heath; *tún,* town. A moor-town; a town built on a moor.

Moss. *Meos,* moss.

Mott. *Mot,* a mote.

Mould. *Molde,* mould, earth, dust.

Mund. *Mund,* a hand, a protection, fence, defense, security.

Munder. *Mund-bora,* from *mund,* protection, and *bora,* a bearer. A bearer of protection; a protector.

Mundy. *Mundig,* from *mundean,* to remember, and *ig,* an adjective termination. Mindful.

N.

Nutt. *Hnut,* a nut.

Nuttall. *Hnut-hule,* from *hnut,* a nut, and *hule,* hull or husk. A nut-hull.

Nutter. *Hnut,* a nut; *ere,* an agent. A nut-gatherer.

O.

Oakey. *A'c,* an oak; *ig,* an adjective termination, Oaky; like oak; hard as oak.

Oakford. *A'c,* an oak; *ford,* ford. The ford of the oak.

Oakley. *A'c-lea,* from *ác,* oak; *lea,* a place. An oak place.

Oat. *A'ta,* an oat.

Oats. *Oat,* Oat; *s* for *sun,* son. Son of Oat.

Oatis. *A'ta,* an oat; *isc,* resembling. Resembling an oat.

Oldham. Eald, old, ancient; *hám*, house. An ancient home. Oldam, contracted form of the name.

Olding. Eald, old; *ing*, expressing action. Growing old.

Otter. Oter, or *otor*, an otter.

Otterson. Oter, an otter; *sun*, son. Son of an otter.

P.

Palmer. Palm, a palm; *ere*, an agent. A palm-bearer.

Park. Parruc, or *pearroc*, a park. Parke, a kindred name.

Parker. Parruc, a park; *ere*, an agent. A keeper of a park.

Parkerson. Parker, Parker, *sun*, son. Son of Parker.

Parkhill, Parruc, a park; *hyll*, a hill. A park hill.

Pearl. Perl, a pearl.

Peak. Peac, or *pic*, a peak, point, top, head. Peck, doubtless, from the same radix.

Perkin. Peter-kin, from Greek *Peter*, a rock; A. S. *cyn*, a relative. Peter's relative.

Perkins. Perkin, Perkin; *s* for *sun*, son. Son of Perkin.

Peters. Greek *Peter*, a rock; *s* for *sun*. Son of Peter; son of a rock. Peterson, from the same roots.

Pinn. Pinn, a pen.

Q.

Quernin. Cwcorn, a mill.

Querner. Cwcorn, a mill; *ere*, an agent. A miller.

R.

Riddle. Hriddel, a sieve, a riddle.

Ridgway. Ricg, a ridge; *wæg*, a way. A ridge-way; a way along a ridge.

Roberts. Rodor-beorht, from *rodor*, heavens, and *beorht*, bright; *s* for *sun*, son. Son of the heavenly bright. Robertson, a lengthened form of the same name.

Robinson. *Robin*, endearing name for Robert; *sun*, son. Son of Robin; son of the heavenly bright. Robbinson, Robbins, of like derivation.

Robson. *Rob*, Robb; *sun*, son. Son of Robb. Robb, contraction of Robbin, title of endearment for Robert—heavenly bright. Robeson, of like kinship.

S.

Scofield. *Sceawe*, a show; *feld*, a field. A show-field. See Scofield, page 99, which contains two errors.

Shourds. *Sceardes*, genitive of *sceard*, a sheard, division. Belonging to a sheard.

Sowden. Anglo-Norman *soudan*, from Moorish *soldan*, a prince. A prince; a sultan.

Sumpter. Anglo-Norman *summere*, a sumpter horse; and *sumpter*, a horse that carries clothes, furniture, etc. Going back to the original, from the Latin *sumo*, I take, *sumptum*, to take, with Anglo-Saxon *ere*, an agent: that is, one that takes or carries.

T.

Thomason. *Thomas*, Thomas; *sun*, son. Son of Thomas. In the Hebrew, *Thomas* signifies a twin. Thompson, of like derivation and meaning.

Tolbert. *Tohl*, or *tól*, a tool; *beorht*, bright. A bright tool.

Tolley. *Tohl-lic*, from *tohl*, a tool, and *lic*, like. Tool-like. Or, from *toh-lic*, compounded of *toh*, tough, clammy, and *lic*, like. Clammy.

www.ingramcontent.com/pod-product-compliance
Lightning Source LLC
Chambersburg PA
CBHW021833230426
43669CB00008B/955